# HILLEL AT MICHIGAN

# HILLEL AT MICHIGAN

## 1926/27–1945

Struggles of Jewish Identity
in a Pivotal Era

By

Andrei S. Markovits
and Kenneth Garner

Published in the United States of America by
Michigan Publishing
Manufactured in the United States of America

DOI: http://dx.doi.org/10.3998/mpub.9719362

ISBN 978-1-60785-403-6 (paper)
ISBN 978-1-60785-404-3 (e-book)

An imprint of Michigan Publishing, Maize Books serves the publishing needs of
the University of Michigan community by making high-quality scholarship widely
available in print and online. It represents a new model for authors seeking to
share their work within and beyond the academy, offering streamlined selection,
production, and distribution processes. Maize Books is intended as a complement
to more formal modes of publication in a wide range of disciplinary areas.

http://www.maizebooks.org

# Contents

# PREFACE AND ACKNOWLEDGMENTS

M y first contact with Hillel occurred on the High Holy Days of 1975. I had just arrived in Cambridge, Massachusetts, in early September to commence my one-year stint at the Center for European Studies at Harvard University. I had friends from my years as a student at Columbia University who lived in nearby Newton, Massachusetts, with whom I would always spend Seders for the following twenty-odd years, but for some reason this was less the case with the High Holy Days—possibly because these friends were Orthodox and I had grown up in a Jewish tradition that in Central Europe, particularly in Hungarian Judaism, was called "Neolog," a sort of amalgam of Conservative and Reform Judaism in North America, to which I felt closer in rituals if not necessarily in spirit. Such differences become virtually meaningless on the two Seder nights with all the food and conviviality, but they assume greater salience in terms of the conduct of services, their melodies, their usage of Hebrew, their intergender seating arrangements, and—most important—their length when it comes to Rosh Hashana and Yom Kippur. Not knowing anybody on the Cambridge side of the Charles River in the fall of 1975, I decided to crash Hillel's Conservative service at Harvard. I was welcomed with open arms and with the warmest of receptions. Above all, it was on that occasion that I met Harvard Hillel's director, Rabbi Ben-Zion Gold, who passed away in April 2016. In the course of those three days of services in the fall of

1975, I became so impressed with Rabbi Gold as a man, a leader, a teacher, a Holocaust survivor, and a Jew that I attended virtually every High Holy Day until the late 1990s at Harvard Hillel's Conservative services, which became so popular that at some point in the early 1980s, they were moved to huge Memorial Hall in Harvard's venerable Sanders Theater, which was regularly packed to the tune of a thousand-plus worshippers on Kol Nidre and other high points (Ne'ila and Shofar blowing) of these two important Jewish holidays.

In notable contrast to the fall of 1975, when I moved to Cambridge as a single twenty-seven-year-old man renting a studio apartment in a run-down building and in need of a Jewish community, in the fall of 1999, I arrived as a fifty-year-old professor with my wife, Kiki, and our golden retriever, Kelly, to a beautiful house located in a lovely neighborhood in Ann Arbor. The moving trucks had just arrived and were still fully loaded when we were most heartily welcomed by a number of neighbors (many, though not all, Jewish) who quickly became our friends, which they still remain. Being a lot more distant in age and career stage from my near-student-about-to-become-postdoc existence in my early Cambridge days also meant that the Hillel at the University of Michigan never attained close to the institutional and integrative role in my life in Ann Arbor that its Harvard counterpart did decades before. Still, Kiki and I have enjoyed Seders at Hillel, we have attended lectures there, and we remain regular financial contributors to this fine institution, though never surpassing the modest tote-bag category. Above all, it has been the constant array of Hillel members, exceptional young people all, who have enriched my intellectual life here at the University of Michigan over the past seventeen years with their regular visits to my office, their wonderful papers, their insightful contributions in class, and their very being as enlightened citizens and thoughtful Jews. And I would be remiss not to mention Michigan Hillel's daily presence in my life, which happens every time I pass the mantle above the fireplace in our living room, which is graced by the "Golden Apple" that I was fortunate to win in 2007, an award annually conferred by student ballot to the best teacher at the University of Michigan's Ann Arbor campus that—thanks to Hillel—has become a staple of the University's academic firmament.

For obvious biographical reasons (born in 1948 as the only child of a Holocaust-ravaged, Hungarian-speaking Jewish family growing up in western Romania, Vienna, and New York), I had devoted parts of my academic career to the study of subjects central to Jewish life, none more so than certain aspects of postwar German but also Austrian—indeed, European—politics, in which issues relating to Jews, particularly anti-Semitism, were central. Even though I had always been deeply interested in American Jewry's history and contemporary affairs, I had never done any serious research or writing on any of its important subjects. This changed abruptly during my four-month stint teaching in the wonderful Michigan-in-Washington Program from early January to late April 2015 when I decided that, upon my return to Ann Arbor in May, I would want to study the history of Jewish students—and Jewish athletes in particular—at my very own University of Michigan.

And that is exactly what happened. On our first Monday back home in Ann Arbor, I drove to the Bentley Library knowing nothing about its resources but knowing full well that this was the one and only place where all my sources lay. The first person I met upon entering this amazing place was the now-retired Karen Jania. And the rest is history, as they say. After telling Karen my vague and completely uninformed ideas, she did not ridicule me or turn away from me but did exactly the opposite: In the most welcoming and encouraging manner possible, she went to work immediately, telling me to contact this and that person and to read this book and that article. She bombarded me with materials and sources, among them *The Hillel News* and the Hillel scrapbooks. My head spinning from all this information, I was headed for lunch when I noticed through a half-opened door Terrence McDonald seated at a fancy desk in a corner office. I suddenly realized that Terry was no longer my long-serving dean but had in the meantime become the director of the Bentley. I knocked on the door and—just as he had done when he was dean—Terry welcomed me here, too, with warmth and openness. When I told him what had brought me to the Bentley Library, he not only expressed genuine interest and real enthusiasm for my project but also promised me that I could always count on him and his staff to help me as best they could. Have they ever! I cannot express with the proper words of gratitude how Terry and the Bentley staff have treated me over the past fifteen months, during which time my two assistants and I have been working on this project. I would like to take this opportunity to thank Charles Sorge and Adam Stone for their excellence in every task that I asked them to accomplish. However, it has been the Bentley staff's immense knowledge and expertise as professional librarians who really know their stuff that has trumped its welcoming spirit and warmth as people and colleagues. And then came the real pièce de résistance: I supplied Terry with the book's manuscript in the hope that he would write one of the two reviews of the work that Maize Books requires. Despite his busy schedule, he graciously accepted. As he was reading through the manuscript, he asked his archivists to go through the manuscript as well and make a list of issues of *The Hillel News* that I missed on account of their not having been available at the University of Michigan when I conducted my initial research. The staff located most of these missing issues in various archives across the country and acquired copies of them that I could then consult at the end of my writing this book, thus all but eliminating any possible lacunae that might perhaps have otherwise lessened the accuracy of the work. This was really special! Tout court, this project would be nowhere without Terry and his Bentley crew. Many thanks to them indeed!

It was at the Bentley Historical Library that I met Kenneth Garner. From our very first meeting, I knew that Ken was special. His knowledge of history, literature, politics, music, theater—in short, his *Bildung*—was exemplary and provided the contours of our early acquaintance. But it was his formidable familiarity with the Bentley and his mastery of its materials that rendered him an indispensable research assistant on this project. However, in the course of working together, it soon became clear to me that Ken had departed from his position as my assistant and had developed into my full-fledged coauthor. But most important, working with Ken for more than a year, he became a dear friend whose work I admire and whose advice I cherish.

Ken and I set out to write a book on Jewish students at the University of Michigan from the University's beginning until 1945. In fact, this project is still very much alive and well, though far from finished. In the course of researching this topic, we inevitably came upon Hillel as arguably this world's most central institution and player. In writing the Hillel chapter for our book, we soon realized that the material was rich enough for something longer. And it was in the course of the summer of 2016 that we decided to convert our Hillel chapter into a small book of its own, devoted solely to the first two decades of this institution's important history at the University of Michigan, thereby shedding some light on a fascinating sliver of American Jewish life in a turbulent era. We hoped that our book would help Hillel celebrate its ninetieth birthday at this University, fully coinciding with the latter's feting its two hundredth. Precisely for that reason, and serving this purpose, we regard the book not only as our presentation and analysis of Hillel's role and existence at the University of Michigan but also as a chronicle of Hillel on the University of Michigan campus, which accounts for our extensive quotations, mainly from *The Hillel News*. We hope and trust that employing this method gives the protagonists their most authentic voices and vivid agency. As such, we see our book as a Festschrift feting Hillel's happy occasion!

Even a relatively low-budget project such as this requires some funding, and once again I am most grateful to the small but immensely helpful research support that the University of Michigan accords me annually via my Deutsch Collegiate and Thurnau professorships.

As I have done with all my writings, this book, too, is dedicated to my beloved Kiki and Cody, without whom none of this would be possible!

*Andrei S. Markovits, Ann Arbor, September 2016*

No research project is ever successful without the help of many people. I would like to thank, first of all, Andy Markovits for bringing me on board for this wonderful journey; for his guidance, encouragement, and insight; and above all, for his unparalleled generosity and warmth. Our working relationship has developed into a fine friendship. A special thanks too to Kiki and Cody Markovits for their gracious hospitality during my many visits. At the Bentley, I would especially like to thank Diane Bachmann and Malgorzata Myc for their research suggestions and for tracking down materials for me. Finally, I must acknowledge my friends and family who have given me much love and support—they are too numerous to mention but too precious to me not to acknowledge.

*Kenneth Garner, Plymouth, September 2016*

*Cowardice asks, "Is it safe?"*
*Expediency asks, "Is it polite?"*
*Vanity asks, "Is it popular?"*
*But Conscience asks, "Is it right?"*

*Hillel News*, October 1941

# Introduction

There is something very telling in the fact that Hillel emanated from the country's Midwest and its great public universities rather than from the East Coast, which has consistently embodied the core of Jewish life in the history of the United States. It was not at the College of the City of New York (CCNY), where, in 1918–19, the student body comprised 78.7 percent Jews; nor at neighboring New York University with its student body consisting of 47.5 percent Jews; and not even at fancy Columbia University, where 21.2 percent of students were Jewish at this time. It wasn't at Harvard (10 percent Jews), Johns Hopkins (16.2 percent Jews), Boston University (9.9 percent Jews), University of Pennsylvania (14.5 percent Jews), or the University of Chicago (18.5 percent Jews). Rather, it was in the Midwest's public university powerhouses—the University of Illinois, with 4.2 percent of the student body being Jewish right after World War I; the University of Wisconsin, with 4.1 percent of the students identified as Jewish; Ohio State University, with 4.5 percent of the students being Jewish; and the University of Michigan, with 4.0 percent—that Hillel organizations were established in 1923, 1924, 1925, and 1926, respectively.[1]

1. Jeff Rubin, *The Road to Renaissance: 1923–2002* (n.p., n.d.), p. 5. The percentages of Jewish students at these universities right after World War I stem from Alfred Jospe, *Jewish Students and Student Services at American Universities: A Statistical and Historical Study* (Washington, DC: B'nai B'rith Hillel Foundation, 1963), pp. 6, 7, 8. Other than Rubin's work, which provides some useful information on Hillel in an

We see two reasons for this development: The first, of course, has to do with the fact that various Jewish organizations preceded Hillel, mainly at East Coast universities, due to the large number of Jewish students there. The first among these was the Zeta Beta Tau fraternity founded under the Hebrew name (*Zion Be-mishpat Tip-padeh*; "Zion shall be redeemed by justice" [Isaiah 1:27]) in New York City in 1898 "to encourage the study of Jewish history and culture among Jewish students, but shortly afterwards converted into a Greek-letter fraternity."[2] The transition from Hebrew to Greek letters signaled to the world very clearly that the young men who had created this organization were at least as interested in its social aspects as they were in its Jewish ones. By switching from Hebrew to Greek, this fraternity conformed fully to the prevailing mode. It was a Jewish entity that embraced the cultural codes of the dominant Gentile world around it. Other

---

otherwise cursory treatment of it in a brochure-like publication full of photographs, and Jospe's *Jewish Students and Student Services*—which, too, offers fine data on Hillel but has the appearance of a type-scripted manuscript rather than that of a published book—we only found one book on Hillel: Alan Webber and Jonathan Sacks, *The B'nai B'rith Hillel Foundation: 1953–1993* (London: B'nai B'rith Hillel, 1993). This book deals almost exclusively with British Hillel. We located one short article on Hillel at Michigan State University by Jennifer Hughey and Jonathan Koenigsberg, "A Rich History and a Bright Future: Hillel at MSU," *Michigan Jewish History* 46 (Fall 2006; Tishrei 5767), pp. 24–27. In the very same issue of this journal, we also encountered an article on pre-Hillel Jewish life at the University of Michigan in which Hillel is mentioned in the article's last two pages. See Barry Stiefel, "Early Jewish Life at the University of Michigan," *Michigan Jewish History* 46 (Fall 2006; Tishrei 5767), pp. 17–23. The next issue of *Michigan Jewish History* featured short articles on Hillel organizations across the state of Michigan, including a retrospective of Hillel of Metropolitan Detroit.

2. Alfred Jospe, "Jewish College Students in the United States," *American Jewish Yearbook* 65 (1964), p. 135. To be sure, Pi Lambda Phi, founded at Yale University in 1895 by three Jewish students, preceded ZBT by three years. But "Pi Lam," as it was called, "was completely non-sectarian and its leadership refused to acknowledge any other classification. Nevertheless, until World War II its non-Jewish members never numbered more than a handful, and it was almost invariably classified as 'Jewish' by the rest of the world." Marianne R. Sanua, "Jewish College Fraternities in the United States, 1895–1968," *Journal of American Ethnic History* (Winter 2000); p. 10.

similar Jewish organizations followed rapidly: "The first professional fraternities, Sigma Epsilon Delta for dental students in 1901, and Phi Delta Epsilon for medical students in 1904. The first sorority, Iota Alpha Pi, came in 1903, as the Jewish girls began to follow their brothers into the collegiate world."[3]

There were other organizations as well, such as Zionist societies at CCNY in 1902; at Harvard and Columbia in 1905; "the University Jewish Literary Society at Minnesota in 1903; Menorah societies at Harvard in 1906 [the first one of its kind] and at Missouri in 1907; the Ivrim at the University of Illinois and the Society for the Study of Jewish Literature at the University of Texas in 1907; the Hebraic Club at Yale in 1909; and the Calipha club for the Study of Jewish Culture and Questions at the University of California in 1910."[4] Most of these organizations merged into the growing Menorah movement founded at Harvard by Henry Hurwitz in 1908, who sought "to build an organization that would promote the serious academic study of Jewish culture in the university and serve as a platform for the nonpartisan discussion of Jewish problems. Hurwitz aimed to liberate the Jewish college student from the feeling that his Judaism diminished his American identity." This was a conflict-laden issue that, as we will see repeatedly in our study, remained central to the lives of Jewish students—indeed, American Jews (or is it Jewish Americans?)—at Michigan and elsewhere throughout much of the twentieth century.[5] "Menorah's primary purpose was intellectual—the study of the history and culture of the Jewish people, so conceived that nothing Jewish should be alien to it. It was to be a nonpartisan and nonsectarian open forum. Nonactivist, as well, it would neither sponsor purely social functions nor engage in philanthropic or social-service activities. Its energies were to be concentrated

3. Lee J. Levinger, *The Jewish Student in America: A Study Made by the Research Bureau of the B'nai B'rith Hillel Foundations* (Cincinnati, OH: B'nai B'rith, 1937), p. 2.

4. Jospe, "Jewish College Students in the United States."

5. Ibid.

upon its cultural purpose."[6] There were other Jewish student organizations besides those in Menorah, among which, perhaps, the Zionist outfit Avukah, founded in Washington, DC, in 1925, became the most prominent. Closely associated with the Zionist Organization of America (ZOA) and Hadassah, this organization—just like Menorah—proliferated among Jewish students on America's campuses, Michigan's included, as we will see. All these organizations shared one important thing: they were almost exclusively student-run and student-dominated institutions with virtually no connection to the Jewish community off campus. Despite Avukah's affiliation with ZOA, the former ran its own affairs completely independent of the latter and indulged in major ideological conflicts between Revisionists and Labor Zionists that was to split Avukah in 1934 and lead to its demise in 1942.

We would be remiss not to mention Marianne R. Sanua's pioneering work on Jewish fraternities and sororities at this juncture, since, as she so convincingly shows, they were most certainly the main places at America's universities at a time when Jewish students could congregate and socialize as Jews unencumbered by a hostile world whose fraternities and sororities, more often than not, remained closed to them.[7] These organizations became crucial places for Jewish students to find a home away from home during their years in college. Moreover, they played a decisive role in the Jewish marriage market, since it was through these fraternities and sororities that young Jewish students had a chance to meet each other. Fraternities and sororities replaced the famed matchmaker of yore for many Jewish students certainly until the end of World War II, which also forms the end of our project. But fraternities and sororities never had the comprehensively cultural, decidedly intellectual, and broadly inclusive social

---

6. Ibid., p. 136.

7. Marianne R. Sanua, *Going Greek: Jewish College Fraternities in the United States, 1895–1945* (Detroit: Wayne State University Press, 2003); and *"Here's to Our Fraternity": One Hundred Years of Zeta Beta Tau, 1898–1998* (Hanover, NH: Brandeis University Press, 1998).

mission and self-understanding that Hillel was to assume. They were closed entities that chose their membership according to certain criteria that—by definition—emphasized some exclusivity, some special characteristic, some particularity that remained incompatible with an all-purpose, big-tent organization of Hillel's model. Moreover, as we will see throughout our study, fraternities and sororities constructed, experienced, and practiced their Jewishness very differently from how Hillel envisioned its, leading to tensions between Hillel on the one hand and the fraternities and sororities on the other throughout the entire period comprising the study.

The second reason for Hillel's Midwestern roots has something to do with Jews' position in society—and society's reaction to Jews—being different in the Midwest from the East Coast. Being fewer in numbers, the fear of Jews losing their Jewish identity—be that mainly of an ethnic, religious, or cultural variety or, as was frequently the case, an undefinable mixture of all three—was more pronounced in the Midwest than on the East Coast. Jewish students at Midwestern universities, virtually all of whom hailed from this region in the early 1920s, had to remain more closely associated with their larger communities outside the walls of academia if they were to continue their active Jewish identity. So a town-gown separation that emerged on the East Coast would have been less viable in the Midwest. But there was another major difference between the Midwest and the East Coast: the role of their respective institutions of higher learning. Whereas private institutions (with few exceptions, most notably CCNY) dominated the East Coast, it was—again, with some exceptions (University of Chicago and Northwestern University)—the large state institutions that characterized higher education in the Midwest. As creations of the Northwest Ordinance (as in the cases of the University of Michigan and Indiana Seminary, later to become Indiana University in Bloomington), but mainly, of course, of the Morrill Land-Grant Act (as in the cases of Michigan State University, the University of Illinois at Urbana-Champaign, the

University of Minnesota, the University of Wisconsin at Madison, and Ohio State University), these Midwestern universities developed a completely different relation to the public trust than their East Coast counterparts. As a result, they featured a much greater sense of obligation to the community whose intellectual and cultural guardianship they assumed. Put differently, the cultural and institutional boundaries that these universities had vis-à-vis the publics of their respective states were much less rigid and formidable than those denoting the identities of private East Coast institutions, especially of the elite variety, which were later to form the Ivy League. Thus, not surprisingly, it was a non-Jewish professor of biblical literature at the University of Illinois named Edward Chauncey Baldwin "who, troubled by the attrition of Jewish knowledge and loyalty which he observed among his Jewish students, pleaded with rabbinical and lay leaders in Illinois to develop"[8] a college program that was to cast a wide net in which Jewishness—however vaguely defined—was to flourish on campus with the active help of the larger American Jewish community. Baldwin asked Rabbi Louis Mann, a prominent leader of the Chicago Jewish community, "'Don't you think the time has come when a Jewish student might educate his mind without losing his soul?'"[9]

If it was not at Baldwin's behest, then it was certainly in cooperation with him and as a consequence of his intellectual influence that Baldwin's University of Illinois colleague Benjamin Frankel, familiar with the three hundred Jewish students at that institution and their often tenuous relationship to Judaism, came to develop at this university in 1923 what was to become the very first Hillel in the world. By all accounts, Rabbi Frankel was the ideal person to found such an all-encompassing organization whose mission it was to include all Jewish students—regardless of political ideology, religious proficiency, or any other intellectual

---

8. Jospe, "Jewish College Students in the United States," p. 139.
9. Rubin, *Road to Renaissance*, p. 4.

disposition or ability—in things Jewish, broadly conceived and implemented. Of warm disposition and respected as a man of great intellect and learning—thus, for example, Abram Sachar credited the birth of this organization to Frankel's "'remarkably expansive, lovable personality, his genius for friendship, his courageous idealism and love for a great cultural heritage'"[10]—Frankel envisioned a place on campus that was to offer Jewish students an emotional home, a social haven, and an intellectual resource during their four years at college. Above all, this structure was to provide a crucial bridge between the university and the outside world, not least in the funding of the former by the latter. For that purpose, Frankel constituted a board of lay leaders from outside the university who were to assist him in his endeavors right from the beginning. Moreover, Frankel included his University of Illinois colleague, the esteemed historian Abram L. Sachar, who would later—upon Frankel's untimely death in 1927 at the age of thirty—become Frankel's successor as the leader of this organization at the University of Illinois in 1928, the first full-time director of such an organization in the country and, in many ways, Hillel's most important national figure of all time. By any measure, Sachar must be seen as one of American Jewry's foremost leaders and most prominent public figures. He had been graduated Phi Beta Kappa from Washington University in St. Louis, received a PhD from Cambridge University, and began his teaching career at the University of Illinois in 1923. In addition to his directorship of the Hillel Foundation at the University of Illinois, Sachar became Hillel's first national director in 1932. As is well known, Sachar became Brandeis University's founding president in 1948, leading it to a world-class research university in his twenty-year tenure. After his retirement as president of Brandeis University in 1968, Sachar continued his active involvement with this institution first as its chancellor and later as its chancellor emeritus. In our research for this book, we also encountered two additional names

10. Ibid., p. 5.

of people who seem to have been very influential in the founding and initial formation of Hillel: Alfred M. Cohen and Boris D. Bogen. According to the University of Michigan's publication *The Hillel News* of October 24, 1929, Alfred M. Cohen, Boris D. Bogen, and Rabbi Ben Frankel were "the three men who made the Hillel Foundation a reality."[11]

Benjamin Frankel decided to name this new entity *Hillel*: "'It was a felicitous choice. Hillel is a symbol of the quest for higher learning. It was a beautiful name, too. It appeared to the Christian fellowship that pioneered the foundation, since Hillel was virtually a contemporary of Jesus. In those days the Jewish community still felt the need for the Christian imprimatur.'"[12] Perhaps most crucially, Frankel and Sachar succeeded in having B'nai B'rith adopt Hillel at the University of Illinois, thus opening the door for a construct in which a nonuniversity-based charitable institution was to fund a good portion of a university-centered entity's activities and existence. Frankel was instrumental in opening the second Hillel at the University of Wisconsin in 1924, with Ohio State's and Michigan's to follow in 1925 and 1926, respectively. It was not until 1939 that Hillel opened its first facility on the East Coast by establishing the Brooklyn College Hillel, which, with an enrollment of eight thousand Jewish students, presented a hitherto unprecedented challenge that Abram Sachar personally oversaw.[13]

Five decisive principles guided the establishment and maintenance of Hillel student organizations. First, bespeaking the

11. *The Hillel News*, Volume IV, Number V, October 24, 1929. Until the issue of December 3, 1930, the paper employs Roman numerals to denote not only every paper's volume number, which is conventional practice, but also its issue's number, which is not.

12. Rubin, *Road to Renaissance*, p. 5. Hillel, of course, was also one of the Jewish people's most pronounced sages and one of its major scholars and teachers, whose name therefore fit the world of higher education as modern society's major locus of learning, research, and teaching.

13. Ibid., p. 7.

seriousness of Frankel's institutional commitment and his acute awareness of the inadequacy of previous amateurish efforts on the organizational firmament of Jewish student life, Frankel insisted that Hillel be run by a permanent professional staff: "Every Foundation operates under the guidance of a Hillel Director, usually a rabbi who combines Jewish academic competence with experience in youth work. Hillel Counselorships—Hillel's extension service units—are served by a rabbi in the community near the campus, an educator or group worker, or a Hillel Director from a nearby Foundation."[14]

The second principle pertains to the broad, indeed ecumenical, nature of Hillel's purpose and mission. All Jewish students, regardless of their theological orientation, sophistication, or ideological predilections, are welcomed by Hillel. The organization is not to address itself to any particular intellectual segment of the campus population. It is not to favor any group or orientation over any other. Hillel "is designed to serve all Jewish students regardless of their backgrounds, Jewish ideologies or denominational preferences, and it seeks to meet student needs on the very intellectual levels on which they may exist. Nor does Hillel sponsor or endorse any partisan view of Jewish life. It is hospitable to every wholesome expression of Jewish interest or concern that may exist in the campus community. Hillel Directors respect genuine differences of conviction but seek to create a sense of community that will eschew divisiveness and relate the Jewish student to the totality of Jewish group experience in time and space."[15]

The third principle pertains to the quality of instruction and discourse set by the organization, which, simply put, must happen on an intellectually high level commensurate with the exigencies and rigor expected at an institution of postsecondary education: "Jewish values must not remain frozen on the Sunday school level. The development of a college approach to Jewish life and

---

14. Jospe, *Jewish Students and Student Services*, p. 30.
15. Ibid., pp. 30, 31.

experience is the raison d'être of a mature program for Jewish college students . . . The Hillel program is designed to fill the vacuum that is created when the immature childhood notions concerning religion and Judaism which many students bring along when they enter college are shattered by the intellectual challenge of the university . . . [The Hillel program] requires the use of educational methods and the development of resources which are geared to the intellectual needs of the academic community."[16]

The fourth principle addresses the synthesis of information and knowledge on the one hand and participation and involvement on the other. While the acquisition of the former is a must in any environment of learning and forms the basis of any communal discourse, without its deployment in moral deeds and actual activities in the real world it might easily disintegrate into abstract, even futile, sterility: "Hence it is a principle of Hillel work to relate the study of Jewish values and ideas to an effort to discover the moral and Jewish basis of actions which students may want, or should be encouraged, to take on basic issues of Jewish or general concern. Discussions of past or present Jewish needs are related to a study of Jewish relief agencies and stimulate the formation of a student campaign for their support. And a study of the values of the prophetic tradition can be applied fruitfully to contemporary issues of social significance and stimulate students to express their convictions in socially responsible action."[17]

The fifth principle demands that students run their own Hillels by electing student leadership groups that help plan and administer the program: "The Director is the guide and counselor, but the students are given the opportunity to share responsibility in Hillel's operation and program development."[18] Students have to staff every committee, students must write all publications, and students decide all featured programs, from dances to lectures,

16. Ibid., p. 31.
17. Ibid., p. 32.
18. Ibid.

from excursions to socials. Students choose whom to invite as guest lecturers and what books and records they want in their Hillel's library. In other words, even though the director and the staff lent a much-needed professionalism to this overall endeavor, Hillel never departed from being a student-centered organization, which it remains firmly to this day.

Lastly, Hillel's financial support broke down as follows: "Seventy percent . . . came from B'nai B'rith, 20 percent from community sources (mainly federations and welfare funds), and the rest from student registration fees and activities income."[19]

The ensuing part of our work will present Hillel at Michigan as a detailed case study. In particular, we will use relevant materials from the two available BHL-UM Hillel boxes as our sources. But, more important, we will harness a close reading of the Hillel publication *The Hillel News*, later renamed *The B'nai B'rith Hillel News* and subsequently *Hillel News*, as our main source to shed light on this important Jewish organization on the University of Michigan campus. While the first copy of this newspaper available to us hails from October 6, 1927, and we thus lack all information pertaining to this Hillel chapter's first few months of existence, and while certain temporal lacunae in the availability of this publication prevented our seamless following of Hillel's minute history during parts of the crucial 1930s and 1940s, we are reasonably certain that the close examination of 154 copies of this content-rich paper published between 1927 and 1945 allows us to gain reasonably good insights as to what issues this organization confronted and how these emanated from—and reflected—Jewish life on the campus of this Midwestern university.

19. Jospe, "Jewish College Students in the United States," p. 140.

# HILLEL AT THE
# UNIVERSITY OF MICHIGAN

We have concentrated our research of all extant boxes at the Bentley Historical Library containing materials of the Hillel Foundation's chapter at the University of Michigan and *The Hillel News* as well as our ensuing narrative into five thematic areas that, of course, overlap in their concerns and topics but that we discern as distinct areas of Hillel's activities and profile. The first—and, in our view, most important—area pertains to Hillel's Jewishness and the construction of its Jewish identity, which includes its relations to Jews and Judaism broadly defined. We group the following themes under this category: Hillel's relations with other Jewish organizations on campus, such as fraternities and sororities; its appeal to Jewish students; discussions as to what constitutes proper Jewish behavior and identity; political issues as they pertain to Jews; all issues related to anti-Semitism; and everything concerning Hillel as an organization both at the University of Michigan and nationwide. The second area pertains to Hillel-University relations. The third concerns Hillel's relations with non-Jewish students and student organizations. The fourth features the role of women in Hillel. And the fifth centers on something best termed "social commitments," meaning Hillel's role in not only providing a forum for plays and actors, choral groups and debating teams, chess, sports, so-called smokers, and dances and balls but also for administering a library and a record collection for its members and the public at large. We think that an analysis of these five areas allows us to capture the main issues that confronted the Hillel Foundation at the University of Michigan from 1926/27 to 1945.

## The Early Years under Foundation Director Adolph Fink

We learn from Barry Stiefel's research that on February 26, 1914, "Jewish students at the University of Michigan officially established their own congregational community, the Jewish Student Congregation. This organization actually predates the more popularly known international student Jewish organization of Hillel."[20] The Jewish Student Congregation at the University of Michigan was the very first of its kind in the United States and was modeled on a similar congregation at the University of Cambridge in England.[21] This organization offered Sunday services and provided social activities for Jewish students, "sometimes in partnership with the Menorah Society."[22] The Jewish Student Congregation also provided a gathering place for Jews living in Ann Arbor who were not affiliated with the University of Michigan and who, until 1916, did not have a place of worship or gathering of their own. In other words, the Jewish Student Congregation preceded Hillel as the very first Jewish organization on the Michigan campus following only the Jewish sorority Alpha Epsilon Phi, which was founded in 1909, and the Inter-Collegiate Menorah Society (founded at Harvard in 1908, as mentioned previously), whose University of Michigan chapter was established in 1910.[23]

According to the annotated chronology for the Hillel chapter at Michigan, "first mention of The Michigan B'nai B'rith

20. Stiefel, "Early Jewish Life at the University of Michigan," p. 17.
21. Ibid.
22. Ibid.
23. Ibid.

Hillel Foundation can be found in the hand-written minutes of the Executive Committee of the Independent Order of B'nai B'rith. 1925—Monday afternoon, December 7, the minutes record that Rabbi Leo M. Franklin of Detroit requested that a B'nai B'rith Foundation be established at the University of Michigan. 1926—December 12, the minutes (in part) read 'At the beginning of the scholastic year, the B'nai B'rith Michigan Hillel Foundation was founded at Ann Arbor.' This would strongly suggest that Hillel was on campus in 1926–1927. However, the University of Michigan index card in the National Hillel Office indicates that service began in 1927."[24] So while it can be safely argued that Hillel at the University of Michigan was founded in late 1926, it is also evident that real operations in any meaningful sense did not commence until 1927. As we will see, Hillel itself seems to have been torn about the date of its origin on the University of Michigan campus; we encountered a number of instances in which the fall of 1926 was mentioned as the founding date, but we saw other occasions in which 1927 appeared as such. It is quite clear, though, that the latter year must have been the Foundation's first truly operational one at the University of Michigan. This is perhaps best reinforced by the fact that the Foundation celebrated its Bar Mitzvah in 1940 and not in 1939.

The first issue of *The Hillel News* that was available to us hails from October 6, 1927, and announces across the entire front page an "Annual Mixer Saturday."[25] Clearly, Hillel's social function was crucial to its identity from the get-go. Since this paper bears the "Volume II" identifier, we assume that there must have been a "Volume I" that most likely published its issues in the first six months of 1927—that is, at some point during what in the University of Michigan's current parlance has come to be known as the "winter semester," which in most other universities in the United

24. "B'nai B'rith Hillel Foundation at the University of Michigan, An Annotated Chronology," BHL-UM, Box 1.
25. *The Hillel News*, Volume II, Number I, October 6, 1927.

States featuring the semester rather than the quarter system as their organizing principle of the academic calendar, operates as "spring semester." We very much doubt that any publication appeared in December of 1926 that could also be seen as the Hillel Foundation's birth at the University of Michigan. In an editorial entitled "Come Around," which features the exhortation "Get the Hillel Habit" repeatedly in its text, we read that "the Foundation has begun its second year of existence as a vital factor in the Jewish student life of the University of Michigan campus. The experiment, which was begun a year ago by the B'nai B'rith organization, has become an institution . . . The Jewish student body's meeting place compares favorably with any of the church guild houses on campus. Make use of it. The best Jewish literature is at your disposal in the Hillel library. A piano and victrola are ready at any moment to entertain. Come around and play bridge, dance or sing . . . Get acquainted. Lose 'that lonesome away-from-home neglected' feeling at the Hillel Open House . . . Make the Hillel a necessary factor in your life and go through your college career with Hillel behind you. GET THE HILLEL HABIT!"[26] It is clear from this passage that Hillel at the time very much considered 1926 to be its beginning at the University of Michigan and that it wanted to attract Jewish students via its social and cultural offerings. These were to remain important parts of the Foundation's identity throughout the period of our study as well as until the present. In a piece entitled "President and Committee Chairmen State Policies," Hillel's aim to reach every Jewish student on the Michigan campus receives pride of place. A social committee was to do everything in its power to attract students by organizing all kinds of activities, including the planning of a musical revue "fashioned after a regular Broadway production and given on a large scale."[27] An education committee was to not only conduct Sunday school for local Jewish children but also be in charge of

26. Ibid. The all capital letters are in the original.
27. Ibid.

acquiring books for the Hillel library. A religion committee was organizing regular Orthodox services on Friday evenings and Reform services on Sunday mornings. It also commenced planning a speaker series. This issue of the paper informs us that a large number of students had already participated in both kinds of services at the beginning of the new semester. Lastly, we read that Ray Baer, the legendary varsity football guard and a teammate of the recently graduated University of Michigan superstar Benny Friedman, "gave a short talk in which he asked the student body to support Hillel with the same enthusiasm in which they support the Michigan football team."[28]

The paper of October 20, 1927, informs us that practices are to begin for Hillel's first musical comedy after tryouts for the cast, which were held in the week of October 1–8, and for the girls' choruses, which occurred between October 7 and 11.[29] While the name of the musical remained a secret at this stage, it is clear from the long list of participants that nearly thirty students were to appear in this show. In an editorial entitled "To the Literati," Hillel promises to publish the work of poets and writers of all kinds in something called *The Literary Comment*, which was to appear in addition to *The Hillel News*. Hillel hoped to rectify the situation on campus and well beyond in which artistic writers of all genres had a hard time getting their work published: "With a Jewish student body of almost 900, the existence of a large number of good writers among them is undoubted. 'The Literary Comment' is one of the few publications on the campus which affords an opportunity to these writers to see their work in print."[30] Even from this single issue of *The Hillel News*, it is more than obvious that the Foundation was immensely eager to satisfy the deep and broad cultural literacy and engagement that the Jewish students on the University of Michigan campus clearly possessed. But in this

28. Ibid.

29. *The Hillel News*, Volume II, Number II, October 20, 1927.

30. Ibid.

issue, we also learn about the Jewish students' interest in many sports, both as participants and—in our view, much more important still—as consumers of such, which gave Jews at the time immense pride, as indeed it continues to do in the present. And it does so for all ethnic groups—minorities in particular—not only Jews.[31] The article bursts with pride in describing the exploits of Ray Baer, Sammy Babcock, and Harold Greenwald on the varsity football team; praises Ralph Cole's and Joe Morris's performances on the varsity golf team; mentions Mannie Schorr, Clarence Batter, Meyer Rosenberg, Richard Fecheimer, and Ralph Miller on the swim team; and delights in touting Victor Berkowitz as the middleweight boxing champion of the campus and Joe Stein as its featherweight title holder. Moreover, "Stewart Schloss, All-Cincinnati high school half-back, and Sid Friedman, Benny's younger brother, are out for freshman football. Stanley Levison and Nimz are working with the freshman swimmers."[32]

In the November 17 issue of *The Hillel News*, crucial matters relating to the Jewish athlete and the ubiquitous brain-brawn divide receive further elaboration. We read: "The Jewish student has always been accepted at liberal institutions throughout the United States as an important factor in the life of the University campus. In scholarship he has been found well up among

---

31. For a detailed discussion of how sports, particularly its stars, provide an immensely important platform of pride for all social groups, see Andrei S. Markovits and Lars Rensmann, *Gaming the World: How Sports Are Reshaping Global Politics and Culture* (Princeton: Princeton University Press, 2010). Just think of the importance of Joe Louis and Muhammad Ali in boxing; Jackie Robinson, Willie Mays, Hank Aaron, and Frank Robinson in baseball; Jim Brown and Doug Williams in football; Bill Russell and Wilt Chamberlain in basketball; Tiger Woods in golf; and Simone Manuel in swimming to the lifting of pride in the African American community. Or think of the parallel phenomena for the Jewish community: its immense growth in pride and delight concerning Hank Greenberg's and Sandy Koufax's incredible exploits in baseball and Mark Spitz's in swimming. Even a temporary manifestation of excellence as exhibited by Jeremy Lin in the NBA's arenas in February 2012 led to something called "Linsanity," which engulfed the Asian American community in a fit of pride that was hitherto unparalleled in its depth and breadth.

32. *The Hillel News*, Volume II, Number II, October 20, 1927.

the leaders, if not often heading the list. In forensic activities he has played an important part. In all branches of the mental college life—publications, politics, the arts—he has made his mark. Yet, in activities requiring exceptional physical strength, the Jew is thought by many to have fallen below his standard. This idea has entrenched itself until it appears unfortunately almost a tradition. Athletic history in the last few years, on the other hand, has shown a steady increase in the participation of Jewish students in sports. The situation at Michigan is typical of what is occurring throughout the country. Friedman, who startled the athletic world with his passing and field generalship for three years, initiated the Hebraic Invasion of athletics at Michigan. This year three regulars who pray to the God of Israel or, lest that statement be too broad, have Jewish leanings, can be listed on the varsity. Baer [who, we learn from another piece in this issue of the paper, had just been named to head an athletic committee at Hillel], Babcock and Greenwald have made their marks . . . The men and women who are making their reputations in these fields are dissipating, in large measure, a rather unfavorable and erroneous impression of Jewish inferiority in that which requires physical excellence."[33] Here, the paper addressed an issue that plagued the Jews as a minority throughout much of their history, primarily in Europe but also in North America—namely, that they remained separate from the majority and its culture by emphasizing intellectual pursuits at the cost of corporeal ones. This, of course, has gone hand in hand with perceiving the Jews as being too urban and thus urbane and cosmopolitan, and thus not sufficiently anchored in the mundane and often physical pursuits of the small-town-based majority that values its ties to the local soil, toil, and its customs. Jews' alleged distance from bodily pursuit and their perceived disdain for physical excellence all to the benefit of their intellectual acuity and mastery of reading, writing, and counting have rendered them in the eyes of many Gentiles an untrusted "other" who think of

33. *The Hillel News*, Volume II, Number IV, November 17, 1927.

themselves as superior compared to their Gentile environment. We do not find it at all surprising that the greater meaning of the prominence and success of Jews in athletics received such a boisterous airing in *The Hillel News* of the time.

In this issue of the paper, we also read about a lecture given by Rabbi I. E. Philo on the topic of Jews seeking solace and a better life by departing from Judaism and joining other religions: "Those who desert Judaism do so to gain social and economic advantage, the rabbi asserted. At least, they do not find more spiritual satisfaction in the creed they may choose."[34] The rabbi gave special consideration to three creeds that he viewed as particularly attractive to Jews but ultimately lacking in giving them the succor and comfort that they sought: Christian Science, Ethical Culture, and Unitarianism.[35] In this same issue, we also learn that the title of the musical that Hillel prepared for a campus-wide showing on December 2 and 3 was *Hello U*, a sort of musical potpourri from its description in the paper.[36]

As we learn from the December 1 issue of *The Hillel News*, the performance of this musical revue was cancelled. After an inspection of the revue's book by Herbert A. Kenyon, assistant professor of French and Spanish in the engineering school and head of the University Dramatics Committee, the play as it stood was deemed unacceptable. The revisions suggested by Professor Kenyon were too extensive, thus making the cancellation of the performance necessary.[37]

In addition, Ray Baer's chairing of the Athletic Committee led to plans for the formation of a ten-team-based inter-Hillel basketball league under the aegis of the University Intramural Athletics Department, which was to include teams of Hillel Foundations, most of which, at this point, were situated at

34. Ibid.
35. Ibid.
36. Ibid.
37. *The Hillel News*, Volume II, Number V, December 1, 1927.

Midwestern universities.[38] This issue of the paper also featured a hearty congratulations to Baer, who had just been named to virtually every All-Conference team imaginable: "Baer is [a] man of whom the Jewish student body on this campus is proud to boast, 'He is one of our own.' Although he is outstanding in football his leadership in other fields is also evident. As a student, he has won a scholarship prize in sociology. As one of that rare combination, student and athlete, we take a justifiable pride in his prowess."[39]

In an editorial entitled "Keep the Faith," the paper apologized for a faux pas that must have been embarrassing: Temple Beth El of Detroit, known for being the house of worship presided over by the eminent Rabbi Leo M. Franklin, invited many Jewish students from the University of Michigan for a Student Day at the temple. Even though a large number of students accepted this invitation and confirmed their presence at the dinner prepared by the temple's sisterhood, "a pitifully small proportion of those who sent in these cards fulfilled their expressed intentions of attending . . . While the *Hillel News* wishes to express its thanks for the excellent program arranged by Temple Beth El, it cannot refrain from remarking upon the fashion in which the Jewish student body of the University of Michigan responded to it. As a remedy for the situation this year, this editorial is useless; as a hint for future behavior, it should prove helpful."[40]

Under the aegis of Hillel's Social Welfare Committee, a weekly Sunday school held at the Beth Israel Community Center was regularly attracting nearly thirty-five boys and girls. The Foundation's Music Committee also became quite active, as did the Book Committee, which acquired, among others, Hugo Bettauer's famous book *The City without Jews*. In this book, Bettauer depicted his home city of Vienna with no Jews, writing that the Gentile

38. Ibid.
39. Ibid.
40. Ibid.

population had forced the Jews there into exile, eerily anticipating what was to become reality barely a dozen years later.[41]

Iowa won the very first inter-Hillel basketball championship after beating Minnesota with a score of eight to five, *The Hillel News* of March 29, 1928, informs us.[42] That score is not a typographical error. Basketball was a very low-scoring game in that era, with the scores increasing somewhat in later decades, though they were still nowhere near the levels that we now see. This has been mainly due to the introduction of the shot clock and the players' much-improved athletic abilities.

The paper also announces the presence of Rabbi Nathan S. Krass, leader of Temple Emanuel in New York City. This place of worship was arguably one of the country's most prominent Reform synagogues and the congregation to which many eminent New York Jews belonged—Adolph S. Ochs, the owner and publisher of the *New York Times*, among them. Perhaps more important than the rabbi's presence was the topic of his lecture: "Psycho-analyzing a Psycho-analyst" was to feature interpretations of Sigmund Freud's work, among others.[43]

Under the headline "Understanding," this issue of *The Hillel News* addresses a theme that has appeared centrally throughout our research: Hillel's difficult relations with Jewish fraternities and sororities. The editorial welcomes an event in which an unnamed Jewish fraternity organized a smoker to which it invited other Jewish fraternities. Apparently, this was a positive rarity in the fractured and hostile world of intrafraternity culture: "This function, which has become an annual event on that fraternity's calendar, goes far to better relations between Jewish organizations."[44] But there remained a serious problem, which the editorial addressed in its

41. Bettauer, a brilliant Viennese investigative journalist who converted from Judaism to Lutheran Protestantism as a young man, paid with his life for his book after being assassinated by an Austrian Nazi in 1925.

42. *The Hillel News*, Volume II, Number X, March 29, 1928.

43. Ibid.

44. Ibid.

subsequent text: "Only one phase of a great problem is attempted here, however—intra-fraternity relations. There is yet another, the establishment of a cordial relationship between the affiliated and the independent student, which is hardly less important. A situation, which was once full of bitterness and antagonism, has been ameliorated, in part by the mingling of fraternity men with independents in the work of the Foundation. An inevitable sympathy has arisen. The Foundation is limited in this work, however, by the number of Jewish students who are active in its different fields. On the Jewish fraternity and sorority does the settlement of the problem rest. From them, as organized groups, must come the initiative."[45]

Another topic that has been absolutely central in our analysis of these documents makes an appearance in two articles of this issue of *The Hillel News*: the role of assimilation as an option and strategy for Jews in America and beyond as part of the larger and constant concern about Jewish identity and its many manifestations. The first piece summarizes a lecture by Rabbi Leo Franklin of Temple Beth El in Detroit, in which the rabbi puts forth an argument for what one could call a modified assimilation as the only viable, indeed desirable, option for Jews: "The solution offered by Rabbi Franklin was a compromise between the two attitudes [assertive Jewishness and complete assimilation]. It is not necessary to loudly proclaim one's Jewishness, nor yet is it necessary to hide it. The Jew can gain the respect of himself and his neighbor by living the Jewish life as it should be lived, decently and courageously."[46]

The second article dealing with assimilation summarized a well-attended discussion led by Rabbi Adolph Fink, the Michigan Hillel Foundation's director, which used the Jews' troubled history in Spain as a gateway to discuss assimilation in the present. This was in the context of Rabbi Fink's teaching a Hillel class every Wednesday evening on the Jews in Spain of the fourteenth

45. Ibid.
46. Ibid.

and fifteenth centuries. The lively discussion's conclusion was that "doubtlessly some individuals may be justified in assimilation, if they suffer a great deal as Jews, but as a group there are too many difficulties and the world would not permit assimilation of all. So, at present, there are proportionately very few who do assimilate."[47]

Although we could not find any evidence as to whether the aforementioned musical *Hello U* was ever performed in public as the Foundation's members had intended, *The Hillel News* of April 26 features all kinds of artistic endeavors on its front page: "'Mary the Third' Performance Set for Next Month," "Dramatics Committee Calls for Synopses of Stunt Show Skits," and "First Musical Recital Staged at Foundation" all appear alongside articles touting the debaters' return to campus from a successful spring contest and a Hillel banquet, which was the "scene of 'April Fool' Spirit."[48]

In a remarkably progressive editorial entitled "The Date System," Hillel picks up on the problematic issue of the stigmatization of women who dare appear with no man by their side for various events: "Library, dance, and theatre dates play an important and justifiable part in university life. But—when the influence of the system extends to a point where a college girl fears loss of social caste if she appears at any kind of mixed function without an attentive male escort at her beck and call, it has gone beyond its limits. Hillel Foundation affairs are intended for men and women. Yet, women are conspicuously absent at most educational and religious functions, seemingly from a fear of appearing unattended. Women are the exception at discussion groups and classes and are absolutely never seen at Friday evening services. Before the recent committee banquet, several feminine members expressed timidity at the prospect of going undated. Appearance in public unescorted was looked upon askance in the Mid-Victorian

47. Ibid.
48. *The Hillel News*, Volume II, Number XI, April 26, 1928.

period. *Today, however is an age of women's rights, and these rights are particularly advocated by college feminists. At every opportunity they are militantly advanced. Freedom of dress, of vocation, of the use of the cigarette are fought for at every step of the way."*[49] We chose to italicize the last three sentences because in both form and content, they could have been written by feminists of the late 1960s and early 1970s, with the possible exception of touting cigarettes. As we will see later in the text, Hillel picked up this topic at a later date as well.

As if to substantiate Hillel's progressive view on women's role in American society, the same issue of *The Hillel News* features an article announcing that a "feminine jurist" is to appear at services: "Judge Mary B. Grossman, of the Cleveland municipal court, will be speaker at the Hillel Sunday services on May 13. Her topic has been announced as 'Law and Human Conduct.' Judge Grossman enjoys the distinction of being one of the few women in the United States holding positions on the bench. Judge Florence Allen, of the state supreme court, is another enjoying the same distinction in Ohio."[50]

The headline of *The Hillel News* of May 10 announced "Ohio State Debate Sunday."[51] Apparently, rivalry with Ohio State extended well beyond the gridiron and was big enough in the debating scene to attract campus-wide attention. The Michigan Hillel's debating pair took the negative side of the question, "Resolved, that the present tendencies of the American Jewish youth are favorable to the future of the Jewish people."[52] Two further points are worthy of mention from this issue of the paper. First, there was the bevy of names belonging to Jewish students who were initiated into honorary societies like Phi Beta Kappa, Phi Kappa Phi, Sigma Xi, Phi Eta Sigma, and Alpha Alpha Delta

49. Ibid.

50. Ibid.

51. *The Hillel News*, Volume II, Number XII, May 10, 1928.

52. Ibid.

for their excellent scholarship and other academic achievements. In addition to these students, others were invited to attend the annual Honors Convocation given by the University and three students were honored in the Law School, with a number of freshmen also rewarded for their scholarly excellence. Second, an editorial entitled "A Word to the Wise" warns Hillel candidates running for the Foundation's presidency—one unnamed individual in particular—to refrain from engaging in any kind of electioneering and campaigning and other "such sordidness" that is strictly forbidden and viewed as unethical. Indeed, the editorial mentioned that Rabbi Fink, as the Foundation's director, had the power to remove such an individual from Hillel's presidency. This power had been invested in him by the Student Executive Council, and the rabbi made clear that he would use it if need be.[53]

The last issue of *The Hillel News* of the academic year 1927–28 exclaimed in a page-covering headline that Richard Meyer, a junior in the Literary College, won the election for student president of the Foundation.[54] Meyer won by a large majority of the record 253 ballots cast in this election. He had been chairman of the Foundation's Social Welfare Committee for the previous two years. The paper also ran a detailed article about Judge Mary B. Grossman's lecture entitled "Law and Human Conduct," which she delivered before services on Sunday morning. The judge's main argument was that "much vice is due to lack of standards, not to infraction of individual standards."[55] The judge traced this to faulty education, which imparted general knowledge "but failed to mold character and teach the rules of life."[56]

This issue's last page informs the reader that the Foundation's baseball team captured the title in the University church league, with the University Intramural Athletic Department awarding

---

53. Ibid.

54. *The Hillel News*, Volume II, Number XIII, May 24, 1928.

55. Ibid.

56. Ibid.

twelve medals to the team's members for this feat. In an article entitled "Committees Conclude Year of Successful Achievement," we get a comprehensive summary of what the Foundation's nine committees had attained during the school year. Perhaps the most important innovation was that the Athletics Committee introduced women's athletics to the community of Jewish students on campus. Hillel organized women's teams in basketball, baseball, and golf. On the academic-intellectual side of things, the Education Committee's achievements could not have been more impressive. Lectures on many aspects of Jewish history and religion appeared prolifically, as did discussion groups on many topics led by the Foundation's director, Rabbi Fink. Prominent faculty members spoke at Hillel, as did the University's president, Clarence Cook Little. Dr. Carl Weller of the University of Michigan's medical school delivered a lecture for men on sex, and national figures such as Abba Hillel Silver came to Ann Arbor to speak to Hillel. In addition, "women's luncheons were instituted for the first time during the second semester."[57]

But far and away the most important piece in this issue of *The Hillel News* was its editorial called "Parting." In it, the paper bade farewell to Irving Yorish, the Michigan Hillel Foundation's first president, and welcomed Richard Meyer as its second. But the editorial also offered some interesting words reflecting on the Foundation's two-year existence on the University of Michigan's campus: "Two years of history will have been written in the records of the Michigan Hillel Foundation within the next few weeks. Two years have been spent in successfully establishing the Foundation as an essential institution for Michigan Jewish students. It has sold itself to the student body in a dignified manner solely on its merits. 'Knock down and drag in' methods have not been used, nor have they been found necessary. The service offered has been sufficient to draw an increasing number of those who might benefit."[58] There

57. Ibid.
58. Ibid.

is no question that Hillel's start on the Michigan campus was auspicious if not spectacular. It clearly had gained a solid foothold in Jewish life on campus, even if its reach could not yet rival that of the fraternities' and sororities'.

At the beginning of the 1928–29 academic year, Hillel sought to convince incoming freshmen that it offered plenty of attractive activities as well as a welcome environment for Jewish students of all stripes. The first issue of *The Hillel News* of that year is a specially designated "Freshman Issue," which begins with a welcome notice from Rabbi Fink that underlined the organization's big-tent aspirations: "The Hillel Foundation is neither Orthodox, Conservative, or Reform in nature. It is merely Jewish, seeking to serve Jewish students of every shade of belief or non-belief. Aiming to weld into one harmonious community the various so-called 'types' and groups, no superficial line is drawn."[59] Throughout the freshman issue, the note that Hillel welcomes all Jews and offers the incoming freshman the promise of belonging to a cohesive, and growing, community is repeatedly sounded: "The Jewish students of the University are eager to know you," Fink enthuses, "and are anxious to make you feel 'at home' on the campus, to give you that comfortable sense of 'belonging.'"[60]

If belonging to the Hillel community was not in and of itself attractive enough, the freshman issue also provides a "catalogue" of activities that Hillel offered the newly arrived freshman, including athletics; debating; dramatics; classes; the literary guild; Avukah, the campus Zionist organization; and Sunday school and Sunday services, among others.[61] If neither the promise of community nor the social activities proved convincing, Hillel provided the enticing prospect of enjoying the company of big-name attractions. The freshman issue announced that it was sponsoring a welcome event for freshman on Sunday, September 23, and that "attempts are

59. *The Hillel News*, Volume II, Number XIV, September 24, 1928.
60. Ibid.
61. Ibid.

being made to secure 'Benny' Friedman, the former all-American quarterback, to give the feature address in the morning."[62]

The mention of Benny Friedman, however, is the only reference to the football great and recent graduate and the only other mention of athletics outside of the aforementioned "catalogue." In the remainder of the issue, Hillel bases its appeal to freshman on its identity as a center for intellectual and social activity. The paper touts that "Hillel Speaking Schedule Shows Imposing Array." The lecture program of the fall 1928 semester advertises, among other things, the return visit of Lewis Browne, an author of a biography on Heinrich Heine, the famous German poet and writer of Jewish origin whose fiction "achieved wide appeal because of their popularization of religious themes."[63] Moreover, a two-column article on the last page highlighted Hillel's already large and growing library that comprised "the cream of Jewish publications" and featured some of the best modern Jewish writers, including Israel Zangwill, Louis Golding, Elias Tobenkin, Frederick Brown, and Grete Stern. Nonetheless, "the subject matter of the collection is far from being limited to Jewish affairs. Sociological problems of interest to youth of all creeds are treated in many volumes."[64] Both the dramatic and the debating teams were being renewed "to a greater extent than last year, it is hoped."[65] Fink himself intended to organize more discussion groups that, in the previous year, had "selected problems of the day, such as intermarriage and the assimilation, for discussion."[66] Fink also intended to offer courses in biblical history and study and a possible third course in "contemporary Jewish affairs."

Thus the fall 1928 freshman issue not only provides a helpful snapshot at the extent to which Hillel had developed as an

62. Ibid.
63. Ibid.
64. Ibid.
65. Ibid.
66. Ibid.

organization in a mere two years but also shows the kind of identity that the Foundation sought to construct for itself. As the issue's editorial indicates, this identity could contain contradictions, or at least, internal tensions. The editorial stresses Hillel's easygoing social culture: "Informality is the order of the day at Hillel Foundation, at all times and under all circumstances. Whether he wishes to play bridge, make use of the library, dance, study or read, the student is welcome at any time the building is open, generally a good share of the daily twenty-four hours."[67] Yet the editorial only features those activities that had an academic or religious purpose: "There are opportunities for practically every student to enter upon a field in which he or she is especially interested. Discussion groups and classes in Jewish history are conducted weekly. Friday night, Saturday and Sunday services are held weekly, and speakers of prominence are secured to deliver addresses at them occasionally. Open Forums are led by men and women of literary and religious note." Indeed, it was only after this list that the editorial finally noted that "regular social events are held. Production of plays and the staging of recitals occupy a prominent place in the program."[68] On the one hand, Hillel held out the promise of fun, socializing, and community, yet on the other hand, it also conveyed a sense of high cultural and intellectual aspirations that could seem at odds with the enticements of bridge-playing, dancing, or meeting stars like Benny Friedman.

Certainly both aspects of the Michigan chapter were evident in the next available issue of *The Hillel News*, that of November 8, 1928. The headline boldly announces a "mixer" for the upcoming Saturday featuring the entertainment of Mike Falk, "well known on this campus as a jazz artist, and connected with Seymour Simons of Detroit orchestra fame."[69] Even so, the announcement is interesting for what it reveals about the social lives of Jewish

67. Ibid.
68. Ibid.
69. *The Hillel News*, Volume III, Number III, November 8, 1928.

women on the campus: "The [Social] Committee is carrying out a plan," it announced, "to provide an escort for every Jewish girl on the campus. Escorts are not to act as partners after they reach the ballroom, however, for with the beginning of the dance it will become a strictly 'stag' affair."[70] The women were seen to require chaperones, which was not unusual in this era but nonetheless reinforced their social subordination to the men. It was also clear that the event was not designed for "pairing up," as it was a strictly a "stag" affair.

Almost the entire remainder of the November 8, 1928, issue is taken up with intellectual and cultural activities. Lewis Browne, a popularizer of Jewish history with several books to his credit, is announced as scheduled to speak on Wednesday, November 21, this being his third campus visit under the auspices of Hillel: "Many will remember his first book, 'Stranger Than Fiction,' in which he portrayed the history of the Jewish race in such an interesting and inimitable style that he has revolutionized the idea of writing history. It is to Mr. Browne, probably more than any other man, that the present day popularity and interest in Jewish events is due."[71] Such hyperbole was obviously designed to attract interest in the event, but the fact that Hillel hosted Browne three times in two years suggests a desire on the organization's part to attract students to its cultural initiatives by featuring a popular rather than an academic historian.

At the very least, this issue well shows that Hillel's initiatives were in high gear by the second month of the fall term. Hillel's Open Forum was featuring a talk by the University of Michigan history professor A. L. Cross, "and a large crowd of students is expected to take advantage to hear him."[72] A sizeable audience had already turned out for the previous forum featuring Professor Robert Wenley of the Philosophy Department, who compared

70. Ibid.

71. Ibid.

72. Ibid.

American and British educational systems. Sunday services had recently hosted Fred Bernstein, a Chicago attorney, Michigan alumnus, and chair of the Advisory Committee on the Hillel Foundations of B'nai B'rith. The committee "has direct charge of the Michigan, Wisconsin, and Illinois Hillel Foundations. Bernstein spoke on the aims and ideas of the B'nai B'rith with the purpose of acquainting his audience with the organization which is sponsoring Hillel."[73]

Forging a sense of Hillel's identity was clearly important to this still-new Michigan chapter. The November 8, 1928, issue of *The Hillel News* contains a second-page entry on "What's What in Hillel" that describes the founding chapter at Illinois, which "blazed the trail which has since been followed in four other universities."[74] Unlike Michigan, the Illinois chapter did not at this time have its own individual house but instead conducted its activities "on the entire second floor of a two-story building." One of the leading lights of the Illinois chapter was, of course, its director, Abram L. Sachar, while Dr. Moses Jung offered instruction in religious education, and Morris Sostin was its associate director and a recent Illinois graduate: "As in Ann Arbor, the Illinois group works in cooperation with the local Jewish community, and the Foundation holds its religious services in the inviting temple of the local congregation."[75] *The Hillel News* promised to feature foundations on other campuses in subsequent issues, promoting a sense of collective identity among the four different Hillel chapters that existed in the country at the time—all, as we know, centered in the Midwest.[76]

In another article of this issue of the paper, chapter pride took precedent. An article that announces the upcoming formation of the next Hillel debating society proudly proclaims that "the men

73. Ibid.
74. Ibid.
75. Ibid.
76. To recapitulate, they were at the University of Illinois, the University of Wisconsin, Ohio State University, and the University of Michigan.

chosen this year will have a high mark to shoot at, to approximate the success of the two previous Foundation teams. In the first of Hillel's establishment at Michigan a trio including Ephraim Gomberg, Philip Krasner, and Emanuel Harris won a unanimous victory over the orators of the Illinois foundation," while "last year Victor Rose and Samuel Kellman represented the Foundation, defeating the Menorah Society of Washington University at St. Louis."[77]

Avukah, the campus Zionist organization, also sought to expand its activities. Members "decided to broaden the scope of the organization with the formation of an Avukah study group . . . Plans for the study group include a program of study on Jewish life since the emancipation period, leading up to political Zionism."[78] As much as *The Hillel News* promoted all these initiatives as part and parcel of the Foundation's growth, other pieces here show how Jewish students were struggling to adapt to University life and to prejudice as well. The editorial discusses the challenge that many students who followed Jewish dietary laws faced on campus, since they "must be served through some medium other than the ordinary campus eating house. And they are being served—to a very limited extent. But the question arises as to whether the facilities being provided in this direction are adequate and satisfactory."[79] The editorial was likely provoked by a petition brought before the Hillel Student Council that asked for the establishment of a Jewish eating house that would use the requisite dietary laws of kashrut.[80] Interestingly, however, the editorial proffers no opinion as to whether such a house should be established, soliciting the advice of the readership: "The answer must come from the Jewish student body itself, from the people intimately concerned in the situation."[81]

77. *The Hillel News*, Volume III, Number III, November 8, 1928.

78. Ibid.

79. Ibid.

80. Ibid.

81. Ibid.

This seems strange given Hillel's consistent and active promotion of Jewish culture and Jewish religious practices on campus. Perhaps there was a concern that a specifically Jewish eating house would be too divergent from many Jews' desire to assimilate on campus; by pointing out the dietary specificities of the Jewish faith, they would risk appearing as "the Other." Serving kosher food in a separate facility might have appeared "too Jewish" to some in the Hillel leadership—perhaps a tad too "in your face" for that era—quite possibly for good reason, given the level of anti-Semitism in southeastern Michigan and American society as a whole at this time.

Although the editorial doesn't specifically mention this matter, another article on page 2, "The Spectator Comments," takes a strongly assimilationist line by denying that there was a specific Jewish voting bloc in the presidential elections of the United States, which occurred that week: "The Jews in this country have pitched their tents in every political camp; and sailed under every political banner."[82] Even though it is not directly spelled out in this issue of *The Hillel News*, the vexed choice between assimilation and cultural specificity—or negotiating some path between them—that beset all of Hillel's existence is clearly implicit. Hillel was growing and devising new and exciting initiatives for its members, but did this help integrate them into the campus community or just reinforce a sense of separateness?

We jump ahead a month to the next extant issue of *The Hillel News*, that of December 6, 1928. On the very front page, we witness the complex terrain that the Foundation was navigating. On the one hand, Hillel was attempting to foster a specifically Jewish community that addressed its members' concerns while also developing their appreciation for their heritage and culture. On the other hand, it was seeking to demonstrate how it was becoming an integral part of the broader Michigan campus community. This issue's main front-page article announces, "National Figures to Speak at

---

82. *The Hillel News*, Volume III, Number V, December 6, 1928.

Sunday Student Services." Hillel had lined up a slate of prominent rabbis from the Eastern United States and Canada during the academic year, the first of which—Rabbi Joseph Fink from the Buffalo, New York, congregation—was going to speak on "Problems Facing American Jewry."[83] Two columns over, *The Hillel News* reports that the Dramatics Committee (which was later to develop into the famed Hillel Players) had selected two one-act plays for a December 19 performance: "The first," the article reports, was "'Greek,' by Edward Heyman . . . a story of fraternities and sororities. It portrays the fraternity life on a campus, showing the complexities, trials and tribulations of fraternity men in a college situation."[84]

Indeed, the December 6, 1928, issue consistently straddles items of specifically Jewish interest and those that demonstrate the Foundation's wider cultural horizons. On pages 1 and 3, *The Hillel News* reports on a performance of Jewish folk songs and dramatic scenes from *The Dybbuk* and *The Deluge* by the Moscow Habimah Players as an occasion to introduce its readership to the term and institution *Habimah*, which surely was not known to most American Jews at the time.[85] Almost as a counterbalance, *The Hillel News* also featured a review of the opera *Rainbow's End*, which appears to be more of a comic and music revue than an opera that debuted at the Whitney and was passing through Ann Arbor to places farther west.[86]

Yet what both sets of activities underscore is the broadening of Hillel's range of programing and the widening of its aspirations.

---

83. Ibid.

84. The second play is only described as a "sophisticated story centering around a plot dominated by clever repartee." See ibid.

85. Ibid. The Habimah was a Hebrew-speaking Moscow-based theater troupe founded in 1907 that was forced underground as a result of Tsarist persecutions in 1913. Upon hearing of their travails, the famous Russian actor Constantin Stanislavsky took the group under his protection, which saved it. Subsequently the troupe resurfaced under the Soviet Union before becoming internationally famous in the 1920s.

86. Ibid.

This issue's editorial expressed both pride and confidence in the growth of the Foundation's activities: "The semester," it says, "has not yet come to its happy end, but already we can point with pride to a long list of unusually worthwhile programs which have been placed before the students. Nothing mediocre has been attempted. Every man appearing has been a leader in his field . . . And even at the risk of appearing over-enthusiastic we must note still further the events scheduled for the future, which include the appearance of Louis Untermeyer, American poet, and many well known leaders in the religious world."[87] Moreover, the editorial even suggests that Hillel's programming of high-cultural events was appealing to the broader student body, not just to Hillel's membership: "There is a definite place for programs of this high type on the campus, for who knows but that these programs may be the reflection of an increased interest on the part of the student body in something finer than the weekly, or nightly movie."[88]

Along with its evident pride in the chapter's growing list of initiatives, this editorial, then, expresses a hope that Hillel's lectures and activities—though tailored to its Jewish members—could have a broader appeal. This squaring of the circle, which suggested that Jewish culture and faith had a role to play outside of the Jewish community, was also the subject of a talk given by Dr. Julian Morganstern of the Hebrew Union College in Cincinnati. Although Jews had been forced into the ghettos of Europe since the fifteenth century, Morganstern argued that "modern Judaism today has a wonderful opportunity to regain a lost opportunity by becoming a leader in the coming religious revival which is facing the world."[89] Morganstern claimed that the Protestant Reformation was "the direct result of the zealous work of the Jews in keeping the spark of knowledge alive."[90] Consequently,

87. Ibid.
88. Ibid.
89. Ibid.
90. Ibid.

Jews had a pivotal role to play in the forthcoming religious revival, as Morganstern saw it, given their intellectual and religious stewardship and the fact that, indeed, "the Jew has not only caught up religiously with the Christian, but is ahead of the Christian fifty years. He pointed to the Reformed Jewish religion as proof of this."[91]

Another Hillel-sponsored speaker, the author Maurice Samuel, spoke about the possibility of ending racial prejudice.[92] What the articles in this issue reveal—as they oscillate between the editorial report on Hillel's activities and the belief (or hope) that these initiatives, and Jewish culture more broadly, had a more universal appeal or import—is both a growing confidence in the organization and an anxiety, somewhat submerged here, about its place within the larger university community. The debate between assimilation and cultural assertiveness will sharpen many years later.

Unfortunately, we do not have any extant issues of *The Hillel News* until March 14, 1929. Yet this issue practically picks up where the last one left off. Indeed, Maurice Samuel, the Zionist author whose talk was featured in the November 6, 1928, issue, here appends "a letter to the Jewish college student" advocating for the creation of a Jewish state in Palestine.[93] What is remarkable about his appeal, however, is his reference to the impact of Jewish thought on non-Jews: "Non-Jews are fascinated (and sometimes irritated) by the enduring quality of the Jewish mind. They are aware that the Jews have produced greatly, there has been a search for the absolute."[94] Samuel invokes the storied names of Albert Einstein and Henri Bergson as seekers of the absolute and states that the building of the Jewish community in Palestine represents the embodiment of this ontological ideal in concrete form. Again,

91. Ibid.
92. Ibid.
93. *The Hillel News*, Volume III, Number IX, March 14, 1929.
94. Ibid.

Samuel seeks to situate a specifically Jewish (in this case, Zionist) program within a broader philosophical stream: "The Jewish will turn Palestine into an idea."[95] This issue of *The Hillel News* also reports on that week's guest speaker at the Sunday services, Rabbi Samuel Goldenson of the Rodef Shalom congregation in Pittsburgh. Goldenson does the opposite of Samuel: whereas Samuel posits the broader philosophical importance of Jewish thought, Goldenson seeks to ground an understanding of Western liberalism partly on the work of the Hebrew prophets: "He believes in religion as a social force," the article reports, "his outlook being based essentially on the doctrines of social justice voiced by the ancient Hebrew prophets—a point of view colored, however, by a profound knowledge of the history of Western though from the time of the earliest Greek philosophers."[96]

In both of these articles, we see the interplay between matters of largely Jewish concern (Jewish history, Zionism) and allusions to their influence among Gentiles and to broader strands of Western thought. Jews could, and should, pursue matters relevant to their faith without necessarily ghettoizing themselves. Indeed, in this spring 1929 issue, *The Hillel News* shows further how the Foundation was becoming more integrated within the campus community while, at the same time, promoting Jewish-centered cultural activities and celebrating their coreligionists' academic success. Hillel sponsored its first booth at the annual Penny Carnival sponsored by the Women's Athletic Association.[97] The Hillel Social Committee began to host open houses this year and, as another article reports, "Thursday afternoon found even a larger number of people visiting the Foundation, and the enthusiasm shown at these initial afternoon open houses indicates that they are to become the most popular function on the Hillel social program."[98]

95. Ibid.
96. Ibid.
97. Ibid.
98. Ibid.

Even more impressively, the Hillel Foundation announces in another article that it was working with the University's Intramural Department to initiate a new sports program where any athletically inclined student could enter a tournament of her or his choice: "Every student will have a wide field to choose from, with tournaments being held in basketball, baseball, handball, swimming, water polo, tennis, golf, foul shooting, bowling and horseshoes."[99] Hillel was taking an especially active role in creating a baseball intramural league: "Independent and fraternity teams may enter the baseball tournament by getting in touch with the Foundation immediately. This league should draw at least thirteen Jewish fraternities, since that number have already signed up for the University intramural league."[100]

As much as the Michigan chapter of Hillel sought to present itself as a valued member of the University community, it also championed its own membership and sought to develop ties with non-Hillel Jews. It boasted about the number of Jewish players on the University's baseball team: "With baseball beginning to draw the attention of the campus, Gerson Reichman, Alfred Freeman, Charles Moyer, and Louis Weintraub are found among the strong-arm men fighting for places on the team. Reichman and Weintraub are practically sure of holding down the catching and third base positions regularly this season, while the other two are making good bids for their posts."[101] The paper championed Jewish intellectual prowess as well: "The recent publication of the list of all 'A' students for last semester shows that eight Jewish students in the Literary School succeeded in maintaining their records for a whole term pure and unblemished by any common 'B,' 'C,' 'D,' or 'E,' by the use of the midnight oil or other forms of oil which have been known to work."[102] But Jewish accomplishments

99. Ibid.

100. Ibid.

101. Ibid.

102. Ibid.

were not limited to those on the Michigan campus: *The Hillel News*'s column "The Spectator Comments" also highlighted note-worthy achievements like the fact that "American Jews spent more than 235 million in 1928 for both sectarian and non-sectarian phi-lanthropy" and that William Fox's acquisition of Loews brought four hundred fifty movie theaters under his control.[103] Finally, this issue promoted outreach efforts to encourage Hillel mem-bers to meet people in the greater Detroit Jewish community. The editorial encouraged members to participate in that year's annual Student's Day, "a sincere effort to foster a bond of inter-est and understanding between Jewish students at the University of Michigan and other educational institutions of the state, and members of the Detroit [Temple Beth El] congregation."[104]

Occasionally, the different initiatives sponsored by Hillel could lead to some amusing contradictions. Thus on the front page of the March 28, 1929, issue of *The Hillel News*, we find a summary of Rabbi Goldenson's talk on liberalism, which had been mentioned in the previous issue. During the talk, the rabbi denounced jazz, seeing in it "an overemphasis of that kind of liberal thinking which is at bottom cheap and false . . . It is a tendency for unnatural accel-eration. Syncopation, another quality of jazz, and all those things which it has influence in the life of today, is 'stunt,' the desire to do the unusual, the bizarre, the irrational."[105] Right above the rabbi's comments, *The Hillel News* placed an announcement for an informal gig featuring Mike Falk's local jazz combo, promising that "for four hours the crowd will 'shake the blues away' to the tuneful tooting of [Falk's] 'Gloom Chasers.'"[106]

Indeed, whereas the fall 1928 issues of *The Hillel News* focused largely on intellectual and religious events and had very little to

---

103. Ibid.

104. The Student's Day program is discussed on the front-page article, "Student's Day, Annual Event, Set For Sunday," in ibid.

105. *The Hillel News*, Volume III, Number X, March 28, 1929.

106. Ibid.

do with sports or entertainment, by March 1929, the coverage was more evenly balanced. Although the paper dutifully reported on upcoming speakers, such as noted scientist Dr. Raphael Isaac's lecture on similarities between modern and ancient Jewish thought for the Open Forum series, it is striking how much space had been ceded to sports and social activities in this late March 1929 issue. Not only was the spring mixer accorded a major headline, but throughout this issue of the paper, we get a stronger sense of Hillel's social life than ever before. In the "On the Campus" column, for example, which had only been introduced that spring, we learn that "a number of Jewish students have played prominent parts in campus dramatics during the past few weeks" in a series of student-authored plays.[107] Pierce Rosenberg was elected to the campus dramatic society, known as Mimes, while Robert Gessner was one of only two seniors chosen to be a representative to the Northern Oratorical League contest in April. Jews were making their mark in athletics as well. Samuel Hart, for example, was the only member of the Michigan hockey team to make the All-Conference hockey team, while several Jewish swimmers were awarded letters.

The Foundation's Social Committee was also making plans to set up a checker league so that "any Jewish student on the campus is eligible to pit his gray matter in this tournament against others in the learned art of jumping pieces from one end of a checkerboard to another."[108] Meanwhile, "spring is in the air," which meant that "bats are appearing on the streets, and Hillel is beginning the organization of a number of baseball leagues in line with its recently adopted athletic program."[109] And for the third year in a row, members of the Phi Delta Epsilon fraternity won Hillel's annual bridge tournament.[110]

107. This and the remainder of the paragraph come from "On the Campus," in ibid.
108. Ibid.
109. Ibid.
110. Ibid.

Yet while the social activities were absorbing more print space in this issue, the editorial itself focused on intellectual matters. The Foundation had, in its first year, produced a literary supplement that had lasted only one issue. The supplement contained "interesting, and perhaps even literary drippings from the pens of Jewish student" and had "aroused some comment and might have been termed an auspicious beginning."[111] Yet it quickly faded into obscurity. Now plans were afoot to resurrect the ghost and "make it a living magazine" whose purpose would be "to provide an opportunity for literary expression for Jewish students on the campus."[112] Indeed, the editorial confidently predicted that there was a wealth of Jewish literary talent lying dormant, just waiting for something like the supplement to provide it with a means of expression: "There is a wealth of literary talent among the Jewish students at Michigan which might thrive if it could only be brought out of hiding." It asserted: "And apparently the difficulty with the Supplement up to the present has been merely a combination of faulty methods of gathering the material and inertia on the part of the campus literary lights."[113]

Despite the persistent upbeat rhetoric, *The Hillel News* occasionally opened a window onto some of the downsides of Jewish students' lives in Ann Arbor. Such was the case in the editorial for the April 28, 1929, issue, which highlighted the perilous living conditions of Jewish students during the summer: "Anyone who has attended a summer school session at Michigan or lived in Ann Arbor during that period," the editorial recounts, "is bound to realize that the Jewish summer school student's life outside of class hours has something vital lacking. The picture of over a hundred Jewish students stranded for two months in a small town, with no way of meeting each other, no way of getting acquainted, no worthwhile way of spending their spare time, no chance of

111. Ibid.
112. Ibid.
113. Ibid.

satisfying any religious wants they may have, should stir up some serious thought."[114] The editorial argues that Hillel should remain open during the summertime to accommodate these stranded Jewish students. Although one could say that the editorial might overstate the problem to better argue its point, it does bring out how lonely many Jewish students felt on campus without the supporting organizations to give them a sense of integration within a broader community. Moreover, Hillel's national/international news column, "The Spectator Comments," reminded readers of the sobering reality of anti-Semitism that many Jews faced. Two hundred Jewish students at Montpelier University walked out on a visiting lecturer when his anti-Semitic activities were made known to the campus. Yet, hearteningly, the item also mentions that "non-Jewish fellow students filed out of the hall when they learned the reason for the Jewish students' departure."[115] Elizabeth Simon, a Hungarian Jewish girl chosen as "Miss Europe" to represent Europe at the Galveston, Texas, International Beauty Contest, withdrew due to the "disagreeable Anti-Semitic outbursts to which she had been subjected since she was chosen."[116] More troublingly, an edict in Yemen required all Jewish children to embrace Islam on pain of death; this conversion policy "is being pursued with almost incredible vigor and cruelty."[117] Although these isolated items in and of themselves should not be taken as indicators of a rising tide of anti-Semitism, they did remind readers of *The Hillel News* that, beyond the leafy confines of Ann Arbor, prejudice and bigotry still abounded.

Otherwise, the April 28, 1929, issue follows in the same vein as its predecessor, striking a balance between the intellectual and high-cultural activities organized or sponsored by the Foundation, with more causal pieces reflecting Jewish students' social

114. *The Hillel News*, Volume III, Number XI, April 28, 1929.

115. Ibid.

116. Ibid.

117. Ibid.

lives and their accomplishments on campus. This issue of the paper introduced a new column, "Off the Campus," to serve as a companion for its "On the Campus" feature. Whereas "On the Campus" focused on noteworthy items involving Michigan's Hillel members, "Off the Campus" reported on issues from all the different sister Hillel chapters. The purpose was not only to keep readers informed but also to foster a shared sense of identity and community across the different foundations. Almost all the news items were social, rather than religious or intellectual, in nature. Thus we learn that at the Illinois foundation, "Vaudeville is being introduced as a part of Hillel entertainment programs . . . Several hundred students were entertained by a series of singing, dancing and comedy skits, which was sponsored by the Hillel Players."[118] Wisconsin's Hillel also had its own Hillel Players, which was "one of the most active organizations in the Wisconsin Foundation."[119] By this point, Michigan Hillel had organized its own Hillel Players, whose members were preparing for an early May production at the Masonic Auditorium at Fourth and William in Ann Arbor.[120]

The April 28, 1929, issue of *The Hillel News* also listed many accomplishments of the Michigan Hillel's women members. Dorothy Touff was celebrated for her election to "one of the highest offices held by women on the campus" as president of the Women's Athletic Association, while thirteen freshman women "received recognition for their ability to pull down A's and B's by election to Alpha Lambda Delta."[121] We also learn from another article that Hillel's open houses continue to be warmly received: "Weekly, more students are learning of this delightful way to kill an afternoon and are dropping in for a cup of tea, a game of bridge, a chat, or what have you."[122] Meanwhile, Hillel's first

118. Ibid.
119. Ibid.
120. Ibid.
121. Ibid.
122. Ibid.

handball tournament was "added for the first time to the list of sports sponsored by the Foundation."[123] The Handball League "has drawn considerable attention and attracted a formidable list of entries."[124] The only real sour note in this scherzo of upbeat social news was the failure of Michigan Hillel to beat the Wisconsin foundation in the annual debating contest.[125]

As Michigan Hillel neared the end of its third year, the articles in *The Hillel News* confidently championed the chapter's growth and recognized that social life (sports, fraternities, clubs) played as much a role in this growth—and how the chapter defined itself—as its religious and cultural programming. Thus the April 28, 1929, issue could, on the same page, describe an upcoming Open Forum talk by Rabbi Solomon Freehof on the question of liberalism in religious faith and note a forthcoming banquet to entertain Hillel workers, where "extreme informality will mark the entire event, with any seriousness to be frowned upon with the same disfavor as an unwelcome mother-in-law."[126] Wisecracking and merrymaking could lie adjacent to sober philosophical and political topics. But perhaps the best indication of the chapter's aspirations was a little blurb published halfway down the front page, "Hillel Questionnaire on Jewish Background Sent Out to Students." The questionnaire was transmitted seemingly on the orders of the University of Michigan Hillel's director, Rabbi Fink, to find out "what the student really believes and to discover, if possible, whether there is any correlation between present beliefs and past training."[127] In essence, Hillel was now seeking to move beyond simply appealing to the whole of the Jewish student body on Michigan's campus and was actively interested—though tentatively, it must be said—in collecting data on Jewish students as

123. Ibid.
124. Ibid.
125. Ibid.
126. Ibid.
127. Ibid.

well; in other words, it was trying to learn important facts about Hillel's clientele.

The questionnaire did arouse "considerable controversy" according to an article in the May 1, 1929, issue of *The Hillel News*.[128] And although the article reports a high level of compliance, it also took pains to limit the importance of the survey: "The study is being made merely to learn the true religious status of students in a large, typical mid-western university," it argues, while Rabbi Fink avers that it "'is a scientific sociological survey to make whatever correlation that may be found between the religious background of the student and the present state of his interests.'"[129] Whatever the intended purposes of the survey were—and we have not located any surviving material beyond these articles about them—its ambition to cover the University of Michigan's entire Jewish student population of the time was clearly ambitious. That this Hillel-initiated study attained a 75 percent participation rate from the Jewish fraternities and sororities at Michigan underscores Michigan Hillel's growing confidence in itself as an organization that claimed (and hoped) to represent *all* Jews on campus. These and similar ambitions were articulated at the Inter-Hillel Convention in Chicago in mid-April.[130] Among the plans for the 1929–30 academic year were the establishment of a national Hillel magazine (a quarterly) that was to feature student contributions, an inter-Hillel oratorical contest, and a national Hillel society comprising the presidents of the different campus foundations. Once again, news items sought to show both how Jews were becoming more integrated into campus life and how they involved themselves in outreach activities. "The Spectator Comments" column reported that an intercollegiate goodwill conference was held at Rollins College in Florida and that "more than 300 students and faculty members of Southern colleges including

128. *The Hillel News*, Volume III, Number XII, May 1, 1929.
129. Ibid.
130. Ibid.

Catholics, Protestants, and Jews met to discuss means of bringing about better relationships and understanding between members of the several religious faiths."[131] One speaker was Rabbi Solomon Goldman, a member of the national Hillel Foundation Commission.[132] Michigan Hillel's director, Rabbi Fink—himself engaged in his own outreach activities—was presiding over a Passover Seder for Jewish prisoners at Jackson Prison, about thirty-five miles west of Ann Arbor.[133] This issue of *The Hillel News* also duly reported the doings in Michigan Hillel's sister foundations but substituted its own "On the Campus" column this time for an article on Passover and its historical background.

Yet the main subject of the final two issues of *The Hillel News* for the 1928–29 academic year was the election for president of the Michigan Hillel Foundation. Three candidates were on the ballot: Philip Stern, a junior in the Literary College and chairman of the Educational Committee; Byron Novitsky, a sophomore in the Literary College and the Foundation's publicity manager; and Morris Zwerdling, a graduating senior from the Literary College who was entering Michigan's Law School in the fall.[134] Not only was Zwerdling the most senior of the candidates; he was also the scion of a prominent Jewish family in Ann Arbor. His father,

131. Ibid.

132. Ibid.

133. Ibid.

134. Ibid. Novitsky would be elected Hillel president for the 1930–31 academic year and would eventually become a prominent attorney in Fort Wayne, Indiana. He was also president of the Fort Wayne Parks Board and president of the St. Joseph Medical Center. In 1966, he was named Jewish Man of the Year in Indiana by the National Post and Jewish Opinion. On Novitsky, see his obituary in the *Indiana Jewish Post and Opinion* 54, no. 22 (February 24, 1988), p. 5. On his becoming the 1966 Jewish Man of the Year, see "Byron Novitsky Selected Jewish Man of the Year," *National Jewish Post and Opinion*, September 9, 1966, p. 1, available at file:///Users/ts505050/Downloads/JPOST-1966-09-09_01.pdf. Morris Zwerdling was graduated from the Law School in 1932 and became a Detroit-based lawyer. His death notice is listed in the University of Michigan Law School's *Law Quadrangle Notes* 19, no. 3 (Spring 1975), p. 38, available at file:///Users/ts505050/Downloads/LSF.0014.001.pdf.

Osias Zwerdling (1878–1977), founded a furrier store in the city in 1904 and became a significant patron of Hillel, helping organize the funding for their buildings well into the post–World War II era.[135] As we mention later in our book with a bit more detail, Osias Zwerdling also became the founder of the Beth Israel Congregation, Ann Arbor's oldest organized community of worship, which celebrated its centennial in 2016. *The Hillel News*'s editorial reminded its readers that while B'nai B'rith had provided a Hillel with a building and a director, "it is up to the student body to provide its own leader, and that leader can make or break the show . . . Hillel's president is its vital spark. As part of the student body he is the Foundation leader closest to the group."[136] Given his senior status and his family's prominence in the Ann Arbor Jewish community, it was perhaps unsurprising that Zwerdling was elected president for the 1929–30 academic year.[137] Along with congratulating the outgoing president, Richard Meyer, *The Hillel News*'s editorial for the week of May 16, 1929, bestowed its fullest confidence on Zwerdling: "That that confidence was not misplaced, he will undoubtedly prove next year."[138]

As the 1928–29 academic year started to wind down, the final issues of *The Hillel News* revealed an organization that had great expectations for future growth and was increasingly adept at staging numerous activities that sought both to foster a strong sense of Jewish identity and community *and* to integrate within the broader Michigan campus culture. The May 1, 1929, issue confidently advised readers to "Expect Packed House for Hillel Presentation of 'Kempy' at Masonic Temple on Wednesday." Using an unabashed amount of promotional hyperbole, this article

135. On Osias Zwerdling, see Helen Aminoff, "The First Jews of Ann Arbor," *Michigan Jewish History* 23, no. 1 (January 1983). See also *Encyclopedia Judaica Online*, s. v. "Ann Arbor, Michigan," http://www.jewishvirtuallibrary.org/jsource/judaica/ejud _0002_0002_0_01122.html.

136. *The Hillel News*, Volume III, Number XII, May 1, 1929.

137. *The Hillel News*, Volume III, Number XIII, May 16, 1929.

138. Ibid.

describes the Hillel Players' upcoming production thus: "'Kempy' gives promise of making Hillel dramatic history and of setting a new landmark for future productions to point at."[139] Perhaps surprisingly, the subsequent issue of *The Hillel News* gave the production a middling review, praising some of the student actors, calling others disappointing, and concluding with a not especially ringing endorsement: "The [Hillel Players] Committee is to be congratulated for the smoothness of the performance and the evident attention to details."[140] The other big development at the end of the 1928–29 year was Avukah, which sponsored a symposium in early May and hosted a national Avukah meeting in Ann Arbor in late June. The May symposium sought to crystallize student opinions on the topic of "Judaism as I See It" in an open forum led by "five prominent Jewish students on the campus," including Richard Meyer, the outgoing Hillel president.[141]

As the following issue of *The Hillel News* recounts, much of the discussion at the May symposium was on how Jewish students saw Judaism differently and the role it played in the construction of their identity.[142] For Meyer, his Jewish identity was simply a fact of his existence: "'There is nothing intrinsic or inherent in Judaism. I am a Jew because my environment has been Jewish, and because the Gentiles won't let me be a Gentile. I don't think there is anything in Judaism which would make me be a Jew if I were not brought up as one.'"[143] For David Cohen, vice president of Michigan Avukah, Judaism was both religious and nationalist: "I began to see that the Orthodox faith was the greatest national-

---

139. *The Hillel News*, Volume III, Number XII, May 1, 1929.

140. *The Hillel News*, Volume III, Number XIII, May 16, 1929. Werner does praise incoming Hillel president Morris Zwerdling's performance as "Pa," writing that "he made the most of the many opportunities offered him by his lines. With the exception of a little stiffness, probably due to his stepping into the role on short notice, his work was above criticism."

141. *The Hillel News*, Volume III, Number XII, May 1, 1929.

142. *The Hillel News*, Volume III, Number XIII, May 16, 1929.

143. Ibid.

izing and unifying force for Jews. By professing Orthodoxy I am steadily reminding myself and others that there does exist a Jewish religion, and that there is a national aspect to Judaism."[144] The final speaker, a junior named Isaac Hoffman, connected Jewish mysticism with a profound sense of realism: "Jewish mysticism as expressed by the old Orthodox Hassids in the Talmud and elsewhere is a desire to accept this world and to appreciate it fully—to beautify it."[145]

The national Avukah meeting, scheduled for the end of June, had an even broader agenda. The meeting was to take up three important issues: "(1) the Palestine project to be undertaken by Avukah, (2) a cultural program based on Jewish life in Palestine today, and (3) a Zionist publication program."[146] This article also serves as something of an introduction to Avukah, describing its mission as "the awakening among the American Jewish youth of a Jewish national consciousness which should be filled with intelligent meaning and which should be a vital spiritual experience. It postulates the philosophy that Jewish nationalism is a way of life, which should be intelligently understood and lived wherever Jews are found."[147] Avukah, moreover, "has steadily grown until now there are about twenty more or less active chapters, representing about forty colleges and universities."[148]

Along with the typical congratulatory messages about Jewish students' achievements and Hillel activities in the "On the Campus" and "Off the Campus" columns, articles on the Hillel Players and Avukah are written in a tone of confident anticipation. One clearly gets a sense that these fledging organizations are growing and on the cusp of greater things. Yet the final extant editorial of the 1928–29 academic year returns to the plight of the Jewish

144. Ibid.
145. Ibid.
146. Ibid.
147. Ibid.
148. Ibid.

summer school student to lobby for a year-round Hillel operation.[149] Again, the emphasis is on the Jewish student's loneliness and sense of isolation, the very thing that Hillel strove to avoid at all cost—indeed, the very reason for Hillel's existence and raison d'être. The article describes "more than a hundred Jewish students suddenly set down in a small town to spend eight long weeks living their own lives, with small chance for Jewish companionship of any sort."[150]

Because the social life of summer school students is not taken into consideration by the powers that be, the article paints a dire picture of Jewish students stranded in a Midwestern college town without any access to companionship: "What are those more than one hundred Jewish students to do with it [spare time], with their only meeting places closed to them? Live eight weeks in the joy of their own companionship? Drown their Jewishness in eight weeks of isolation from everything and everyone Jewish?"[151] The implication of this argument is stark: however much Jewish life had developed at the University of Michigan by then, Jews remained a distinct minority of the greater Ann Arbor population. Consequently, the cultivation of Jewish student life in Ann Arbor was strictly a fall through winter affair. By keeping Hillel open over the summer months, the Foundation would become "a center from which the Jewish student's social life, his spare time activity may radiate during the eight weeks he is stranded in Ann Arbor."[152] According to the editorial, the initial proposal generated a considerable degree of interest among a number of students, "and queries have been many as to the possibility of carrying out such a project."[153]

---

149. It was actually a double editorial, the second of which was the congratulatory note to the outgoing and incoming Hillel presidents.

150. *The Hillel News*, Volume III, Number XIII, May 16, 1929.

151. Ibid.

152. Ibid.

153. Ibid.

The 1928–29 academic year, then, witnessed Hillel's growing presence as a member of the broader campus community with the organization of the Hillel Players, with its involvement in intramural sports, and its proliferating social activities. Of course the Foundation furthered its mission to provide a sense of community and intellectual growth to the Jewish students that it served. Behind the often-confident tone of many of these articles, however, there still remained a sense—even if only indirectly stated—that no matter how things were improving for Jews at the University of Michigan, they still were outsiders in the University's community, never mind Ann Arbor's. One can experience this in Hillel president Richard Meyer's comment that Gentiles won't let him be a Gentile, in *The Hillel News*'s advocacy for a year-round Hillel to support the Jewish summer student "stranded" in Ann Arbor, and in the reports of anti-Semitism's national presence (though not at the University of Michigan). Nonetheless, the overall impression produced by *The Hillel News* articles from 1928 to 29 is that this was a happy time for Hillel: its members enjoyed the luxury of being part of a growing organization, new initiatives and activities were constantly introduced to extend students' opportunities for participating in the cultural life of the Foundation, and the roster of invited speakers and guests provided a steady dialogue on Jewish history and Jewish identity for those who wished to partake of them. Like the University of Michigan as a whole, and like campuses nationwide, Hillel in 1928–29 basked in the autumnal glow of the final year before the Depression hit and began to upend many of its members' aspirations—both for Hillel and for their own college careers.

Commencing the academic year 1929–30, the October 3, 1929, issue of *The Hillel News* features articles that address all the areas that we in this study have deemed central to Hillel's identity and existence. Thus, in his welcoming address of the class of 1933, Rabbi Adolph H. Fink, Michigan Hillel's first director, addresses a crucial issue that was to remain central for Hillel throughout our considered time period: students' Jewish identities. He exhorted the incoming freshmen "not to emphasize their Jewish activities to the exclusion of campus activities, nor, on the other hand, to avoid all things Jewish."[154] This balancing act between the Scylla of ghettoization on the one hand and the Charybdis of assimilation on the other has remained perhaps the most salient topic for American Jews to this day. In an editorial entitled "Mixing," the paper makes it clear that Hillel wants Jewish students to experience their Jewishness in a social way among others. In fact, the editorial uses the mixer to highlight the essence of Hillel: "The purpose of the Mixer is the purpose of the Foundation—to bring the Jewish students at Michigan together on a social basis. Of course, the Foundation is more than a social meeting house, but it represents social equality based on the strength of social bonds, a common race and religion."[155] An adjacent editorial entitled "Avukah" (Hebrew word for "torch") explains the goals and purpose of this Zionist organization, using the very term to shed light "amidst the chaos and darkness of American Jewish life." Avukah assures the students that "its idea of Zionism is not, however, limited by Palestinism. It sees in Zionism revitalizing of Jewish life."[156]

The subsequent issue of *The Hillel News* of October 17, 1929, features two very interesting items. The first, entitled "Christian and Jew," is a verbatim reprint from the University of Wisconsin's *Hillel Review*. The text is a review of a "Symposium for Better Understanding" entitled *Christian and Jew* and edited by Isaac Landman.[157] We learn that "most of the Christian writers seem quite conscious of the fact that most of the readers will be Jewish. Many of them, therefore, seem to be afraid of expressing themselves freely. Thus, many limit their essays to abstract discussions of liberty, tolerance, inter-dependence of human beings, and the forces that are drawing human beings together. Many of the Jewish writers rehash the

154. *The Hillel News*, Volume IV, Number II, October 3, 1929.
155. Ibid.
156. Ibid.
157. *The Hillel News*, Volume IV, Number IV, October 17, 1929.

causes of anti-Semitism. Here are some of the more outstanding ideas presented in the symposium. John Erskine seems to think that anti-Semitism is negligible in the schools and colleges. As a former professor at Columbia University, he might be expected to know better. Columbia has been called the home of the 'intellectual pogrom' . . . Elmer Davis opposes what there is of Jewish solidarity. He favors assimilation placing most of the responsibility of making changes upon the Jew. Zona Gale, charming liberal that she is, starts out in an even more charming way by saying 'I am singularly ill-equipped to write on radical prejudice, for I have none and, moreover, I cannot get the point of view of those who have . . . Channing Pollock calls the Jews too self-conscious, too sensitive to criticism. He believes that the results of the prejudice against the Jew in America is negligible.'"[158] This symposium clearly addressed questions that were central to Hillel from its very beginning and were featured throughout the duration of our study and, of course, well beyond into our contemporary period: how much anti-Semitism existed in America, what were its reasons, who were its main carriers, and what, if any, remedies leading at least to its weakening, if not complete eradication, existed? It is not quite clear why the University of Michigan's Hillel found this particular Wisconsin review such an important voice on this topic to reprint it word for word. But we would repeatedly encounter the themes that emerged in this symposium, including the idea that Columbia University's anti-Semitism must have been most pronounced because, as we will later see in our book, a study of how Jewish students viewed their environment at a large number of American universities published in 1939 placed Columbia in the "severely anti-Semitic" category, the study's worst. Thus being known as the home of the "intellectual pogrom" may sound a tad harsh to us today but seems to have had a solid grounding at the time.

The second noteworthy item in this issue of *The Hillel News* appears in "The Spectator Comments" rubric under the title "The

---

158. Ibid.

Future of American Judaism—A Contest."[159] This is an announcement of a writing competition financed by Julius Rosenwald of Chicago in which prizes up to $1,500 could be won for fifteen- to thirty-five-thousand-word essays responding to the following prompt: "For the fullest spiritual development of the individual Jew and the most effective functioning of the Jewish Community in America, how can Jewish life best adjust itself to and influence modern life with respect to (a) beliefs and theories; (b) institutions; the home, the synagogue, the school and other communal agencies; and (c) Jewish education: for the child, the youth and adult?"[160] The deadline was December 31, 1930! On a lighter note, we also read that a "Hillel Mixer Introduces Charming Jewish Co-Eds to Michigan Campus."[161]

In the October 24 issue of *The Hillel News*, we encounter a congratulatory editorial honoring Alfred M. Cohen's seventieth birthday. Attentive readers will recognize him as one of the founders of Hillel. By becoming president of B'nai B'rith in 1925, Cohen had "an opportunity to forward the work of the Hillel Foundation, which his keen mind realized as an organization sorely needed and destined for great success on the American campus."[162] We are also informed that "the current issue of the B'nai B'rith magazine contains the story of the work of the past year at the four oldest Foundations. The article entitled 'Looking Back on Hillel,' is written by the Foundations heads. Dr. Sachar of Illinois, Rabbi Landman of Wisconsin, Rabbi Levinger at Ohio State, and our own Rabbi Fink. The composite story reveals a very successful year in all divisions of Hillel work, religious, dramatic, social, and cultural, with Michigan ably holding its own."[163] And, of course, the Hillel Library welcomed new books by authors such as Walter

159. Ibid.

160. Ibid.

161. Ibid.

162. *The Hillel News*, Volume IV, Number V, October 24, 1929.

163. Ibid.

Lippman, Lion Feuchtwanger, I. L. Peretz, Sholom Alehem, and Max Brod, to name just a few.

*The Hillel News* of November 21, 1929, informs us that Lewis Browne, famous Jewish writer and lecturer "and one of the outstanding of the modern biographers," spoke to Michigan students on the topic of "Credulous America."[164] Born in London, Browne was the author of two "lucid books" on religion, *Stranger than Fiction* and *The Believing World*. We mentioned the former's content previously. A captivating speaker who addressed capacity crowds on his two previous visits to the University of Michigan campus, Browne was a particularly interesting person in that he was an ordained rabbi who had become estranged from the rabbinate and resigned from it, yet he remained very committed to Jewish concerns.[165] In addition to Browne, the Episcopalian Dr. Frank Gavin discussed the relationship between Judaism and Christianity under the combined auspices of the Hillel Foundation and the St. Andrews Episcopal Church: "Mr. Gavin has been vitally interested in things Jewish all his life. He is a graduate of the University of Cincinnati and while taking his degree there, attended classes at Hebrew Union College, a Reform Jewish Theological Seminary."[166] The long editorial entitled "Everything to Gain" is one of the many attempts by Hillel to tout its advantages in terms of being a fine social environment of succor and hearth—not only a great purveyor of culture but also a discoverer of hidden talents. At Hillel, "out of the dark recesses of the unknown appear debaters of merit, committee workers, athletes, journalists, dancers, musicians and what nots. The unfortunate side of the matter resides in the fact that not enough of this hidden talent is uncovered so that its potentialities may be employed for advancement of the interests of the Jewish group at the University . . . For the college man and woman here it means a chance for physical, men-

---

164. *The Hillel News*, Volume IV, Number IX, November 21, 1929.
165. Ibid.
166. Ibid.

tal and moral broadening, of a nature which the University cannot and does not attempt to provide. Why not try your hand at Hillel work? *You have nothing to lose and everything to gain.*"[167] Yet another attempt to market Hillel to all Jewish students on campus! We encountered many such efforts in the course of our work. On a lighter note, we are informed that a Foundation basketball tournament involving fifteen teams was about to commence.[168]

In *The Hillel News* of November 27, 1929, Hillel's outreach to organizations of other faiths features prominently. Thus we learn that on Thanksgiving Day, Rabbi Fink, Hillel's director, was to participate in the Baptist Church in a communal service featuring him and the church's minister, with the sermon delivered by the minister of the Presbyterian Church in town. In an editorial on page 2, we learn of the extant and long-lasting tension between Hillel and the Jewish fraternities at the University of Michigan, another recurring theme throughout our study. At the core of this is Hillel's worry that its mission on campus remains hampered not so much by an antipathy toward the Foundation on the part of Jewish students but rather by a clear indifference and disinterestedness relating to Hillel's activities, even its existence. For it was "this very thought which was in the back of the Heads of the Foundation founders in the country. The terrible realization that Jewish students were disinterested in things Jewish was the spur which pricked their imaginations and caused them to establish Jewish focal points at American colleges."[169] In some way, Hillel's activists viewed Jewish fraternities as major culprits in perpetuating this apathy on the part of Jewish students.

On page 3 of this issue, we encounter two articles characterizing the contradictory role of women in Hillel, Jewish life, the University of Michigan, and American society as a whole. On the one hand, we read a short article on the planning of a women's party headlined

---

167. Ibid. Italics in the original.

168. Ibid.

169. *The Hillel News*, Volume IV, Number X, November 27, 1929.

by "Plans Are Maturing for Hillel Hen Party" in which the "girls" are asked to "underline December 12 on your date calendars and tell the men you'll be too happy to see them some other night."[170] Right next to this is an announcement that Florence Frankel "will lead a discussion of Achad Ha'am's first three essays" in the Achad Ha'am study group, which "carries on all its discussions in modern Hebrew."[171] The paper from January 23, 1930, featured an article on the expansion of the Hillel Basketball League, which would be composed of "two divisions with a like number of teams in each . . . The members of the championship team will receive gold basketballs awarded by the Hillel Foundation."[172] This issue of *The Hillel News* was the first in a number that touted the fifth anniversary of the Hebrew University's founding in Jerusalem, which was to be celebrated in April 1930: "The Hillel Foundation, we understand, will employ the occasion to bring the work of the University to the attention of students at Michigan."[173]

Ecumenical themes feature in the December 5, 1929, issue of *The Hillel News*. Dr. Gavin's forthcoming lecture, already mentioned in *The Hillel News* of November 21, receives front-page prominence with a much more detailed account of Dr. Gavin's expertise in the subject of Christian-Jewish relations.[174] We are informed that Dr. Gavin holds doctorates from Harvard and Columbia in addition to his aforementioned education both at the University of Cincinnati and at that city's Hebrew Union College. His lecture entitled "The Jewish Background of Early Christianity" featured an issue that has proved sensitive to both Christians and Jews over the ages. In an editorial called "Good Will," the text reads: "Probably the first Good Will banquet ever held on such a large scale in an American university will be given under the

170. Ibid.

171. Ibid.

172. *The Hillel News*, Volume IV, Number XV, January 23, 1930.

173. Ibid.

174. *The Hillel News*, Volume IV, Number XI, December 5, 1929.

sponsorship of the Michigan Union, Wednesday evening, December 18. The various members of the three main religions, Catholicism, Protestantism, and Judaism, will mingle at the dining table in an effort to perpetuate the friendly feelings between [sic] the three groups. The Union is sponsor of the banquet and invites all students, faculty members, and townspeople to participate . . . President Ruthven, the main speaker of the evening, will be making his first appearance before a large cosmopolitan group of students since he entered upon the presidency of the University this fall . . . Father Babcock of the Catholic Church, Rabbi Fink of the Hillel Foundation and a Protestant minister will officially bridge the gap between [sic] the various religions in interesting talks."[175] This was a coming-out of sorts for President Alexander Ruthven, whom we will encounter on numerous occasions throughout our study. Tellingly, it was in connection with a theme that remained dear to Ruthven's heart throughout his presidency at the University of Michigan and that formed his overall vision for constituting the proper character that a university of Michigan's caliber and stature required as guidance of its educational mission and rule of its ethical principle—namely, the understanding and collaboration among the three great religions of Western civilization: Catholicism, Protestantism, and Judaism.

Continuing with the ecumenical and interreligious theme of this issue of *The Hillel News*, we also learn that "representatives of all denominations, gathered together in this first general Thanksgiving convocation, were led in prayer by the various directors of spiritual activity on the campus including Rabbi A. H. Fink, Rev. Merle H. Anderson of the Presbyterian church, and the Rev. R. Edward Saules of the Baptist church."[176] The paper also announced that on November 24, Justice Louis D. Brandeis had broken "the silence he had maintained for thirteen years regarding Zionism" by committing himself wholeheartedly

175. Ibid.
176. Ibid.

to this idea and movement in a keynote address that he delivered at the Hotel Mayflower in Washington, DC.[177]

The theme of ecumenicalism spilled over into the last issue of *The Hillel News* preceding the Christmas holiday. We are informed on the front page of the December 12, 1929, edition of the paper that a "Campus Good Will Banquet" was planned by the Michigan Union.[178] "In the same spirit that prompted the communal Thanksgiving services, the Michigan Union is standing sponsor to a Good Will banquet, Tuesday, December 17 at 6:15 PM in the Michigan Union Ballroom."[179] Once again, the speakers announced were President Alexander Ruthven, the three aforementioned representatives of the three major denominations, and also Mayor Edward W. Staebler who was going to address the assembled representing the city of Ann Arbor.[180]

In the editorial called "Campus Opinion," we once again bear witness to the complexity of the dating issue that clearly beset Hillel at this time. A rarely signed editorial, in this case by initials J. H. S., argues that closing the doors to those who do not wish to "date" on open house nights "defeats the purpose for which they were established. The Open House, as its very name implies, is an event to which everyone interested should be cordially invited. Its purpose ought to be that of providing social contacts for all who desire them. The Open House affairs should endeavor particularly to provide a congenial group for the formation of new friendships. They should be mixers where the more reticent individuals can be induced to meet others, and push out of the shell of shyness which deprives them of social enjoyment. Unless the Hillel Open House can achieve these things, they are of little use."[181] Juxtaposing this opinion seems to be the Federation's official line, which

177. Ibid.
178. *The Hillel News*, Volume IV, Number XII, December 12, 1929.
179. Ibid.
180. Ibid.
181. Ibid.

apparently only admitted students with "dates" to attend these open house events: "It is undoubtedly true that the 'date' affairs have proved very enjoyable to those who have put in an appearance the past few Sundays. It is also true that the stag affairs have brought a preponderance of men."[182] Once again, however, we see Hillel's sensitivity to this matter by "throwing open" the pages of *The Hillel News* for discussing this issue so "that a complete and representative opinion may be reached."[183]

On page 4 of this issue of the paper, we are treated to a particularly edgy subject that the aforementioned Dr. Frank Gavin raised openly in his lecture. The speaker "created a furor by an expose of the discrimination practiced by medical schools in the East. Dr. Gavin made a complete investigation of the number of Jewish students who were allowed to enter these schools and found that scores were kept out solely because they were Jews. The total number admitted to these schools, he found, is very small. He revealed that many Jewish students were forced to go abroad each year to study medicine because of this discrimination. A Jewish student is forced to apply to about five medical schools to obtain entrance in contrast to the one or two schools to which Christian students apply, the minister reported. Dr. Gavin made this report to the Good-Will Committee of the Federal Council of Churches in New York."[184] As is well known, and as we will demonstrate in our further work on Jews at the University of Michigan (which is to appear in late 2017 or early 2018), such blatant discrimination was not contained to the country's East Coast and was common to all its regions, the Midwest included. Indeed, the University of Michigan's medical school also partook in this discriminatory practice.

The ecumenical activities continued into 1930. The January 16 issue of *The Hillel News* informs us that Rabbi Fink addressed the

182. Ibid.
183. Ibid.
184. Ibid.

Women's Alliance of the Unitarian Church on the subject of "Chassidism" on January 10.[185] Even in the themes of plays picked by the Hillel Players we can detect an ecumenical bent. Indeed, the next play that the Players were going to perform had nothing Jewish about it and was deeply anchored in eighteenth-century Catholicism, demonstrating the wide intellectual reach of this troupe and, at least indirectly, of the Hillel Foundation itself: "More than fifty students responded to the call for tryouts for the next Hillel Players production, *Caponsacchi*, a three-act drama . . . set in the eighteenth century and centered around an affair in which the monk, Caponsacchi, and the wife of an Italian layman of Rome become entangled."[186] We also learn in this issue that Rabbi Fink and "Reverend Harris, Director of Harris Hall and one of the rectors of St. Andrews Episcopal Church" formed a group of Jewish and Episcopal students "to study the always interesting subject of Judaism and Christianity. The subject of Jewish-Gentile relations is now one of the most important problems facing America today and according to Rabbi Fink it can be solved 'and good will made a reality only through knowledge' first of your own religion and then the religion of others."[187] There were going to be twelve weekly meetings throughout the coming term lasting into the first week of May. Under the headline "A Gesture of Good Will," this issue of the paper offered an editorial supporting this interfaith activity wholeheartedly: "This very novel idea is probably the first constructive attempt on the Michigan campus to bring Jews and Gentiles together distinctly for the purpose of seeing their common intellectual and religious heritage."[188]

Religion remains the theme in the ensuing editorial. Under the headline "Religious Hillel," the paper feels the necessity to tout Hillel as a religious organization as well. In Hillel's quest to become

185. *The Hillel News*, Volume IV, Number XIV, January 16, 1930.
186. Ibid.
187. Ibid.
188. Ibid.

a social and cultural big-tent gathering place for all Jewish students on campus, there emerged the concern that to some Jewish students, the Foundation may have come to deemphasize—not to say diminish or neglect—the religious aspects of Jewish life. It was time to tout Hillel's contributions to Jewish religion on the Michigan campus and to recenter that aspect of the Foundation's image and mission in addition to its intellectual, cultural, and social ones: "It is easy to over-look the religious side of Hillel if one becomes overwhelmed by other interests. But religiously Hillel is doing big things. Friday and Sunday services, orthodox and reform respectively, are held weekly; every afternoon a Kiddush service is given at the Foundation and on the high holy days appropriate services are conducted. Rabbi Fink, visiting rabbis, and ministers as well as student speakers address these congregations. It is encouraging to see that a number of Hillelites make it a regular practice to attend services. The number is slowly but steadily increasing as students come to realize that Hillel offers them spiritual opportunities in addition to the social and intellectual ones which it sponsors. The college age it has often been said, is the age in which to form habits. Jewish students on campus should use the Hillel services to form those religious habits which will give them the fullest spiritual development in later life."[189]

The Hillel News from February 20, 1930, also includes plenty of articles on all the aforementioned areas of interest, excepting that of women. Thus the front page of the publication announces, "Offering Jewish students an opportunity to meet Dr. Alexander Ruthven, President of the University, the educational committee has arranged for an informal luncheon to be held at the Michigan Union Women's dining room, Thursday noon, February 27."[190] On the same page, we are also informed that James Waterman Wise, son of the famous Rabbi Stephen S. Wise, and "famous critic and poet" Untermeyer will come to Ann Arbor on March 6 and 10,

189. Ibid.
190. *The Hillel News*, Volume IV, Number XVI, February 20, 1930.

respectively, to present lectures to Hillelites. Lastly, the paper announces that "plans [are] complete for couple dance to be held March 1."[191]

On page 2, we encounter an editorial that opines that entering Michigan in the second semester is particularly difficult and much harder than in the first semester. It announces that Michigan Hillel Foundation Director Rabbi Adolph H. Fink will speak to such second-semester entrants to the University about adjustment problems and how best to overcome them. On the same page, we also note that a joint Jewish and Gentile religious study group organized by Rabbi Fink and Reverend Thomas Harris "to study the history of Judaism and Christianity in their relation to each other" will hold its first meeting of the semester on Wednesday at the Hillel Foundation.[192] Lastly, on page 4, the newspaper announces that the Hillel debaters will clash with their counterparts from the University of Illinois in Detroit at Temple Beth El and that the bridge contest attracts a large list of entries.[193]

In the very next issue, there appears a complaint voicing Hillel's disappointment regarding the lack of participation by the Jewish fraternities in writing something for a newly instituted venue in the paper called "On the Campus": "An attempt has been made to secure for this column all available information about activities of Jewish students on campus. Every fraternity was notified of the existence of this column and numerous solicitations of news were attempted but results were discouraging."[194] The tension caused by Hillel's intellectual and educational mandate and its disdain for the fraternities' mainly social role on campus is best expressed by the following sentiment in this piece: "Accomplishments in University circles rather than trivial social items or personals are the type of material desired. There will be no guarantee of publi-

191. Ibid.
192. Ibid.
193. Ibid.
194. *The Hillel News*, Volume IV, Number XVII, February 27, 1930.

cation of any articles submitted but everything deemed worthy will be printed."[195] The conflict between Hillel's self-perception and its assessment of fraternities could not be expressed in any clearer manner. Here we have evidence of an interesting unsolved intra-Hillel tension regarding the Federation's relationship to Jewish fraternities. While on the one hand, Hillel saw its mission very much as a social one—in other words, as an organization offering Jewish students the opportunity to thrive communally in a place in which they feel comfortable and can live and express their Jewish identity in whatever manner they so choose—on the other hand, Hillel somehow found the social dimension of the fraternities shallow and, in a way, not sufficiently Jewish.

In an editorial entitled "Your Move!" Hillel implores freshmen in particular to join the various committees (educational, social welfare, social, publication, among others) of the Foundation that plan its life on campus. The paper once again announces President Ruthven's forthcoming address to students at the luncheon.[196]

The ensuing issue of the paper features a front-page article on the Hillel Players, a drama group that was to be featured in many an issue of *The Hillel News* and of which Hillel remained clearly proud. Many of this group's performances, just like in this case, occurred in the Lydia Mendelssohn Theatre, a prime and coveted venue on campus for plays, musicals, operettas, and operas to this day. The Hillel Players surely were among the most effective campus-wide ambassadors for Hillel's presence at the University. They were completely unique among campus organizations in that they were the only drama group that was entirely student run and directed. Each academic year, they presented one major production that was either student written or authored by a well-known playwright and already successfully performed on stages in New York, Chicago, and/or Detroit. Often the Hillel Players' performances featured socially significant themes. They performed

195. Ibid.
196. Ibid.

mainly at the Lydia Mendelssohn Theatre, almost always in March or April.

*The Hillel News* of March 6, 1930, features a fascinating article under the headline "Ruthven Urges Loyalty at Hillel Luncheon" that recounts how the president inveighed against the malicious gossip about Michigan, "which is seized eagerly by newspapers everywhere," and exhorts the students not to accept this gossip as truth and to "condemn the administration without an adequate knowledge."[197] The editorial, appearing most often on page 2 of the paper, is devoted solely to Hillel's forming the aforementioned Religious Committee to deal with the obviously contentious matter as to how much and what kind of religious activities should be featured in Hillel. From the editorial's text, it is clear that the main problem confronting the Foundation on this important matter was "not student skepticism or organized and carefully thought out disbelief in religious matters but rather student apathy and disinterestedness."[198]

Other than congratulating George Abramovitz for sinking thirty-eight consecutive foul shots and lauding six students from the Literary College (the equivalent to what is now the College of Literature, Science and the Arts [LS&A]) and three from the medical school for having received all As in the past semester, the most notable article in this issue of *The Hillel News* was a detailed summary of poet and critic Louis Untermeyer's talk at the University under Hillel's auspices in which he inveighed against Jews' invoking the existence of anti-Semitism in America (he thought it was

197. *The Hillel News*, Volume IV, Number XVIII, March 6, 1930. Far and away the most frustrating incident in what otherwise was a wonderful research experience compiling this book was our futile attempt to ascertain to what "malicious gossip about Michigan" President Ruthven was referring. Even though he added that this gossip was "seized eagerly by newspapers everywhere," our detailed examination of *The Michigan Daily*, *The Ann Arbor News*, *The New York Times*, and the Detroit and Chicago presses revealed absolutely nothing even vaguely resembling Ruthven's assertions or worries. So we simply do not know what exactly President Ruthven meant.

198. Ibid.

bogus): "I dislike the 'professional Jew,'" he said, especially in literature, where he chided the work of Ludwig Lewisohn in particular as well as that of other authors "who capitalize on these imaginary sufferings of their race."[199] Most of the "persecution" of the Jews, according to Untermeyer, is "due to the attitude that the Jews themselves take."[200] Untermeyer said that the African American poet Langston Hughes had a similar interpretation of the "negro problem" in the United States as the Jews had of their predicament, though unlike the Jews, "'Hughes, however, has a saving sense of humor, his material is more original and he has much more reason for complaining.'"[201] Alas, we could not find any published reactions to this article or to Untermeyer's talk, which surely must have raised some controversy and ruffled some feathers, though we are also certain that many Jews in his audience and well beyond on the Michigan campus and in American society agreed with him. And many still do. Interestingly, with Jews as compared to other minorities, it is their overidentification with being Jewish that is coded as reactionary and dismissed as playing the victim and being the "professional Jew," whereas assimilation is extolled as the progressive option, the enlightened way. Thus, unlike with African Americans, where assimilationists are derided as "Uncle Toms" and those who express "blackness" are prized for courage and rectitude, the exact opposite pertained to Jews in the 1920s and 1930s and remained so until the late 1960s when a new form of Jewish identity, one that defined itself at least orthogonally—if not in clear opposition—to dominant white America, emerged. It was spawned by the student revolts on the campuses of America's leading universities, with the University of Michigan as a major force. But the fact remains that even today, Jews are quickly blamed for excessive tribalism, which is often associated with a certain particularism

199. *The Hillel News*, Volume IV, Number XIX, March 13, 1930.

200. Ibid.

201. Ibid.

that is viewed as conservative, even reactionary, if it remains confined to Jews and does not also exhibit a considerable dosage of ostensible universalism, whereas the exact opposite is the case with other minorities where their identification with and pride in their particular group is always coded as progressive.

The ensuing seven issues of *The Hillel News* feature articles on a number of interdenominational matters ("Indian Educator Will Talk Here This Afternoon," "Bishop to Talk on Hebrew Books," "Inter-guild Dinner to Be Given by Wesleyan Guild on April 27"); numerous pieces on the Hebrew University; a debate on the value and necessity for Hillel to have its own facility accompanied by a sincere gratitude to the University for allowing Hillel to use University facilities campus-wide; and the appearance of a number of women in leadership positions listed on the masthead of the publication, with Josephine Stern, who was to become the University of Michigan's first Hopwood Prize winner in 1931, among them.

One topic from the April 3, 1930, issue of *The Hillel News* is worthy of special mention: the Foundation's need for its own space. In a signed editorial entitled "A New Foundation," Byron Novitsky, vice president of the Hillel Student Council, makes the emphatic case for the first time in arguing that Hillel possess its own building and facilities in order to maximize its many missions on campus: "The problem of building a new home for the Hillel Foundation is not a new one. I cannot understand why up to this time it has not caused greater discussion among those interested . . . In the fall of 1926, the date of Hillel's establishment on this campus, the site at 615 E. University was thought satisfactory as a temporary home . . . We have existed in this same place for almost four years during which time the Hillel Foundation has outgrown its home. We cannot function here as we should. We are cramped for space, and the foundation is suffering because of it."[202] Novitsky goes on to describe how the Foundation can only host one function at a time because there exists no room

202. *The Hillel News*, Volume IV, Number XXII, April 3, 1930.

for more and how the available space is often much too crowded when popular speakers come to address the students or during open house on Tuesday and Thursday afternoons and Sunday evenings. Many of Hillel's functions had to be held elsewhere on campus, quite often in the Women's League Building (now Michigan League): "As a result of this, the Jewish students do not connect any of the above events [speakers, lectures, drama and music performances, and social occasions such as dances] with the Hillel Foundation since all of them are away from its home. It is quite true that the affairs are held under the auspices of the Foundation and the students are aware of it. However, the spirit which has grown up with the Hillel in is present handicapped condition would develop a great deal faster and reach the heights we dream of a great deal sooner, if there were a place where all things carried on could be performed in the atmosphere provided by the Hillel Foundation. A spirit, a Hillel spirit, would be created with greater intensity, and our objectives would grow nearer and clearer to us ... In a new and more comfortable home in which we could house all our activities, the Foundation might grow to satisfy all our hopes and ideals for future Judaism."[203]

On May 22, 1930, *The Hillel News* published its last issue of the academic year, in which an editorial entitled "Another Year Gone" offers a useful summary of the year's highlights and problems. The editorial commences by stating that establishing a concrete tally of successes and failures for an organization of Hillel's kind is "hopeless when the work is not of a material nature. Hillel's value is outside the realm of numbers or weights of measures; it is abstract."[204] Still, a bevy of positives were worthy of mention: "[Hillel] is offering more and more to the Jewish students on the campus. This year has seen the development of a program of athletics more extensive than any yet attempted ... The loan fund has been established ... The Hillel Players has made its debut

203. Ibid.

204. *The Hillel News*, Volume IV, Number XXVI, May 22, 1930.

in an outstanding production . . . The Movement for a building suitable for housing Hillel activities has gathered momentum . . . These are merely the most noticeable advances; others of as great importance but of greater subtlety have also been inaugurated."[205]

But then the editorial changes course by stating in the very next sentence, "Still all is not well. The intensity of the support given to Hillel is tremendous but too few individuals are contributing to it. Interest in the foundation is manifest in many, but still not enough. If it is true (and we hold it to be so) that the future of Judaism depends upon the abilities and attitudes of those who are now the Jewish college students, then upon the success or failure of the Hillel Foundation rests the future of Judaism."[206] Pretty heady stuff, this! Thus the editorial concludes by exhorting Jewish students to "'roll up your sleeves. See, here is work to be done. You are the first generation of Jews to hold aloof from the worthy endeavors of your co-religionists. Come on.'"[207]

Immediately following this editorial is another entitled "An Appreciation," in which the Foundation thanks the University of Michigan for the many ways in which it has supported Hillel's presence on campus, from providing its faculty members as speakers to opening its many facilities for Hillel to hold its activities in them: "The Hillel Foundation feels the tremendous debt it owes Michigan and can never hope to completely express its appreciation and thanks for the infinite amount of aid which it has received."[208] These two editorials provide great insights into Hillel's overall mission among Jewish college students and the American Jewish community at large on the one hand and its relationship to the University as its host on the other.

Lastly, we find an article on page 7 of this issue—a rarity, since virtually all others never exceeded four pages—entitled

205. Ibid.
206. Ibid.
207. Ibid.
208. Ibid.

"Successful Year Sees Growth of Hillel Movement: Foundations Increase in Influence on Many of the Country's College Campuses."[209] We read: "The passing school year is without a doubt the most successful in Hillel history, bearing out more clearly than ever the wisdom of the vision and efforts of the late Rabbi Benjamin Frankel, who conceived and founded the first Hillel Foundation at the University of Illinois. The number of Foundations was increased to eight: at the Universities of Illinois, Wisconsin, Michigan, Ohio State, Cornell, Southern California, West Virginia and Texas. In all the number of students participating in their activities increased, and the scope of work broadened."[210] The article then proceeds to highlight noteworthy events from some of these Hillel chapters, giving "the baby member of the group, the Foundation at the University of Texas," a particularly lengthy passage.[211]

## Exit Adolph Fink, Enter Bernard Heller

The academic year 1930–31 began with the departure of Rabbi Adolph H. Fink, who arrived in Ann Arbor from the University of Illinois where he had served as assistant director of the Hillel Foundation for one year (1925–26) in 1926 to open the Foundation at the University of Michigan as the fourth such organization in the country. His successor was Rabbi Bernard Heller, who joined the University of Michigan from Scranton, Pennsylvania, where he served as the rabbi of Madison Avenue Temple for twelve years. The same issue of *The Hillel News* that announced the leadership change at Hillel ran an editorial entitled "A Bright Future" in which Hillel touts its achievements in the hope of attracting freshmen to join who are "new on the campus with but few friends and little companionship"—both of which, the piece asserts, the Foundation offers galore. But in the editorial entitled

209. Ibid.
210. Ibid.
211. Ibid.

"Help Wanted," which follows the previous one in short order, Hillel admits that "the most difficult obstacle that the Foundation has had to overcome is indifference—indifference to the purposes and accomplishments of the organization, and indifference to the organization itself."[212]

In a passage of self-criticism, the piece then berates its own failures but promises "to listen to suggestions, and to adopt them if they are worth adoption . . . We are trying our hardest to improve the Federation, and you can make our task much easier if you let us know what you think is wrong with the organization."[213] It appears to us that this was a lot of chest beating and blaming organizational shortcomings for the real issue confronting Hillel then and in subsequent years, perhaps even today: many Jewish students in the United States constructed and lived their Judaism in ways that did not accommodate Hillel. The paper congratulates Florence Frankel, a prominent and active Hillel member, for being named to the Law Review at the University of Michigan's Law School, an honor that "few women in the University have attained in recent years." The piece is introduced by the sentence "Again, the women are coming to the fore,"[214] which could well have been the headline of the next issue of *The Hillel News* in which there is a first-page story announcing that three women were elected as officers of the Student Council, with Beatrice Ehrlich chosen as its secretary. Touting Hillel's social dimension, an editorial entitled "The Heller Banquet" urges students to attend this function, which surpasses mixers on many dimensions—not least, of course, offering a space for "Jewish students to get together and become acquainted."[215]

Rabbi Heller seemed to have hit the ground running with an activist approach featuring his own involvement on a number of

212. *The Hillel News*, Volume V, Number I, October 8, 1930.
213. Ibid.
214. Ibid.
215. *The Hillel News*, Volume V, Number II, October 15, 1930.

fronts. He commenced regular Sunday Reformed services, a feature of the Reform practice of Judaism foregoing the traditional Sabbath celebrated by its Orthodox and Conservative practitioners, testifying to the preponderance among the University of Michigan's Jewish student body that adhered to the Reform movement in contrast to the other two; he began teaching a course on Judaism; he encouraged Avukah, the student Zionist organization, to offer a class at Hillel on the history of Zionism; and he seemed to be committed to broadening the religious offerings at Hillel on both an intellectual and a practical level. Under the title "New Plan for Services," *The Hillel News*'s editorial mentions that "the Hillel Foundation is dedicated to the 'social, cultural, and religious' welfare of Jewish students. In the past the former two have been amply provided; the latter has evoked a feeble response. We feel that the three are at least of equal importance."[216] It is likely that Rabbi Heller introduced various religious practices common to the Reform movement precisely as a way to attract Jewish students who appeared to show little, if any, interest in expressing their Jewishness in religious ways, which Heller believed was part of Hillel's mission.

The five remaining issues of *The Hillel News* until the end of calendar year 1930 featured two large topics, each representing one cluster that we delineated above: the first pertained to Hillel's role regarding gender; the second featured important questions pertaining to Jewish identity and Hillel's role therein. As to the former, a short announcement on the front page of *The Hillel News* of October 30, 1930, entitled "Houses Which Accept Jewish Girls Listed" mentions how such a list will hopefully alleviate "many of the difficulties encountered by incoming Jewish girls in the past."[217]

In Marianne Sanua's first-rate study of Jewish fraternities, in which she argues that, among many reasons, the lack of available

216. *The Hillel News*, Volume V, Number III, October 22, 1930.
217. *The Hillel News*, Volume V, Number IV, October 30, 1930.

housing for Jewish young people on account of blatant discrimination against them was so important to these fraternities' proliferation at American universities of the 1910s, 1920s, and 1930s,
Sanua says, "Residential discrimination against Jews in small college towns, which had long been a serious obstacle, intensified [in
the 1920s]. As early as 1925, the Dean of Women at the University
of Michigan had informed a visiting Alpha Epsilon Phi representative that 'the problem of housing Jewish girls becomes harder
every year.'"[218]

On the same page of *The Hillel News*, we read that a "Women's
Gathering" was to be held on November 12: "The members of
the committee want this affair to mean as much to the women
as the Smoker means to the men."[219] But perhaps much more
important was a note authored in the November 5, 1930, issue
of *The Hillel News* entitled "A Plea for More Women at Open
Houses by a Woman," signed by a K. J. F., in which the author
argues eloquently that the reason for the paucity of women at Hillel at any given afternoon when a visitor would find thirty men
and five women had everything to do with the women's sense that
the men viewed any visit by women to Hillel as an attempt to land
a date rather than to avail themselves of the fine opportunities,
such as the exquisite books and great music collection, that the
Foundation offered.[220] The author makes it clear that this pervasive male attitude of seeing women as predators who use their
going to Hillel only to meet men rather than to enjoy the Foundation's fine cultural offerings or its amenities makes women avoid
going to Hillel just to hang out and have a good time. She ends
her piece by exhorting her sisters to attend this week's tea in large
numbers to show that women, just like men, are fully entitled to
benefit from Hillel's cultural as well as convivial offerings without being seen as predators and threats to men's peace of mind.

218. Sanua, "Jewish College Fraternities in the United States," p. 15.
219. *The Hillel News*, Volume V, Number IV, October 30, 1930.
220. *The Hillel News*, Volume V, Number V, November 5, 1930.

This then led *The Hillel News* to respond with a full-blown editorial in the paper's subsequent issue of November 12, 1930. Entitled "Women," the editorial dismisses the letter writer's reasoning and labels her argument that men see women's coming to Hillel as merely a way to "catch dates" as "a gross and silly overstatement of the situation."[221] The editorial then proceeds to argue that one of Hillel's many roles is indeed to have Jewish men and women meet, which, in fact, constitutes one of the founding reasons for Hillel's creation. The editorial then presents at length the passage in Hillel's founding document that speaks of Hillel "as a place 'where Jewish men and women on the campus might meet and share common interests . . . in short, instill in them a greater Jewish consciousness, replacing the isolation or absorption in the large student body that was previously the situation.'" The editorial emphasizes that there should be no reason lectures on Zionism or Yiddish or Jewish history should be any less interesting and relevant to Jewish women than they are to Jewish men. And for good measure, the editorial ends by asking the reader to look up to the top of the page where women's names appear prominently on the newspaper's masthead. All good, all fine, but the editorial completely failed to address the real fact of and possible reasons for the extant gender imparity at Hillel that the author raised in her original contribution. There is no reason such disparity should exist, the editorial concludes, but it does, which the response ultimately fails to address.

The other large issue pertains to matters of Jewish identity. In an editorial entitled "A Heritage," *The Hillel News* touts the quality of its library collection as a crucial way for the students to connect with their Judaism, which, in many cases, has been all but lost: "Jewish students have often been told that theirs is the greatest heritage in the world, and, in the same breath that the future of Judaism rests upon their shoulders. And just as frequently has it been charged that they know less of their history and their people

221. *The Hillel News*, Volume V, Number VI, November 12, 1930.

than any other group. In these problems the Hillel Foundation
has its roots."[222] The editorial then continues to mention that the
Foundation offers a bevy of lectures and events designed precisely
for fulfilling this mission but that it realizes time constraints
upon students make it often impossible for them to attend these.
Instead, the editorial argues, the Foundation's library is chock-full
of books in "histories, poetry, fiction, exposition and discourses,
and biographies" that will enhance the student's knowledge of and
interest in many facets of Judaism: "Here is an opportunity for
Jewish students to learn more of their past and to keep abreast of
the present."[223]

Three major topics that have remained as central to all of Jewish life today as they were then appeared in issues of *The Hillel
News* in late 1930: the role of religion and its practice, the deeper
meanings of Judaism and why it even exists, and discourses about
Orthodoxy, Reformism, and Zionism. As to the former, the best
presentation appears in an editorial entitled "Why?" Published
in *The Hillel News* of November 5, 1930, the piece makes clear
the frustration that the Hillel leadership must have had with not
being able to calibrate the proper texture of religious services that
would appeal to a large number of the just-announced nine hundred Jewish students on the University of Michigan campus: "For
some reason there seems to have grown up a tradition among Jewish students on the campus that services are to be avoided."[224] The
Foundation had instituted Sunday morning services at 11:15 a.m.
precisely to attract the most number of students. Still, an insuf-
ficient number, at least to satisfy Hillel's expectations, seemed to
appear. The editorial assures the students that services are not
there to preach to them about the putative defective ways of their
lives. Services are not preachy and lecturing. Nor are they a form
of intellectual discourse on the compelling topics of the day. Nor

222. *The Hillel News*, Volume V, Number IV, October 30, 1930.
223. Ibid.
224. *The Hillel News*, Volume V, Number V, November 5, 1930.

is the addition of the Hillel Choral Group, recently formed at the Foundation, an attempt to imitate a Christian choir that sings at the students as some must have complained. Clearly, the position of services remained amorphous for the students then as they often continue to do in the present. The editorial concludes with the platitudinous sentence that services "fill a spiritual and inspirational place in his [the student's] life that no other function or experience can replace."[225]

In a fascinating editorial entitled "Why Religion?" *The Hillel News* of November 19, 1930, summarizes the main points that Rabbi Bernard Heller was to address at Sunday services, which were to be followed with much greater elaboration in his class on Judaism. Planned as the first installment of a two-part series with the ensuing topic being "Why Judaism?" (see presentation that follows), Hillel and its director addressed arguably the most central theme preoccupying most, if not all, Jewish students on the Michigan campus at the time: "These religious questions are being considered by students constantly. Raised in orthodox homes and taught to hold orthodox dogma as absolute truth, they soon come into contact with numerous conflicting ideas. These merely serve to throw them into mental confusion, taking the ground from under their feet, and putting nothing in its place. Finding nothing immediately to align themselves with, they often take the attitude that all religion is without a rational and pragmatic foundation, and call themselves atheists or agnostics. This is especially true of the Jew, and is prevalent among many of the Jewish students on campus."[226] The editorial continues: "Most Jewish students know little of the past history and culture of their people. The origin and reason for religious practices and ceremonies have never been made known to them. Accordingly, when they find no immediate and pressing cause they abandon them, and thinking that these constitute all there is to religion, call themselves agnostics.

225. Ibid.
226. *The Hillel News*, Volume V, Number 7, November 19, 1930.

Religion is not all ritual. When scientists, statesmen, and men of intellectual achievement and renown continue to align themselves with organized religion, there must be some firm basis for it. Students might well learn what it is. The world has always had religion and has regarded it as essential to the welfare of mankind. Can it be overthrown with a mere gesture and without deep and serious thought based upon a thorough knowledge of the facts? And if it cannot, 'Why Judaism?' in preference to Unitarianism, Christian Science, Seventh Day Adventist, or any other faith?"[227] While the editorial never provides any answers to these insightful questions, and we have no idea as to how Rabbi Heller responded to his own queries in his course on Judaism, it is evident that these were *the* topics comprising the core issues of Jewish identity at the time and quite possibly today as well: What is the religious component of being Jewish? What degree of knowledge about Jewish history and religion should one have as a Jew? Is the mere practice of rituals not vacuous and thus susceptible to leading to a departure from Judaism, since, with no content beyond such rituals, the religion and identity surrounding it appear superficial and even burdensome in a world quite hostile to Jews? What road could be easier to assimilation than the jettisoning of meaningless rituals! We found the list of religions mentioned in the editorial quite interesting, since it did not include the two main religions: Protestantism and Catholicism. We strongly suspect that Hillel at this stage was worried about Jewish students converting not to Unitarianism, Christian Science, or Seventh Day Adventism but rather to various expressions of left-wing radicalism that had come to attain popularity on campus at this time.

A companion piece featuring important matters concerning Jewish identity appears in this issue of *The Hillel News* announcing a lecture by Professor John H. Muyskens of the Linguistics and Speech Departments on the subject of "Habitual Jewish Apology." Muyskens argued that there appeared to be a growing view that

227. Ibid.

the Bible was not divine and contained a good many errors. But, so he submitted, "'religion, to exist, must have an innate feeling which goes beyond the mechanism of rituals. But in the process of transmission this innate quality is lost and replaced by definite outward principles. We do want to be Jews, but we want to know why. If we are to make sacrifices for being Jews, we ought to get back what Judaism means. Let us have a complete reconstruction. Let us evolve a certain set of principles, convince ourselves that these principles are right, and then pass them on to the next generation for their use as a Jewish creed.'"[228]

In another editorial entitled "Smoking," the newspaper explains why a nonsmoking policy had been established by the Foundation on its premises. "The reasons are these: There are on the campus a number of Orthodox students as well as Reformed, using the Foundation, and to them, smoking on the Sabbath is of course very un-Jewish, and decidedly against the grain. Students may find it hard to appreciate this situation unless they have been raised in Orthodox homes and have learned to hold such traditions in reverence . . . Jews are as a rule quick to courteously respect the views and traditions of non-Jews. Why not the same respect to the Jew?"[229] Of course, the issue here is about such marginalia as smoking. But the underlying matter goes a lot deeper because the editorial addresses three points that remained at the Foundation's core throughout the period of our study: the proper integration of all Jewish students in Hillel, Jews' role and demeanor toward the outside world, and, in turn, the outside world's relations to and reflections on Jews.

We also learn from this issue of *The Hillel News* that Rabbi Heller donated 150 copies of his own books to the burgeoning Hillel library. The books covered a wide array of fields, from psychology to religion, from philosophy to politics. Their authors included an eclectic array, such as Bertrand Russell, Will Durant,

228. Ibid.
229. Ibid.

William James, Mary Baker Eddy, and George Santayana, demonstrating the catholicity in taste and breadth in interest that the Hillel readership clearly had.[230] Additionally, the Foundation director informed the students that his personal library would be open to them anytime they wanted to avail themselves of it.

The issue of *The Hillel News* of November 26, 1930, informs us that the aforementioned Josephine Stern was to give a public lecture on "The Jewish Youth Movement in America," once again underlining this woman's central role at the Hillel Foundation and among Jewish students at the University of Michigan at this time.[231] In an editorial entitled "Gift," *The Hillel News* thanks Rabbi Heller for his extensive generosity not only for giving the Foundation 150 copies of his books but also for opening up his personal library to students, which appeared to have particular value at crunch times when term papers and theses were due. Students had a hard time getting the books they needed from the University of Michigan libraries, with one of their major grievances being "that professors get first choice of books in the University library and it is a long time before they [the students] get them."[232] There also appears in this issue of the paper a fine review of Shalom Ash's tragedy *Sabbatai Zevi*, featuring the famous Sephardic rabbi and cabalist of the seventeenth century who claimed to be the Messiah. In another editorial entitled "Music," we get a sense of how important—as we have come to see throughout this book—music was to Hillel's daily life: "Of all the innovations that have been instituted at the Foundation this year, perhaps none is more noteworthy than the formation of the Hillel Choral Group to study and sing Jewish music. It is a significant stride toward the cultural goal which the Foundation has set for itself and which it is attaining more and more every day. In orthodox families Jewish and Hebrew music still holds an important place, and children

230. Ibid.

231. *The Hillel News*, Volume V, Number 8, November 26, 1930.

232. Ibid.

soon pick up these traditional hymns and festive lyrics. But until recently it was confined more or less to them. The only other place to hear it was in the temple, and with the religious apathy prevalent among a good many, it may be safe to assume that they knew little about it."[233] The editorial then continues to detail the growing popularity of Jewish music in American culture by mentioning the example of the Irish tenor Peter Higgins who, having sung "Eili Eili" over a nationwide radio program, was inundated with so much positive mail that he had to repeat it one week later. The editorial emphasizes the deep spiritual meaning of Jewish music by invoking the famous chant of "Kol Nidre" that commences the holiest of Jewish holidays, Yom Kippur: "The plaintive charm of that melody seems to embody the whole history of a race through thousands of years of struggle and hardship. To attempt to describe it would be futile. There is nothing else like it."[234]

But, by extolling the creation of the Hillel Choral Group, the Foundation not only fetes Jewish music but also accords all music a central place in culture and education: "One hardly thinks of the word culture without immediately associating it with music. Anyone without a knowledge and appreciation of the latter has sadly neglected his education."[235] Confirming this precise point is a short announcement in the paper that in addition to the Hillel Choral Group, various instrumental ensembles are also being organized by Hillel members all over campus. Music's centrality in Hillel's outlook could not be rendered more explicit than by these views and deeds.

In a lecture entitled "Why Judaism," Rabbi Heller mentions that the word *Judaism* is found "neither in Yiddish nor in Hebrew, and does not refer to a creed, church, sect, or denomination. Instead, it means a culture, a way of life, a hope and an ideal. Consequently

233. Ibid.
234. Ibid.
235. Ibid.

the question really means, 'Why be Jewish?'"[236] After presenting some rather weak and tautological arguments, such as Jewishness "will perform for you the basic function of religion in a way that no other can" mainly because it "emancipates the individual from the material things that tie him down," Heller ends his contribution by invoking the universalizing qualities embodied by Jews whom he liberally substitutes for Judaism.[237] For that purpose, he concludes by citing Ludwig Lewisohn from his *The Island Within*: "'The Jews as a people should persist because the world needs a challenging minority. The prevalent and dangerous tendency of standardization in thought and habits can only spell stagnation. As a questioning minority, the Jews can perform a great service to the world.'"[238] In other words, Jews' role—and presumably that of Judaism as well—is to provide a critical voice in the world, to be its democratizing agents, to perform the role of opposition and antinomy, and never to worry about its own particularistic problems. It was precisely this restlessness, this universalistic antinomy here extolled by Rabbi Heller, for which the Nazis and many others on Europe's *voelkisch* far right despised the Jews as *zersetzende Seelen*—as corrosive souls wallowing in trouble and causing the disintegration of the harmonic lives of the organic, non-Jewish, Gentile, and Aryan *Volk*.

Lastly, Jacob De Haas, a Zionist leader, presented a lecture on political Zionism to students on December 10, 1930, under the auspices of Hillel and Avukah, in which he characterized Orthodox Judaism as a form of passive resistance and Reform Judaism as passivity with no resistance. Only Zionism, he argued, provided the active resistance Jews would need to avail themselves increasingly in the future. Interestingly, on the very same page of *The Hillel News*, Adolf Hitler's name appears for the first time in the newspaper. The Nazi leader was mentioned in a lecture

236. *The Hillel News*, Volume V, Number 9, December 3, 1930.
237. Ibid.
238. Ibid.

on socialism presented by Preston W. Slosson, professor in the Department of History at the University of Michigan.[239]

The second semester of the 1930–31 academic year witnessed a continued debate about the role of religion in Jewish identity. Editorials named "Religious Emphasis," "Ignorance and Indifference," "Judaism Analyzed," and Rabbi Heller's chiding (though not denouncing) of Darwinian theory for not being able to explain crucial facets of the miracle and marvel that is the human condition continued to inform life at Hillel. The extolling of the genius of Albert Einstein and the favorable mention of his Zionism received coverage, as did a fine retrospective by a departing senior who extolled Hillel's ninth semester at the University of Michigan and noted that its tenth coincided with his own graduation from the University. Oddly written in the third-person singular, the author thanks Hillel for having provided him not only with true inspiration but also with a fine sense of belonging over the past four years. He also mentions that he cannot help but feel that many of his acquaintances who could and should have joined Hillel in their freshman year, like the author did, would have had a much happier experience at Michigan.

Three items central to Hillel's role and identity as a fulcrum of social life for Jewish students on the University of Michigan campus as well as the centrality of its educational mission appear in the issue of *The Hillel News* from January 9, 1931: the annual dance, Hillel's offering all kinds of tutoring help for the impending final examinations, and the role of Hebrew at the Foundation at this time.[240] Commencing with the dance, an editorial called "Annual Dance" exhorts students to come to it because

239. *The Hillel News*, Volume V, Number 10, December 16, 1930. Preston Slosson was one of the most popular professors at the University of Michigan at that time. According to the "Memorial" section of the LSA Minutes and the University of Michigan Faculty History Project, "for four decades his [Slosson's] freshman and more advanced surveys of modern Europe were among the most popular courses in the University."

240. *The Hillel News*, Volume V, Number 11, January 9, 1931.

it "is the social highlight of the Hillel program. It is the one big opportunity of the year for Jewish students to meet informally for the express purpose of 'having a good time.' As such it is different from any other Hillel event, and certainly from any other campus dance. Here one is almost certain to know everyone else, lending an atmosphere that is lacking in practically every affair held at a large university."[241] With these words, Hillel expresses three of its priorities very clearly. First, it is a "serious" institution with very high intellectual standards in which all activities—other than this dance—have some kind of educational angle and scholarly purpose. Second, this dance underlines Hillel's social mission of being a fun place in addition to an intellectually demanding one. Third, with its annual dance, the Foundation also offers a safe place on the Michigan campus for Jewish students to mix and mingle among each other apart from the pressures of the outside, non-Jewish world: "The fact that it [the dance] will be informal should meet with unanimous approval. When originally announced as a formal dance complaints immediately poured in that it would be restrictive and would force many to stay away who would otherwise attend. These persons should have no objections now. One further consideration should be mentioned. It will probably be the last opportunity for social recreation until after final examinations."[242]

This leads us to a brief presentation of Hillel's initiative, announced in this issue of *The Hillel News*, that the Foundation's Social Welfare Committee has arranged to tutor any student who needs help in her or his preparations for the incumbent final examinations: "A notice has been placed on the Hillel Bulletin Board under which those students who desire tutoring may sign their names and also the subject. The subjects in which tutoring will be offered will be those of more popular demand, numbering about six. It is expected that there will be about fifteen or twenty

241. Ibid.
242. Ibid.

students for each of these subjects. No doubt these will be among the subjects selected: French I and II, Political Science, Sociology 51 and a History course. Others will be added upon demand. The tutors will be composed mainly of professors and some advanced students who are very graciously rendering their services on the expectation that students will take advantage of such an opportune offer."[243] The article ends with an exhortation that no professors, we are sure, appreciated at the time, nor would they today: "Will all those students having old examination questions kindly contribute them to the Hillel file by leaving them with either Victor Rose or Hazel Greenwald. This file is at the disposal of any student."[244]

As to the teaching of Hebrew, for which there appeared to be some demand, the Foundation directed all those interested to the University, which "offers two years of Hebrew, consisting of instruction in grammar and practice in reading, taught by very competent scholars. The so-called 'scientific Hebrew' is used (the Hebrew actually spoken in Palestine today) instead of the dialects which have appeared through use in many European countries. Especially valuable is the grammar, for while many know how to read Hebrew and perhaps understand some of it, they lack a thorough knowledge of the construction and are thus unable to adequately handle the language. In the University Hebrew is handled much like other language courses, giving one thorough grounding in the conjugation, sentence and word structure, proper pronunciation, and vocabulary."[245] This was to change in later years when, as we will see, Hillel came to teach Hebrew because the Foundation rued the fact that the overwhelming number of Jewish students at the University of Michigan studied all kinds of languages—from French to German, from Spanish to Latin—but failed to enroll in the fine Hebrew classes offered by

243. Ibid.
244. Ibid.
245. Ibid.

the University, in which most of the small number of registered students were not Jewish.

The growth of the Hillel library continued unabated. The books' themes ranged from every possible aspect of Judaica to global literature, from music to poetry. Magazines included *The Atlantic Monthly*, *Harper's Time*, *Reader's Digest*, *The Nation*, *The New Republic*, *The Christian Century* (which was a Jewish magazine), *The American Hebrew*, and *The Reform Advocate*, among many others. In a front-page article entitled "Many Books Added to Hillel Library" published in *The Hillel News* of January 15, 1931, one cannot help but be truly impressed by the quality and bevy of books that found their way to the Foundation's library toward the end of that fall semester.[246] The author writes, "The Foundation library has recently added a number of new books to its shelves. Though examinations are just around the corner [exams for the fall semester were held after Christmas at that time] and text books are amply taking care of all literary interests students may have at the present time, the books will undoubtedly see much use as soon as the impending scholastic formalities (?) [*sic*] have passed. The new books have added variety as well as numbers to the library. Topics range from 'The life of the Bee' to 'Religion in a Changing World.' A number of the volumes have been 'best sellers.'"[247] But books such as *Disraeli and Gladstone*, *Mother India*, and *The Rise of the House of Rothschild* were just a few of the titles one can easily categorize as highbrow.

Hillel's interfaith activities persisted. Thus we learn that Rabbi Heller and Reverend Fisher, minister of the local Methodist Church of Ann Arbor, will "preach a joint sermon at the regular Sunday evening service of the latter church, January 18 . . . Their topic will be 'Einstein's Cosmic Religion.' The service promises to be one of the most unique held in Ann Arbor this year."[248] This topic seems

---

246. *The Hillel News*, Volume V, Number 11, January 15, 1931.

247. Ibid.

248. Ibid.

to have fit with Rabbi Heller's interest and expertise, which, as we learn from another piece in this issue of the paper, centers on the relationship between science and religion, on which he held a sermon at Sunday morning services on January 11.

An interesting editorial entitled "Dr. Slawson" announces the presence on campus of Dr. John Slawson, director of the Jewish Charities in Detroit, who will speak on "'Problems of the Modern American Community.' And of special interest to Jewish students is the fact that Dr. Slawson is directing the program in Detroit to properly adjust Jews to a wholesome social situation, and eliminate poverty and dependency from among them . . . Most Jewish students on the campus probably know something of the problems confronting immigrant Jews on their arrival in America. Their efforts to become economically established, to adjust to a strange language, different customs, and a new mode of life, are probably not unfamiliar to many. Some of these do not immediately succeed, and need sympathetic aid if demoralization is to be prevented . . . Students should need no urging to be at the League chapel Sunday morning. The advice instead is, more appropriately, come early if you want a seat."[249] This, we believe, was the only instance in which we saw the paper address the issue of Jewish immigration to the United States. We found its silence on this topic quite telling of the need to downplay one's immigrant roots and origins. While this was in no way tantamount to denying one's Jewish identity or opting for a seamless assimilation into Anglo-dominated American society and culture, it did bespeak a clear attempt to create a Jewish identity all its own in this "new world," in the *goldene medine*, away from that of the "old country." Let us also remember that with many of the Jewish students hailing from immigrant families, their class position was quite different from what it was to become in ensuing decades. Rather than being doctors, lawyers, and university professors, these students' fathers were typically shop keepers, small merchants, or

249. Ibid.

even laborers, with their mothers being housewives or working some kind of low-paying, low-status service job to complement the family's meager income.

To Hillel's credit, the services on Sunday, March 22, were conducted exclusively by women. Led by Florence Frankel, member of the Law Review at the University of Michigan Law School, this event was to raise issues concerning women's role and position in Jewish life in contemporary America. Here is the article announcing this forthcoming event. Note the worried language written from a male perspective: "The woman, at one time, was crowded out of ordinary life. She was submerged in her family and cared little for religion. It is in this modern day, however, that the woman has asserted her rights. She has forced her way to the fore and seems destined to take her place in the front in almost all fields, science, politics, and business. Religion alone still seems to be safe. But is it?"[250]

But gauging from what Frankel said in her speech to her audience, men's worries should have been allayed: "However, she said that marriage continues to be their [the women's] chief interest and that the average Jewish girl who goes to college at the present time does so either with the thought of raising her value in the marriage market or of preparing for a career that will be a stopgap between school and marriage."[251]

A fascinating editorial labeled "Prejudice" addressed a major issue preoccupying Jews at the time and in the present. According to Professor Angell of the Department of Sociology at the University of Michigan, "the greatest percentage of mal-adjusted students on the campus were Jewish, that is that the Jewish share in the number of mal-adjusted students is far out of proportion to the eight hundred odd Jewish students on the campus. This is a decidedly abnormal condition, and one which reflects somewhat upon the Hillel Foundation as the only visible indiscriminating

---

250. *The Hillel News*, Volume V, Number 16, March 18, 1931.
251. *The Hillel News*, Volume V, Number 17, March 25, 1931.

organization for Jewish students here at the University."[252] Interestingly, the editorial then blames this maladjustment of Jewish students not so much on external factors, such as discrimination against Jews and anti-Semitism—which, the piece concedes, still exists but is "slipping the way of all antiquities of an understanding civilization"—but on another prejudice that "is attempting to grasp for the power of the old one [prejudice] and is trying to squirm its destructive way through modern young Jewish life. We Jewish students cannot deny that there is an obscure yet prevalent feeling of internal prejudice which lurks in our midst. Our aged grandparents would stubbornly deny the existence of any such thing but those who daily wander through the world of modern Jewish youth are entirely aware of its presence."[253] The culprit: Jewish prejudice against and disdain toward other Jews. The editorial concludes, "Suffice it to say that it exists, and should be blotted out." And the best, possibly only, place to do so would be the Hillel Foundation. In other words, the intra-Jewish tensions of status anxiety, the ever-present but unresolved issues surrounding the desirability or scourge of assimilation, the difficulty of finding the right balance of religiosity—to name but a few crucial conflicts besetting virtually every American Jews' existence then (and even now)—seemed to have taken their psychological toll on the mental well-being of many Jewish students at the University of Michigan in the early 1930s.

But on the whole, and these major problems notwithstanding, things seemed to be going positively for Hillel and Jewish students at the University of Michigan at this time. Under the headline "Unfortunate," an editorial in *The Hillel News* of May 20, 1931, the last issue of that academic year, bemoans the fact that some students chose to smoke at the Hillel Formal dance in a University building where smoking was not allowed, which then led the University to revoke the usage of this building for future

252. *The Hillel News*, Volume V, Number 18, April 1, 1931.
253. Ibid.

Hillel occasions. The reason we found this editorial of particular interest was the effusive language with which the Hillel leadership speaks of the University's welcoming attitude and generous gestures toward Hillel. It cites the frequent usage of University buildings for various Hillel functions, the many members of its faculty that lecture at Hillel events free of any remuneration, and numerous other benefits that the University extends to Hillel: "The Foundation has been extremely fortunate throughout its existence in the fact that the University, both through its administrative officers and faculty, have constantly exhibited a very friendly attitude [toward Hillel] and have aided it [Hillel] on many occasions."[254] The editorial mentions that the students were probably not aware of the smoking ban but affirms immediately that ignorance cannot be an excuse for malfeasance. Hillel's public apology to the University for violating University rules and regulations on the part of some of the Foundation's members appears to be contrite and genuine.

The fall semester of 1931 commenced with immense optimism. First and foremost, Hillel celebrated its occupancy of an entire building "with tall white stately pillars"[255] that lent the Foundation a hitherto unknown presence of authority and stature, not to mention fine new facilities in which to hold its events and offer its members a great space to meet. Instrumental in this move were Mr. and Mrs. Osias Zwerdling, arguably the most important Jewish family in Ann Arbor, who had very close personal as well as institutional ties to the University of Michigan.[256] Also influential were Professor and Mrs. I. Leo Sharfman who, without a doubt, represented far and away the most active University of Michigan

254. *The Hillel News*, Volume V, Number 2, May 20, 1931.

255. *The Hillel News*, Volume VI, Number 1, October 8, 1931.

256. It was in the Zwerdlings' home, celebrating the High Holy Days of Rosh Hashana (New Year) and Yom Kippur (Day of Atonement) in 1916, from which Beth Israel, Ann Arbor's oldest Jewish synagogue and organized congregation, emerged, thus making Beth Israel Hillel's predecessor and senior by exactly one decade. A number of celebratory events throughout 2016 commemorated Beth Israel's centennial.

faculty in all matters Jewish on campus throughout the 1930s and beyond.

In an editorial entitled "High Hopes," *The Hillel News* announces to its readers that the forthcoming academic year will see a proliferation of cultural events at the Foundation that will surpass anything it had offered in the past. This included visiting faculty members giving lectures both at the Foundation and at the various fraternity and sorority houses, clearly bespeaking an increasing effort in the collaboration between Hillel and the Jewish fraternities and sororities on campus. There would also be dances, teas, an expansion of classes offered on varied topics, and an augmentation of the burgeoning library with the acquisition of the valuable collection owned by the late Louis Marshall, which he bequeathed to the Foundation.[257]

The following issue of *The Hillel News* presents all these new and exciting things to the freshmen in an editorial simply called "Freshmen" and concretizes its claims by listing the presence of two new courses at the Foundation taught by University faculty: a philosophy course on "Jewish Ethics" and a course on present Jewish problems taught by a "graduate fellow" in the Department of Economics.[258] In addition, a bevy of new all-women programs demonstrated Hillel's attempts to include women in its purview.[259]

The presence of the venerable Boston Symphony for a concert at Hill Auditorium on October 27 led the omnipresent and multitalented Josephine Stern to commence on Sunday, October 25, something called "Hillel Musicales" (sort of music appreciation sessions), which were to continue every Sunday afternoon thereafter, featuring the Foundation's extensive record holdings of classical music. First, students listened to these pieces together, and then they discussed them led by Stern's expertise.[260] As has

257. *The Hillel News*, Volume VI, Number 1, October 8, 1931.

258. *The Hillel News*, Volume VI, Number 2, October 14, 1931.

259. Ibid.

260. *The Hillel News*, Volume VI, Number 3, October 21, 1931.

become obvious throughout this study, we were immensely impressed by the Hillel students' high level of cultural sophistication in terms of their avid consumption of world-class literature and classical music. Thus we think that it is not by chance that Hillel referred to some of these organized music sessions by the nomenclature of "pop concerts." To wit, here are two notes hailing from the fall of 1936 that announce such pop concerts: "The first semi-monthly pop concert will be given Sunday, October 25, at 2:30PM at the Foundation. Brahms Symphony 1 and Debussy's 'Afternoon of a Faun' will be played. The second in a series of pop concerts will be given at the Foundation on Sunday, November 8 at 2:30PM . . . The fourth in a series of pop concerts will include Mendelsohn's Violin Concerto and Schumann's Quintette."[261] Amazingly, Brahms's, Debussy's, Mendelsohn's, and Schumann's music qualified as "pop" for students in those years.

Telling of the obvious rapprochement between Hillel and the Jewish sororities and fraternities at this juncture, *The Hillel News* announced in an editorial labeled "Afternoon Teas" that the Foundation's Social Committee had transferred the handling of afternoon teas to the University's sororities and fraternities: "It is also the purpose of the Hillel Foundation to act as the center for Jewish life for Michigan students. It can be readily seen that for the accomplishment of this aim, the Foundation must form a close relationship with Michigan's fraternities and sororities."[262]

In *The Hillel News* of October 28, we encounter for the first time any mention of the economic depression. This happens in the odd context of asking for an extra quarter in the entrance fee to a Hillel dance (going from $1 to $1.25), which the organizers, as did the editorial, hoped would not detain anybody from participating despite the hardships that the Depression imposed on students. On the same page, there is a short notice on the passing of the

261. Hillel Scrapbooks, 1936–37, BHL-UM Hillel, Box 1.
262. *The Hillel News*, Volume VI, Number 3, October 21, 1931.

great Austrian writer Arthur Schnitzler on October 22 at the age of sixty-nine. Schnitzler's brilliant plays addressed anti-Semitism in the Vienna of his time.[263] The last four issues of the paper published in the fall semester of 1931 tout the immense richness and "diversification"[264] of the Foundation's cultural offerings, which, via the growing number of classes offered at the Foundation, provide a "rare opportunity"[265] for any student to avail her- or himself of diving into topics such as ethics, medicine, literature, politics, and economics.

In addition to this concerted effort to expand the Foundation's cultural offerings and its attempt to include the fraternities and sororities in Hillel's nodal role of representing Jewish life on campus, the most salient activity that fall was the loan drive, in which Hillel attempted to persuade every Jewish student on the University of Michigan campus to donate at least one dollar to a fund that was to help students hit by the Depression.[266] This Hillel loan fund must have lasted at least one year because it is yet again featured in a Hillel editorial literally one year after the fund's creation. In this editorial, called "The Loan Fund," Hillel makes the fund's purpose and nature crystal clear by stating that "it is the purpose of the Loan Fund to aid these students, to become a buffer which will tide them over these critical periods in their college careers. It must be realized that the Fund is not fundamentally a charitable organization. It is what its name implies a 'loan' fund into which the money is returned by students who have been helped by it. This fixture eliminates the usual stigma which is attached to an outright acceptance of money, and adds to the general success of the Fund in its purpose."[267]

263. *The Hillel News*, Volume VI, Number 4, October 28, 1931.

264. *The B'nai B'rith Hillel News*, Volume VI, Number 6, November 11, 1931. Starting with this issue, *The Hillel News* assumes this modification in its title, which lasts until the issue of May 27, 1936.

265. *The Hillel News*, Volume VI, Number 5, November 4, 1931.

266. *The B'nai B'rith Hillel News*, Volume VI, Number 7, November 18, 1931.

267. *The B'nai B'rith Hillel News*, Volume VII, Number 4, November 30, 1932.

The featuring of cultural events that was so evident in the fall term of this academic year intensified during the spring term of 1932. There was a well-attended forum on intermarriage. Josephine Stern was the main speaker at a major event featuring the work of Spinoza, arguably one of the greatest Jewish philosophers of all time. After presenting the play *Caponsacchi*, written by Arthur Frederick Goodrich and Rose A. Palmer, to campus-wide acclaim in 1930—a play, incidentally, that no amateur company had ever performed anywhere in the country—the Hillel Players staged an equally taxing production entitled *Death Takes a Holiday* (music and lyrics by Maury Yeston, based on a book by Peter Stone and Thomas Meehan), which, too, was widely hailed by the entire University of Michigan community. Both of these performances were presented at the University of Michigan's well-known Lydia Mendelssohn Theatre. Women, notably Josephine Stern among them, of course, continued their prominence at the Foundation's Sunday religious services. And the Foundation organized a large exhibit of paintings and sketches by Jewish artists whose work had attained lesser prominence among the Jewish public than that of their creative colleagues working in other media such as music, drama, and literature. Lectures on Jews and medicine were presented in which topics such as Jewish attitudes toward autopsy, evolution, eugenics, and science were analyzed, as were medicine's relations to such particularly Jewish topics as dietary laws and *schechita* (kashrut).

The appointment of Benjamin Nathan Cardozo as an associate justice to the United States Supreme Court became not only a topic for a Foundation-sponsored and well-attended public forum; it also led *The Hillel News* to write a very optimistic editorial called "Prejudice Weakening" in which the paper depicts a trajectory in America that has been positive for the Jews, leading them from a society that discriminated against them openly and sharply to one that now accepts them and has muted, if not totally silenced, its voices of hatred and discrimination: "In 1932 we feel that the sharp edge of the blade of anti-Jewish prejudice has been dulled to a significant degree, and we may cite the case of Judge Cardoza [sic] as glaring evidence of this fact."[268]

In the same issue, we find the first longish article on the dangers of Hitler's rise to Jews in Europe. That world seemed to be far from the world of America, which—at least gauging by the aforementioned piece in the paper—seemed to be a place of bliss for its Jews. Indeed, in the issue of The Hillel News of April 21, there appears a celebratory note on Hindenburg's victory over Hitler in Germany's presidential election.[269]

Tellingly, The Hillel News began the fall semester 1932 with a powerful editorial entitled "What Hillel Means." The piece commences by detailing how most American Jews, certainly American Jewish students, experienced their Judaism: it all starts with learning its manners, mores, form, and content from their parents' and communities' practice of it, a phase that the editorial interestingly describes as "rather juvenile contacts" with Judaism. To be sure, the editorial does not dismiss or ridicule these as useless or infantile or immature, asserting that later in life, one returns precisely to these roots as a form of succor and comfort. But in between these two, shall we say, less-sophisticated phases of one's Jewish life, a rich middle of learning, living, experiencing, and growing occurs for which no organization constitutes a better hub than Hillel. In addition to listing all the fine concrete items that Hillel offers to all students on campus (Jewish and non-Jewish), among which mention is made of the Hillel Players, the Foundation's excellent library featuring books on Judaica as well as beyond, its classes on many topics centered on Judaism, and, of course, its rich social activities (such as dances and mixers) involving fraternities and sororities, the editorial invokes the educational and moral authority of Robert Maynard Hutchins. The

---

268. *The B'nai B'rith Hillel News*, Volume VI, Number 16, March 10, 1932. For reasons that seem somewhat puzzling, even embarrassing, to us, the editorial consistently calls Justice Cardozo "Cardoza."

269. *The B'nai B'rith Hillel News*, Volume VI, Number 20, April 21, 1932.

famous president of the University of Chicago, for whom a college education was only partially about books and lectures and laboratories, claimed that "the development of character"[270] was much more important.

Under a rubric called "The Jew Today," we read a short note about the travails besetting Jews in Germany and "the adjacent countries" followed by two relatively short and contrasting pieces. The first praises life in America for Jews in general, and the second lists Jews who had made their mark in American politics, most notably in this case contesting seats in the United States Congress in the forthcoming election of November 1932.[271]

But Hillel's worries about reaching Jewish students the way the Foundation viewed as optimal remained extant. Rabbi Heller bemoaned the fact that B'nai B'rith's spending about $80,000 per year needed to be amortized by more than mere attendance at dances, teas, and similar social activities. Such intellectually lightweight pursuits have their time and space, but Hillel's mission centers on acquainting Jewish students with "the glorious history, literature and philosophy" of the Jewish people: "It is with this aim in view that classes are offered, services are held, and lectures are given. A sincere Hillelite is one who distinguishes the more significant from the less significant activities and directs his interests and energies accordingly, to the former as well as the latter."[272]

Appropriately, an editorial entitled "Classes" published in the same issue of *The Hillel News* touts the difference between regular classes offered at the University and those offered by Hillel. Tout court, the attraction of the latter vis-à-vis the former manifests itself in that the former are compulsory and hence often met with the students' boredom, bordering on disinterest—even "an attitude of antagonism for both course and instructor."[273] This,

270. *The B'nai B'rith Hillel News*, Volume VII, Number 1, October 14, 1932.

271. Ibid.

272. *The B'nai B'rith Hillel News*, Volume VII, Number 2, November 4, 1932.

273. Ibid.

according to the editorial, is clearly not the case with Hillel classes, in which the topics are of great interest to the students, and their relationship with the instructors are based on mutual love for the topics and the personal acquaintance between teacher and student. In "The Jew Today" rubric, the paper proudly presents that Colonel Herbert H. Lehman and Judge Henry Horner are running for governorships of New York State and Illinois, respectively.

*The Hillel News*'s exhortations to make the Foundation more than a place for social gathering continue in the subsequent issue of the paper with two editorials entitled "Debating" and "Services." In the former, the paper's editors praise the intellectual values of debating and how becoming involved in that activity enhances one's horizons of knowledge and fosters oratorical and leadership skills. In the latter, the tone of frustration with the lack of student involvement and participation becomes marked: "[A] recurring gap of vacant seats greet those who speak at services. It is useless to bluntly ask why. One cannot answer a question involving what appears to be a fundamental flaw in Jewish collegiate life in a few sentences. The flaw can be described, however, as a peculiar lacking of spiritual interest which seems to forge itself into the make-up of individuals as they reach their college age, a decided indifference to one of the most powerful of history's and the world's forces, that of religion."[274] In this version of "The Jew Today," the paper warmly congratulates the victorious Governor Horner of Illinois and Governor Lehman of New York and mentions the beginning of the eighth academic year at the Hebrew University in Jerusalem.

In the ensuing three copies of *The Hillel News* available from that academic year, we see passages that continue to address a clear malaise Hillel seems to experience with its role in the lives of Jewish students on the University of Michigan campus. In an editorial entitled "Spiritual Prosperity" published on March 15, 1933, we read that while Hillel's efforts and results "have not been

---

274. *The B'nai Brith Hillel News*, Volume VII, Number 3, November 18, 1932.

thoroughly disappointing, [they] have not been up to the standard that might be expected . . . Without attempting to take away any credit from those who have worked, it is clear that something is wrong."[275] Despite the bevy of activities and resources that the Foundation has to offer the student body, there seems to be a lack of interest and commitment on the part of the latter toward the former. After listing these, the editorial concludes on a rather glum note: "Students as a whole are thoughtless. It is inconceivable that anyone could or would willfully deny the benefits of the Hillel Foundation . . . not only to himself but to the student body as a whole. This simply means that the Jewish student is not thinking, that he is careless in his judgment of values. Stop and think, view values in their true proportion and then actively join in the functions of Hillel."[276]

In a more confident tone, the paper's huge front-page headline reads "Players Will Present The Dybbuk: Famed Play to Be Enacted at the Laboratory Theater."[277] This turned out to become one of the Hillel Players' most successful productions in their illustrious work over the two decades under consideration in our study. Indeed, this particular Hillel Players' production of *The Dybbuk* attained national attention. Thus *The Pittsburgh Press* of April 16, 1933, ran an article on Sylvan Simon—twenty-three-year-old graduate of the Pittsburgh-based Schenley High School—who, in addition to his postgraduate studies at the University of Michigan's Law School, was also assistant director of the University's broadcasting department: "His acting and directing with the Hillel Players of the University in an English translation of the Yiddish play 'The Dybbuk' has resulted in praise for the production from many sources . . . By augmenting the English translation of Dimitri Komonosov with pantomime and suggestion through the use of expression and lighting, the Michigan students have won

275. *The B'nai B'rith Hillel News*, Volume VII, Number 6, March 15, 1933.
276. Ibid.
277. Ibid.

praise for their simple and clear rendition. Encouraged by the acclaim, the Hillel group plans to send Mr. Simon and the leading actors of the group on the road."[278] So things were not all bad and gloomy. There were clear moments of pride for the Foundation even in what seemed to be trying days.

That things were on an upswing by the end of that academic year is well revealed in an editorial called "Looking Back" published on May 3, 1933: "When school opened in September, the attitude toward the Hillel Foundation was one of morbid disinterest. However, since then, a small group of zealots headed by President Wermer and Rabbi Heller has managed to make Hillel affairs a topic of interest and concern to a large number of students."[279] The paper also lists thirty-seven names of Hillel members that received various academic honors that year, which includes eleven elected to Phi Beta Kappa (Josephine Stern among them, of course). Nothing short of impressive!

Academic year 1933–34 commenced with Hillel's first concerted membership drive on campus. To Hillel's delight, all fraternities and sororities supported this pledge, leading to 104 of their members joining Hillel. These students belonged to 8 fraternities and 2 sororities and paid a dollar each for a year's membership in Hillel. With an additional 100 unaffiliated students joining the Foundation in October 1934, Hillel secured about two-thirds of the membership that it desired.[280] This increased collaboration between Hillel and Jewish students in the Greek system and received further mention in subsequent issues of *The Hillel News*, which reported a membership of 300 by November 23 of that year.[281]

Thus, for example, we are also informed in that very same issue of the paper that Zeta Beta Tau, the oldest and most prestigious Jewish fraternity, was awarded "the Cecil Lambert Memorial

278. Donald B. Hirsch, "Local Youth Directs Play," *Pittsburgh Press*, April 16, 1933.

279. *The B'nai B'rith Hillel News*, Volume VII, Number 7, May 3, 1933.

280. *The B'nai B'rith Hillel News*, Volume VIII, Number 1, October 24, 1933.

281. *The B'nai B'rith Hillel News*, Volume VIII, Number 2, November 23, 1933.

Trophy for being first in scholarship for the third time since the cup was donated."[282] Even though there is no mention of this, we think it safe to assume that this trophy was under the purview of the Foundation, thereby demonstrating an institutional link between Hillel as the adjudicator of this award and the fraternities as its recipient. Perhaps less admirable from our current moral standards was the fact that the topic for the very first public intra-Hillel debate consisted of the resolution that a woman's charm varied inversely with her size, with three men arguing on the affirmative side and three women on the negating one.[283]

Despite these collaborative efforts between Hillel and the fraternities, tensions between the two parties did not disappear. In a rather forcefully worded piece under the rubric "Director's Column," Rabbi Heller attacks what he sees as the Jewish fraternities' dominant belief that Hillel only exists on campus to take care of Jewish students that are unaffiliated with fraternities: "This view, it is true, is less prevalent now than it was a few years ago. There is, however, still a significant number who hold on to that opinion. The truth of the matter, however, is that the fraternity man stands in as great, if not greater, need of Hillel Foundation than does the so-called independent."[284] And then comes Rabbi Heller's decisive punchline: "It is an indisputable fact that many men belong to Jewish fraternities mostly because the doors to Gentile fraternities are shut to them. Their Jewish association is a negative one—the mere product of existing social discrimination. The Hillel Foundation, through its religious and cultural work, wishes to convert that negative association or gregariousness into one that will be based on idealistic and spiritual motives and interests."[285] Lest the rabbi's stark differentiation between the negative association of fraternities and the positive association of Hillel be

282. Ibid.

283. Ibid.

284. *The B'nai B'rith Hillel News*, Volume VIII, Number 3, February 15, 1934.

285. Ibid.

misconstrued, he invokes "the danger of provincialism" that the world of fraternities bestows on its members and contrasts this to Hillel's milieu, which "includes Jewish students of diverse social, economic, and religious backgrounds and beliefs."[286]

Apropos Hillel's diversity, in the very same issue of the paper, there is an announcement under the headline "Hillel Foundation Is Real Jewish Center of Culture" that Hillel will be a coorganizer of the Spring Parley, the important all-campus activity. The Spring Parleys were an initiative by the Ruthven administration to foster dialogue between students and faculty on important themes and issues. Established in 1930, the first year of Alexander Ruthven's presidency, they were administered from 1932 by the Reverend Edward Blakeman, head of the University of Michigan's Office of Religious Education. Each year, a committee of faculty and students would decide on the theme and subtopics of that spring's parley. Any student could attend the Spring Parleys, which were generally held over a weekend in April or May, and pose questions to the faculty on the topic at hand. In effect, the parleys functioned as a means for the University, and the Ruthven administration, to channel student concerns and grievances into a structured and disciplined format. Blakeman's archives contain the notebooks for the parleys from 1931 to 1942 and, indeed, they appear to have been discontinued due to World War II. They were never revived after the war.

Hillel's concerted attempt to become the undisputed center of Jewish life on the Michigan campus continued unabated, as the editorial in *The Hillel News* of March 15 makes amply clear. Written most likely by Rowena Goldstein, the University of Michigan Hillel's first female president and entitled "Make Hillel Yours," the piece does not mince words: "Numerous efforts to coordinate the Jewish populace on the Michigan Campus have come to dismal but undeniable failure. We who constitute this group are all characterized by a curious lack of interest, a bored complacency, a

286. Ibid.

disinterestedness that we mistakenly construe as characteristic of worldliness. We are content to withdraw into a lethargic smugness and assume ourselves that 'the thing will take care of itself.'"[287] The editorial then continues to argue that this inactivity and studied aloofness is not only unbecoming of Michigan students but actually perilous for Jews, given "current happenings."[288] It then concludes that under "a new administration [that] has assumed the control of the Foundation," Hillel hopes to attract every Jewish student, "including the worldly ones who seem to fear that a show of interest [in things Jewish and Hillel] will betray a spark of life incompatible with 'savoir faire.'"[289] This, the editorial concludes, is crucial, otherwise this new Hillel "administration's attempts, just as attempts in the past, will prove worthless."[290]

In the April 16, 1934, issue of *The Hillel News*, we learn that President Alexander G. Ruthven enthusiastically supported the impending showing of "The Romance of a People" at the Olympia in Detroit. Depicting two thousand years of Jewish history, this was a massive theatrical production with more than two thousand people first performed on July 3, 1933 (Jewish Day), at the Chicago World's Fair as a direct response to Nazi violence in Europe and growing anti-Semitism in the United States. Virtually this entire issue of *The Hillel News* was devoted to discussions of this pageant that was shown in New York, Philadelphia, and Cleveland—in addition to Chicago—before its arrival in Detroit: "'It is a privilege to welcome this production and to congratulate those who have created it and are bringing it to Detroit,'" said President Ruthven, as quoted on the front page of *The Hillel News*.[291] Only Rabbi Heller's "Director's Column" dealt with a different, though related, topic—namely, how being Jewish in

287. *The B'nai Brith Hillel News*, Volume VIII, Number 4, March 15, 1934.
288. Ibid.
289. Ibid.
290. Ibid.
291. *The B'nai B'rith Hillel News*, Volume VIII, Number 5, April 16, 1934.

America, though much more secure than anywhere else in the world, did not absolve the Jews of being a minority, which meant being always perceived as different, always observed, always judged. As such, hiding behind the wall of assimilation was futile, as was an attempt to disengage from being praised or reviled as a Jew in an absolving "I-want-neither-the-honey-nor-the-stings" opting out, which simply never helps.[292] Hiding one's Jewishness, so the rabbi argued, is doomed to fail. This, of course, also meant that "in sportsmanlike fashion, [one must] be willing, it seems to me, to share the responsibility of the actions of those whom he [the Jew] would not consider a credit to his race or religion . . . The course, therefore, which the more ideal and refined Jew should pursue is not attempt to exclude himself from the group even as a matter of self-protection."[293]

The issue of Jews' standing on the University of Michigan campus must have entered a more acute, heightened, perhaps even precarious, stage by the fall of 1934, as a number of articles in *The Hillel News* of November 3 reveal. First, there appears a front-page appeal to all the Jewish fraternities and sororities to join Hillel with the added incentive of being offered a yearly free subscription to one of three publications: (1) *B'nai B'rith Magazine*, (2) *Menorah Journal*, and (3) *Opinion*. (We have no idea how attractive an incentive these publications would have been to a Jewish undergraduate in 1934.) Then the "Director's Column" is a word-for-word rerun of Rabbi Heller's piece published in the April 16 issue of the paper. Lastly, there is a triumphant editorial entitled "Jews on Campus" in which Hillel not only delights in the more than 900 students on campus who declared themselves Jewish but also assumes that of the 2,000 students who did not declare any religious affiliation, 500 must be Jewish, thus leading the tally of all Jews at Michigan to 1,400 students.[294]

292. Ibid.
293. Ibid.
294. *The B'nai B'rith Hillel News*, Volume IX, Number 1, November 3, 1934.

However, in the very same editorial in which Hillel delights at such a fine number of Jews on campus (it remains totally unclear by what logic and metric Hillel arrived at the conclusion that "of this 2,000, it may be conservatively estimated that 500 are Jewish"[295]), there is a lengthy discussion about how the presence of a large and concentrated number of Jews leads to anti-Semitism. Even though unsigned, we assume that this editorial hails from Rabbi Heller because the first-person singular appears: "I can venture to say that if there were but a few persons of Jewish blood on this Campus, there would be absolutely no problems for us to face. However, as it is at present, we must face facts and regardless of what we would like we cannot help but see that this problem [i.e., anti-Semitism] really exists." It is evident that Rabbi Heller seemed not to know the well-established global and, alas, timeless syndrome of anti-Semitism without Jews. Anti-Semitism's presence and practice seem to have been independent of the quantity of Jews living in a given society. Be that as it may, here is how the Foundation's director continues his telling piece: "Every Jew is judged by the action of his coreligionists. It must be remembered at all times that we are Jews and as such must conduct ourselves as befitting the name. We must remember that we are in a peculiar position and should at all times act in such a manner that will reflect only glory in our race. Let it not be said that any Jew conducted himself on this Campus in a manner unbefitting a gentleman. Only in this way can we hope to stem any anti-Semitism that may be arising on the Campus of this University."[296]

Despite their broad generalizations about the status of Jews in Gentile society, Heller's editorial comments were tied to a worrisome set of developments, as he saw them. Put simply, Hillel and the Jewish fraternities and sororities were not the only organizations on campus by 1934 to be associated with Judaism. By then, a chapter of the National Student League (NSL), a

---

295. Ibid.
296. Ibid.

Communist-directed student radical organization founded in 1931 at CCNY—perhaps the most Jewishly identified postsecondary institution in the United States of that era—had been established at Michigan.[297] Furthermore, given its New York origins, its function as a front organization for the Young Communist League, and the visibility of Jewish students in its leadership roles, NSL's Michigan chapter was very quickly castigated by conservative students as a redoubt of East Coast Jewish radicalism.[298] As the NSL's Michigan chapter became increasingly visible in its political agitation, Heller, and Hillel more generally, were concerned that a growing number of students at the University of Michigan and the larger public beyond the campus proper would attribute such radical political activity to *all* Jews. Hence Heller's editorial clearly sought not only to minimize the impact of the NSL's activities on Jewish life on campus but also to remind radical Jews of the effects that their actions had on the broader Jewish community.

Immediately following the aforementioned editorial, there appears another one entitled "The Jewish Emotional Tragedy" in which the text bemoans the mutual disdain and contempt that reformed Jews and their Orthodox brethren feel for each other. But when calamity strikes—as seems to be the case with Hitler in Germany—Jews unite for better or worse and help each other. But there still exist outliers, whom the piece labels "renegade Jews," toward whom the bitterness and enmity of the Jewish community for their not joining it and for their aloofness from it remain real.[299] And to make matters more complete still, there appears a short, untitled piece featuring the cosmopolitanism of the "Wan-

297. For the founding of the National Student League, see Robert Cohen, *When the Old Left Was Young: Student Radicals and America's First Mass Student Movement, 1929–1941* (New York: Oxford University Press, 1993), esp. ch. 2.

298. See, for example, Guy M. Whipple Jr., "What Is the National Student League? Statistical Analysis Makes a Reply," *Michigan Daily*, March 31, 1935, in which the author claims that "the conservatives of the campus have charged the N.S.L. variously with being a narrow sect of Eastern Semites."

299. *The B'nai B'rith Hillel News*, Volume IX, Number 1, November 3, 1934.

dering Jew" who, throughout the centuries, was the bastion of Jewish scholarship and whose intellectual contributions might be threatened by a successful assimilation.[300]

The newspaper's December 3, 1934, issue continues to delight in Hillel's successful membership drive while still bemoaning that too many of the fraternity and sorority members choose not to join Hillel and opt to conduct their social lives elsewhere on campus. One editorial reveals its content in its title: "Join the Hillel." The other, labeled "Attend Hillel Dance," states that "we must face the facts, fraternities and sororities do develop cliques." Then it pleads that unlike last year when only a few couples joined the annual Hillel dance, this year all Jewish students on campus, be they associated with fraternities and sororities or unaffiliated with either, must attend this festivity.[301]

The paper's issue of March 10, 1935, once again features discontent with the University of Michigan's ten Jewish fraternities and two Jewish sororities. But, for once, the editorial bemoans not so much the fact that this world is either rivalrous with Hillel or dismissive of it but rather the situation that its internecine fights are childish and counterproductive. The editorial, entitled "An Open Challenge," reads as follows: "There are on the University of Michigan campus 10 Jewish fraternities and two Jewish sororities. These organized Jewish groups represent a considerable proportion of the Jewish student body. They could, if the proper spirit of cooperation existed between them, exert a powerful influence on this campus. But the spirit, instead of being one of cooperation, is one of rivalry and

---

300. Ibid.

301. *The B'nai B'rith Hillel News*, Volume IX, Number 2, December 3, 1934. In an announcement under the headline "The Social Whirl," we read something that is very strange from our current vantage point: We are informed that Michigan students joined their Ohio State counterparts in celebrating "the Ohio victory over the Wolverines" at various dances and other "formals" in fraternities and elsewhere: "Michiganites were not bowed in sorrow, as some might expect, but joined in crashing the formals . . . and informal dance held by the Z.B.T.'s, the Phi Epsilon Phi house party; and the A. E. Phi open house and buffet supper."

jealousy. The fraternities are openly antagonistic; no love is lost between the two sororities . . . The situation can only be termed, to use a slang expression, 'rotten' . . . The fraternity men and sorority women have developed the art of cutting each others' throats with the sweetest voices and actions. For the sake of the Jewish student body as a whole, we must learn the meaning of 'Co-operation.'"[302]

In a subsequent editorial called "Change of Policy," the paper announces that henceforth it will regularly run stories that ought to be of great interest and relevance to Jewish students, even though these stories might have nothing to do with the University or even with the United States. But *The Hillel News* will feature them because it deems such stories relevant to all Jews. A case in point occurs in a column on the same page labeled "Max Warburg's Farewell Speech." This is the speech that the renowned Hamburg banker and shipping magnate delivered to his assembled colleagues of high finance, politics, and the maritime business at a fancy dinner held honoring his forced retirement by the Nazis. In this famous instance, in which Warburg was to remain silent throughout the sumptuous dinner while being bombastically hailed and falsely feted for his many accomplishments by his powerful peers, Warburg—to the surprise of all—stood up from his seat at his table at the beginning of the banquet and delivered a speech about himself and his immense contributions to the German shipping industry and to the country's economy as a whole that he knew nobody of the assembled would or could ever give on account of his being a Jew. Upon finishing, he folded his napkin and departed the icy stares and stunned silence of the assembled.

The newspaper's copy of April 15, 1935, provided three related and personally signed contributions that we regard as among the most important of our research on Hillel. Lending the topic's urgency a definitive stylistic point, Rabbi Bernard Heller's

---

302. *The B'nai B'rith Hillel News*, Volume IX, Number 3, March 19, 1935.

"Director's Column," which almost always appeared on page 2 of the paper, was featured on this issue's front page, prominently occupying its left column. It is here that the Foundation's director voiced his opinion on the profoundly sensitive topic that preoccupied the Michigan campus at this time: the increasingly fraught relationship between the Michigan chapter of the NSL—which was perceived in conservative circles to be a Jewish-led organization—and the Ruthven administration. The chapter had grown increasingly vocal in its political activities during the 1934–35 academic year. Along with its pacifist platform, the NSL found itself a leading participant in a broad campus-wide campaign against Michigan football coach Harry Kipke, who decided not even to dress, let alone play, the team's only African American member, running back Willis Ward, for the game against Georgia Tech in the fall of 1934 as per the Southern school's demands that Michigan not have any African American players on its side when the two teams took the field.[303] Continuing its radical activities in the remainder of the fall 1934 term and resuming them in the winter and spring of 1935, NSL invited a British Communist economist, John Strachey, to speak on campus in March of that year. Moreover, NSL also organized a walk-out of classes in support of the national NSL's annual antiwar demonstration in April 1935. In response to these actions, Ruthven chose to dismiss summarily four NSL members—all of whom were Jewish students from the

---

303. The Willis Ward story has many fascinating angles: Future president Gerald Ford's fury concerning Kipke's decision, allegedly leading Ford not wanting to play in the game at all; Michigan's abysmal 1934 football season, in which its victory against Georgia Tech was its only one that year following the winning of the Big Ten and national championships in 1932 and 1933; Ward's scoring all of Michigan's twelve points throughout the remainder of the season after the Georgia Tech game, with no other Michigan player scoring any; Ward's depression after that football season and his disillusionment with Michigan football and sports; and, of course, Ward's being an All-American athlete in track and field, in which he even beat the legendary Jesse Owens of Ohio State in a one-hundred-yard dash in a Big Ten meet.

New York and New Jersey area—in July 1935. They were William Fish from Newark, New Jersey; Joseph Feldman from New York City; David Cohen from Trenton, New Jersey; and Leon Osview from Elizabeth, New Jersey. In addition to these four dismissed students, there were two others that were suspended in 1935: Edith Folkoff and Leo Luskin. All students, with the possible exception of Edith Folkoff, were Jewish. Of the dismissed students, only "Osview obtained an interview with President Alexander G. Ruthven, and was permitted to resume his studies after an unqualified promise of better behavior in the future . . . President Ruthven remained firm in his decision against readmission of Fish, Feldman and Cohen."[304]

In its campus publication, *Student News*, NSL's Michigan chapter pointed out that the four dismissed students were all Jewish and from the East Coast, and Ruthven himself, in a letter to University counsel George Burke, indicates that this was a factor in his decision.[305] The turmoil surrounding this incident led a talented Jewish student from New York named Arthur Miller to write his second play. Called *Honors at Dawn*, this play in three acts, for which Miller won his second Hopwood Award in 1937, takes place at a large Midwestern university where a radical student's activities in support of striking workers at a factory in the university's vicinity are stymied by his treacherous brother who succumbs to the financial blackmail initiated by the university's president and its dean at the behest of the factory's owner and his personnel manager.[306]

In this politically heightened context, the Hillel Foundation's director found it an absolute necessity to address the sensitive issue of Jewish student radicalism at the University of Michigan

304. R. Ray Baker, "Radicals Agitate to Make Public Issue of Episode at University," Hillel Scrapbooks, BHL-UM Hillel, Box 2.

305. See the letter from Ruthven to Burke in the Bentley Historical Library, Alexander Ruthven Papers, Box 58, Folder 13.

306. Arthur Miller, *Honors at Dawn*, typescript copy, University of Michigan Library.

on the front page of the Foundation's publication. The leading sentence of the untitled piece frames the contribution's tone and substance perfectly: "Idealism to be effective must be coupled with prudence."[307] Rabbi Heller continues, "Jewish students who are inclined to be radical in their social, political, and economic philosophy ought, it seems to me, to ponder a great deal over this bit of practical wisdom. I hope I will not be misunderstood as exhorting the student with deep and sincere convictions to abjure those convictions out of regard for expediency or a fear of the opprobrium of those who differ from them. If one feels that he must be radical, by all means let him be radical. Nor do I want him to be a clandestine or a 'morrano' type of radical. What distresses me, however, is the tendency of these Jewish students to protrude themselves to the leadership or forefront of such groups."[308] Rabbi Heller then offers his reasons for admonishing Jewish leadership in politically radical organizations on campus and abetting or even approving of Jewish participation among the rank and file of such causes. First, the rabbi avers, the movement would prove much more popular among students on campus were its leaders not readily identified as Jews. And second, the overrepresentation of Jews among the leaders of radical movements poses a problem for all Jews on campus because, as the rabbi clearly states, "Jews do suffer by each other's actions."[309]

Both reasons bespeak a clear worry of anti-Semitism on campus and the rabbi's—and thus Hillel's—mission to protect Jews and offer them a world in which their being exposed to anti-Semitism be a bit curtailed rather than exacerbated as, per Rabbi Heller's (and many others') views, the presence of Jewish activism for radical (in this case Communist) causes inevitably does. The rabbi concludes his editorial by stating that "there are many

307. *The B'nai B'rith Hillel News*, Volume IX, Number 4, April 15, 1935.

308. Ibid. It is fascinating that Rabbi Heller uses the term *morrano*, instead of the correct *marrano*, in this context, referring to the Jews who tried to escape the Spanish Inquisition by renouncing their Judaism officially but adhering to it clandestinely.

309. Ibid.

who are disposed to see in the desire of Jews to be at the head and the helm of such movements a propensity to exhibitionism. One may not agree with such a version. It should, however, impel many of us to a greater degree of self-analysis and a more rigorous scrutiny of our motivations."[310]

The bottom line is that for Rabbi Heller, it is a pity that Jews become radical leaders and thus embarrass and discomfort and endanger the larger Jewish community. If they cannot help but join radical causes, it would be best were they to do so sotto voce. Thus it is not surprising to find out that Rabbi Heller at least understood, if not welcomed or supported, President Ruthven's decision to punish students for their radical activism on campus. Above all, Heller clearly rejected any notions that anti-Semitism in any form might have entered into Ruthven's decision. He also drew an indelible line between Hillel and the radical students. Thus "Rabbi Bernard Heller, director of the Hillel Foundation and religious counselor to the Jewish students, says he does not believe that 'religious or racial considerations entered into Dr. Ruthven's decision. Furthermore the young men studiously avoided identification or affiliation with the Hillel Foundation. I can't recall their ever participating in any of the religious or cultural activities sponsored by the foundation. It is not unlikely that their aloofness was prompted by the belief, current in radical circles, that their only valid associations must be based on class consciousness and issues [sic]. Granted that the general charges of the president are true, then his action is not unwarranted. Attendance at the University of Michigan—especially to non-residents of the state—seems to me to be not a right but a privilege which is conditioned on the proper interest and demeanor of the students. One may not agree with the administration's conception of what is proper interest and demeanor, but I do not believe one can disagree with the principle involved. It becomes, then, a

310. Ibid.

matter for the regents, the legislature, or the people of the state to decide—but not the courts.'"[311]

On page 2 of the same issue of *The Hillel News* there appear two opposing pieces under the overarching headline "The Jewish Problem and How to Solve It." A reprint of an address delivered by Justice Louis D. Brandeis delivered in 1915 represents the Zionist "exit" option for the solution of the Jewish Problem, whereas the anti-Zionist-assimilation-to-America "loyalty" option is articulated by the reprint of an interview of Joseph M. Preskauer that he gave to the *World-Telegram* on February 5, 1935.[312] Missing in these two opposing versions, we believe, is the "voice" option that Albert O. Hirschman so brilliantly presents not only as a course of action but also as a frame of strategic thinking (exit, voice, and loyalty) for people, organizations, and institutions in a complex society.[313]

The third piece of interest in this issue of *The Hillel News* also concerns the situation of Jews in America. An editorial quotes a letter by Franklin Delano Roosevelt written to Philip Slomovitz, editor of the *Detroit Jewish Chronicle*, in which the president tries to lay to rest for good the constant insinuations in Europe and North America of the time—and even today as still expressed in right-radical and neo-Nazi circles in Germany and Austria—that he was of Jewish ancestry: "'In the dim distant past,' writes President Roosevelt, 'they (the ancestors) may have been Jews or Catholics or Protestants—what I am more interested in is whether they were good citizens and believers in God—I hope they were both.' It is this paragraph that makes the Roosevelt letter to Mr. Slomovitz a historical document."[314]

Of the four copies of *The Hillel News* from the academic year 1935–36 that we found in the archives of the Bentley Library, it seems

---

311. Baker, "Radicals Agitate to Make Public Issue of Episode at University."

312. *The B'nai B'rith Hillel News*, Volume IX, Number 4, April 15, 1935.

313. Albert O. Hirschman, *Exit, Voice and Loyalty: Responses to Decline in Firms, Organizations, and States* (Cambridge: Harvard University Press, 1970).

314. *The B'nai B'rith Hillel News*, Volume IX, Number 4, April 15, 1935.

clear that issues relating to the Jewish people beyond the University of Michigan assumed greater salience. Thus, for example, in the paper of November 1, 1935, there is an appeal for all Jewish students on campus to join Hillel and pay a newly instituted membership fee of one dollar, which would give all students a free subscription to *The Hillel News* and free access to all of Hillel's activities and facilities, including the newly established Dr. Louis Weiss Library featuring a bevy of English-language books on Jewish topics. Once again showing his respect for and commitment to Hillel on the University of Michigan campus, President Alexander Ruthven was among the dignitaries who spoke at this library's inauguration.[315]

We also encounter in this issue of the paper a detailed account of institutions in the United States having called for a boycott of the Berlin Olympics to be held in the summer of 1936: "Backing the Columbia Spectator, the Teachers College News and the Student Board of Columbia College, Dean Herbert E. Hawkes of Columbia College has come out in favor of an American boycott of the 1936 Olympic Games in Berlin . . . Labor rebukes Germany . . . Christian Churches: No . . . Allegheny A.A.U. Speaks . . . on record as favoring American withdrawal from the Olympics unless the Nazi government proves it is not discriminating against Jewish and Catholic athletes."[316]

The next issue of *The Hillel News*, not appearing until February of 1936, mentions how the Nazis denounced Albert Einstein as the "apostle of Jewish physics." We also learn that following the enlightened policies instituted by Kemal Pasha (known as Ataturk) in Turkey, Mirza Reza Phalevi, Shah of Persia, decreed that all Jewish ghettos be abandoned in Persia (subsequently known as Iran) and the Jews no longer be forced to wear the distinctive garb that they had to for centuries.[317]

315. "Dedicate Weiss Library Sunday," Hillel Scrapbooks, 1935–36, BHL-UM Hillel, Box 2.

316. *The B'nai B'rith Hillel News*, Volume X, Number 1, November 1, 1935.

317. *The B'nai B'rith Hillel News*, Volume X, Number 2, February 27, 1936.

The next issue of the paper featured an editorial called "Boycott Heidelberg" that appeared alongside two full-page columns under the headline "Reunion in Heidelberg?" In these, we are informed that the Yale faculty urges a ban to attend the Heidelberg festivities; that Harvard accepts the invitation to attend them; that English universities such as Oxford, Cambridge, Birmingham, London, Manchester, and Liverpool all decline to send delegates to Heidelberg; and that various petitions were signed at Columbia and Cornell to have the respective universities not send representatives to the festivities in Heidelberg celebrating the 550th anniversary of the founding of that university. Together with several leading American universities, the University of Michigan, too, was invited to participate in the anniversary celebration of Heidelberg University, the third-oldest university of the German-speaking world following those of Prague and Vienna. This invitation caused quite a commotion at Michigan, just like it did at most other universities, leading to intense discussions among all constituents on campus—faculty, students, administrators. Under the title "Boycott Heidelberg," Hillel's position—not surprisingly—could not have been clearer: "We are astonished that American educators, so frequent in their denunciation of Nazism, [are] becoming so 'impartial' when faced with an opportunity to serve the cause of human freedom. Hitler has destroyed German learning; he has openly challenged the research and experience of years of scholarship, and has driven men of achievement and ability from German universities . . . Will American universities now join in the Heidelberg festivities—to commemorate the death of German learning? Or will they repudiate this latest attempt by the Nazi party to hide its cruelties by celebrating the anniversary of what was—before Hitler—a great center of knowledge?"[318] The only telling matter here is the fact that in its impassioned plea, the editorial never mentions the University of Michigan and

---

318. *The B'nai B'rith Hillel News*, Volume X, Number 3, March 31, 1936.

its leadership in particular, preferring not to implicate either by leaving it all vaguely in the realm of "American universities" at large. President Ruthven received significant correspondence from Jewish organizations and even Jewish members of his own faculty, such as longtime economics chair I. Leo Sharfman, protesting Ruthven's decision to send a faculty delegation to Heidelberg.[319] The letters reveal a kind of collective incredulity that the president was unwilling to consider the symbolic importance of sending an official University of Michigan delegation to an event sponsored by a Nazified university.

A fine case in point is a public letter written by "George L. Abernathy, Grad." published on March 11. Under the header "Heidelberg Decision," Abernathy writes to the editor: "I regret very much that the University of Michigan has found it desirable to accept the invitation to be represented at the 550th anniversary of the founding of the University of Heidelberg. My regret is not based on the fear that the National Socialist Party will try to convert the anniversary celebration into a political rally, but on considerations of principle . . . The invitation from Heidelberg forces the universities of the world to come to some decision as to whether they wish to remain true to their liberal heritage [that the author in an earlier part of his letter identifies with 'the primacy of reason,' 'the development of international technology and scientific culture,' 'the value of freedom and individuality,' and 'the faith in progress and humanitarianism'], or whether they wish to embrace a new philosophy of totalitarianism, racialism and nationalism. The British universities have chosen the former . . . Why has the University of Michigan accepted the Heidelberg invitation? Was it just a thoughtless and conventional acceptance? Or was it an implicit repudiation of the ideals of American university life? If it was the former, it is not too late to reconsider and to

319. The letters can be found in the Bentley Historical Library, Alexander Ruthven Correspondence Archive, Box 53, Folder 18.

cancel the acceptance. If it was the latter, it is of sufficient importance to warrant much wider discussion by the entire university
community—students, faculty, and administration."[320]

Although it is difficult to gauge whether Ruthven's insensitiv-
ity to Jewish concerns in this matter had any long-term reper-
cussions, it does suggest some strain between the president and
his Jewish constituency despite the president's rather awkward
view that his approval of Michigan's delegation to Heidelberg
had nothing to do with his personal sentiments about Nazism.
Perhaps part of this tension was exacerbated by a short piece in
*The New York Times* published on the Heidelberg controversy
in which President Ruthven was mentioned. The piece, untitled
and undated, reads: "The University of Michigan authorities today
confirmed a previous announcement that two university delegates would attend the celebration of the 550th anniversary of
Heidelberg University in June. This announcement was made
despite the fact that the Nazi political machine would assume an
important role in the celebration. President Alexander G. Ruthven of the University of Michigan stated that he believed that
Germany's presecuting [*sic*] of the Jews and Catholics had been
no worse than Italy's treatment of the Ethiopians, and recalled
that academicians from all parts of the world attended similar
scholastic ceremonies in Rome a year ago, which were presided
over by Premier Benito Mussolini."[321] Apart from the slight factual
error that Italy's war against Ethiopia had not yet commenced
when these ceremonies occurred in Rome in the summer of 1935,
Ruthven claimed to a number of people that he had been mis-
quoted, his views distorted and misrepresented—perhaps even
deviously so—by someone he trusted. This was made particularly clear in Ruthven's reply to Rabbi Bernard Heller, the Hillel
Foundation director at Michigan, who wrote a letter to Ruthven

320. "Heidelberg Decision," Hillel Scrapbooks, 1935–36, BHL-UM Hillel, Box 2.
321. Bentley Historical Library, Alexander Ruthven Correspondence Archive, Box
53, Folder 18.

expressing the dismay these remarks had caused people in the Jewish community who felt that Ruthven's attitude was clearly contrary to what they wanted the University of Michigan's policy and action to be.

Yet what also emerges in the tone of the exchange between Heller and Ruthven is the obvious goodwill, trust, and close relations that these two men shared with each other and how much both cared about the University of Michigan's public image and reputation. Here is Heller's letter of May 11, 1936, to Ruthven: "My dear Dr. Ruthven: The enclosed is one of the very many letters that I have received with reference to an interview which a newspaper account claims to have obtained from you. I must confess that I am at a loss to know what reply to make to such inquiries. If you care to be of aid to me in this matter, I shall be very happy to avail myself of it, especially if it will redound to the best interests of the University and to the esteem which I know you were held by many of the writers."[322] And here are excerpts from Ruthven's reply to Heller written on May 19, 1936: "My dear Rabbi Heller: I am really surprised for, confidentially, the situation is as follows. I said to one or two friends, in the course of general conversation something I remember saying to you. It was that I was surprised the University had not been criticized when it certified delegates to Rome a year ago. Someone, and I do not want to mention who it was, evidently told this to the papers or to some reporter with the statement that I was using this as a justification for certifying staff members to the Heidelberg celebration. This, of course, is ridiculous and a rather disheartening experience. I refuse to comment any more on the whole matter. If my record is not sufficient to indicate my breadth of interest, then certainly nothing that I can say will be of any avail."[323] While Ruthven may not have fully understood the importance of sending Michigan faculty to Heidelberg, Hillel—certainly at Director Heller's behest—did not

322. Ibid.
323. Ibid.

perceive this controversy sufficiently grave to address it beyond its aforementioned editorial entitled "Boycott Heidelberg," which made Hillel's stance clear in a general way without, however, embarrassing President Ruthven in the University of Michigan's particular case.

The next issue of the paper, published on May 27, 1936, featured an across-the-page headline in bold letters the like of which we had not encountered in any of the paper's preceding copies: "Hillel Foundation to Raise $3,000." This was part of a national drive by the American Jewish Joint Distribution Committee to help the Jews in Germany, if possible, and—better still—to help them depart from Germany. In addition to the article on the paper's front page and the editorial labeled "Support the Drive!" there were a number of other instances in this copy of *The Hillel News* where its readers were urged to contribute to this important cause. None was clearer in its exhortatory voice than an entry under the "Reflections . . ." column, which was written in all capital letters: "IT IS THE DUTY, IN OUR OPINION, FOR EACH AND EVERY JEWISH STUDENT TO CONTRIBUTE TO THE JOINT DISTRIBUTION DRIVE. REMEMBER THAT A PRICE OF A FEW SHOWS WILL FEED A FAMILY FOR A WEEK. LET'S GO OVER THE $3,000 QUOTA."[324]

Alas, we could not find any copies of *The Hillel News* for the academic year 1936–37 or for the fall semester of 1937. We could not locate any issues of Volume XI or the first few of Volume XII.

However, we did find a few items relevant to our themes in the boxes at Bentley Library housing the Hillel scrapbooks for 1936–37 and one containing "loose materials." It is clear that Hillel's irritation with what it perceived to be the Jewish fraternities' and sororities' persistent parochialism and their reluctance to engage with and in Hillel remained salient in this period as well: "Because of the dangers of provincialism and parochialism arising from the limited contacts afforded by fraternities and

---

324. *The B'nai B'rith Hillel News*, Volume X, Number 4, May 27, 1936.

sororities, a need has arisen for student movements whose objectives counteract this tendency, Dr. Bernard Heller told 70 persons Sunday night at the Hillel Foundation."[325]

This was not the first time that this Hillel Foundation director, like his predecessor as well as successors, expressed his irritation with the Jewish fraternities' and sororities' reluctance to engage with Hillel to a degree that was to the latter's liking. Of course, there were consistent contacts, and the quality of relations ebbed and flowed. But somehow, Hillel could not rid itself of viewing the fraternities' and sororities' lived Jewishness as shallow, parochial, even provincial—much too concerned with solely experiencing Judaism's social dimensions, while neglecting its intellectual and "deeper" meanings.

On other relevant matters, "Francis A. Hensen, widely known anti-Nazi and formerly executive secretary of the Emergency Committee on Aid of Political Prisoners from Nazism, who recently returned from a trip through the Reich on a fake press pass," not only spoke on the Catholic, Communist, and Social Democratic underground in Nazi Germany but anticipated "that these groups will lead in rebuilding Germany upon ashes of the Reich." Hensen predicted this to happen much sooner than it did, leading a newspaper to summarize his lecture with the headline "Hitler's Reign Is Almost Over."[326] Were that only to have been the case!

In a series on "Jews in Science," Samuel A. Goudsmit, professor of physics at the University of Michigan, delivered a lecture on Albert Einstein, whose name *The Hillel News* mentioned with some frequency throughout the two decades spanning our study.[327] It is also clear that Hillel students at the University of Michigan

325. "Heller Scores 'Provincialism' of Fraternities," Hillel Scrapbooks, Loose Materials, BHL-UM Hillel, Box 1.

326. "Hitler's Reign Is Almost Over," Hillel Scrapbooks, 1936–37, BHL-UM Hillel, Box 1.

327. "Goudsmit Lecture to Be on Einstein," Hillel Scrapbooks, 1936–37, BHL-UM Hillel, Box 1.

were in no way bothered by Richard Wagner's rabid anti-Semitism in terms of having that affect their appreciation for his music. Thus, in one of the regular music afternoons at the Foundation, students enjoyed excerpts from Wagner's major operas, such as *Lohengrin, Siegfried, Die Walkuere, Goetterdaemmerung*, and *Tristan und Isolde*.[328]

Far and away the greatest loss by not having copies of *The Hillel News* for this period was our missing out on what probably were detailed discussions and lengthy reviews of the Hillel Players' presentation of Arthur Miller's play *They Too Arise*, which was awarded the Hopwood and the Theresa Hepburn Awards in 1936. The Players presented this play at the University's Lydia Mendelssohn Theatre, where they had become regulars throughout the decade of the 1930s.[329] According to one report, "'They Too Arise,' the prize-winning play of Arthur Miller, '38 . . . is one of those plays which by its sensitive character treatment sends you out of the theatre with the warm feeling of having been in good company. The material of the play . . . is a middle-class Jewish family in New York, the father a small cloak manufacturer. The play alternates between the scenes in the home and at the factory with economic stress and a strike creating a dramatic progression."[330] Another report stated: "Arthur M. Miller, twenty-one-year-old junior at the University of Michigan, came home from a final examination in a history course Monday afternoon to find himself winner

328. "Hillel Concert Today to Offer Wagner Music," Hillel Scrapbooks, 1936–37, BHL-UM Hillel, Box 1.

329. We read the play under the title *No Villain*, which is available in a typescript copy at the University of Michigan's library but was—at least to our knowledge—never performed again until sometime in the winter of 2015–16 when, "in a tiny theater nestled above the Old Red Lion Pub" in London, Sean Turner, a twenty-nine-year-old director, revived the play using the *No Villain* name, not *They Too Arise*, which was the play's name when the Hillel Players performed it in March 1937. Christopher D. Shea, "Arthur Miller's 'Lost' Play: His First," *New York Times*, December 12, 2015.

330. "'Richness' of Miller's Play Is Lauded," Hillel Scrapbooks, 1936–37, BHL-UM Hillel, Box 1.

of a $1,250 scholarship award from the Bureau of New Plays in New York for his dramatization of an industrial strike, 'They Too Arise.'"[331]

Our next issue hails from March 1938, in which we noticed two stylistic changes. First, the paper's name had changed from the previous *The B'nai B'rith Hillel News* and the preceding *The Hillel News* to *Hillel News*. Moreover, while in all earlier issues an exact day of the month denoted the date of publication, now only the month appeared without any day.

As usual, issues of what best defined Jewish identity (in all its facets, from religiosity to nationalism, from culture to politics) remained central to Hillel. To wit, in addition to an editorial explaining the most basic tenets of Zionism, yet also making it clear that "we do not mean to urge the cause of Zionism upon anyone," Rabbi Heller uses his "Director's Column" to delineate the rich history of internecine fighting among the Jewish people over centuries. He employs this as a setup to plead with his constituents to attend Friday evening services, "which will be traditional in structure and yet esthetic and appealing even to the liberal-minded Jew. We consider it silly and stupid either to insist that all worshippers pray with donner or doffed headwear. We allow each to follow his own predilections. We love the Hebrew of the liturgy but we refuse to consider ourselves derelict when we translate certain prayers into the vernacular. Jews have occasion to plead for tolerance and liberalism on the part of Gentiles. They vibrate their pleas if they manifest an attitude of intolerance and bigotry to fellow-Jews, who may be disposed to adhere to customs which do not chime in with theirs."[332]

In its ever-present quest to enhance its stature and relevance to all Jewish students on the University of Michigan campus, Hillel announced a massive reorganization plan in April 1938. All extant committees experienced enlargement in terms of their

---

331. "Student, Down 50 Cents, Wins $1,250 Drama Award. U. of M. Junior Quits Dishwasher's Job as Celebration," Hillel Scrapbooks, 1936–37, BHL-UM Hillel, Box 1.

332. *Hillel News*, Volume XII, Number 3, March 1938.

membership, and a few new ones emerged, yielding the following ten: Social Welfare Committee, Book Club Committee, Classes Committee, *Hillel News*, Forensics Committee (commissioned to commence planning on a thousand-mile debate itinerary across the United States to be made the following academic year by the Hillel debate team), Library Committee, Religious Committee, Art Committee, Forum Committee, Music Committee, and Social Committee.[333]

In an editorial entitled "Hillel Reorganizes," which accompanied the announcement of Hillel's reorganization effort, the reasons for such become clear. They are centered on what the editorial—in this case, signed by Nathaniel Holtzman, Hillel's just-elected new president—preciously calls "mischievous inertia," a sort of passive-aggressive identification with one's Jewishness: "Nowhere is it appreciated that the antipathy of students to their race is not the only operating motive that impels even this elementary promotion of Jewish identity and activity. Most important of all it is the mischievous inertia of those of you who consent to your Judaism but refuse to assert and express it, a dilemma which perverts the reality of sound living that has given rise to this new implementation . . . A structure in itself is without purpose or meaning. It can obtain its necessary vitality only by harnessing the creative capacities of those it would comprehend. For this there must be an admission of the failure of mechanical indifference and the abhorrence of positive antipathy . . . Hillel is the only organization that can do anything really substantial for Jews as Jews."[334]

In an ensuing and, in this case, unsigned editorial entitled "The Jewish Problem Again," which was written as a response to a lecture at Hillel by Ludwig Lewisohn, an ardent Zionist whose passionate advocacy of Zionism's exit option being the only viable strategy for survival for Jews in the United States and elsewhere

333. *Hillel News*, Volume XII, Number 4, April 1938.
334. Ibid.

in the Diaspora clearly caused much controversy. Some of the students did not share the speaker's Zionist convictions and believed that the Jews' fate was better served by their adaptation to, even assimilation in, America. The argument emerged that the best protection for the Jews lay in strong and lasting democratic institutions that would always successfully oppose forces such as fascism that were the Jews' worst enemies: "The salvation of the Jew depends on the salvation of democracy. The Jew and the Gentile have a common cause, our bond. Let the differences in the fatherhood of God be obliterated in the brotherhood of man."[335] In other words, reject the exit option in favor of a mixture of the loyalty option (adaptation and assimilation) but with a modicum of the voice option as well (in the form of being outspoken proponents for democratic institutions and avid opponents of fascism).

The panegyric on democracy continued in the subsequent issue of *Hillel News* in which a speech by Jonah B. Wise—the national chairman of the American Jewish Joint Distribution Committee—equating democracy with Moses received prominent mention. Only democracy can be the Jewish people's savior from a situation in which "there is not one, there are a number of Egypts."[336]

The Foundation's director, Rabbi Bernard Heller, devoted his entire "Director's Column" to the horrors befalling Jews in Germany and Poland. In that context, Rabbi Heller reprimands the Ann Arbor Jewish community, including the Jewish students at the University of Michigan, for underachieving in its donations to the Joint Distribution Committee, whose help to Europe's Jews in need literally meant life or death for thousands, if not millions, of people. According to Heller, Ann Arbor's Jewish population, including the University of Michigan's Jewish students, hovered at around 1,400 people at the time, the equivalent to the Jewish population of El Paso, Texas. However, whereas the

335. Ibid.
336. *Hillel News*, Volume XII, Number 5, April 1938.

latter oversubscribed its quota of a $10,000 donation as its contribution to the Joint Distribution Committee's national drive, Ann Arbor was having difficulties reaching its quota of a relatively paltry $1,600. Indeed, places like Orlando, Florida, and Fall River, Massachusetts—also with Jewish populations comparable to Ann Arbor's—far surpassed their respective quotas. To be sure, students cannot be expected to donate amounts comparable to those of money-earning adults. Still, the apathy on the part of at least some portion of the University of Michigan's Jewish student body appeared palpable and irksome to writers in *Hillel News*: "If after reading reports and explanations of the drive and its purposes . . . the Jewish students do not respond with vigorous support, there is little this writer can say here that will be of any influence," signed by Morton Jampel.[337]

That academic year's last issue of *Hillel News* was brimming with confidence and delight. Apparently, the major organizational restructuring assumed during the course of the year bore the desired fruit: the classes offered by Hillel created wide student interest, the $1,600 quota stipulated by the Joint Distribution Committee to aid the Jews of Europe was exceeded by $800, a new Sunday evening lecture series drew large crowds, noted speakers and socials highlighted Friday services that were much better attended than previously, and many new books joined the Hillel Library by authors as varied as Thomas Mann, Lion Feuchtwanger, Thomas Hardy, and Elmer Rice, to mention but a few. An editorial entitled "Thanks a Million" penned by Morton Jampel extolled all these positive developments and attributed much of their existence to Rabbi Bernard Heller in a tone that sounded eerily like a good-bye: "But the same influence that saw to it that the Foundation achieved its present height of success will prevent it from sliding backward. We are naturally referring to Dr. Bernard Heller. We hesitate to use such a trite phrase as 'hero unsung' but no other describes Rabbi Heller. We feel we are not misinterpreting the consensus of

---

337. Ibid.

student opinion when we say were it not for Dr. Heller the Foundation would not be where it is today."[338]

The first issue of *Hillel News* welcoming the new—and old—students to the fall semester of October 1938 ran an editorial with the title "Welcome Home," which, we find, most aptly and succinctly characterized what the Hillel Foundation at the University of Michigan hoped to embody: "In a sense it is a paradox to extend an invitation to you [to participate in various activities], since the invitation comes in the last analysis from you. Hillel is simply the crystallization of the existing community of Jewish students on this campus. It is the framework, so to speak, of the community that would exist in chaotic form even without it. So when we invite you to participate in Hillel we are merely urging you to take your rightful place in the community to which you already belong. An invitation to express your Jewish interests through the agency of Hillel is not a call to join a few narrow predigested activities. It means that you are given an opportunity to experience here and develop here all the factors which enter into the eddy and swirl of living as a Jew in the modern world. As a democratic Jewish community center Hillel can invite you to help it be a cross-section of the Jewish life outside. Here for the first time many of you will have the opportunity to come in contact in social intercourse with many Jewish patterns of living which you may not have encountered before and which may be suitable to the mosaics of your lives. Welcome, then, to the complex structure of which you are a vital part. Welcome to your own."[339] As is only appropriate, we read elsewhere in the paper that Hillel commenced this new academic year with a mixer in which "smooth seniors and foolish frosh rub elbows on the stag line to cut in on the many fair damsels . . . at the Union, with Charlie Zwick and his band furnishing the jam."[340] The article ends as follows: "The

338. *Hillel News*, Volume XII, Number 6, May 1938.
339. *Hillel News*, Volume XII, Number 7, October 1938.
340. Ibid.

following Thursday, October 20, after everyone has been well Mixed, the first of the weekly Teas will be held at the Foundation. These events are expected to make Thursday afternoons a popular social hour at the Foundation when one and all may gather for a bit of music, be it Count Basie or Count Beethoven, a bit of intellectual discussion with someone young and pretty, a bit of meeting new faces, and last but not least a bit of tea, as only it can be prepared by our Social Committee."[341] From Count Basie to Count Beethoven just about aptly characterizes the Hillel community's musical catholicity at this time!

In a column appropriately labeled "Outside Eden," the paper informs its readers of the brutal realities that beset the world away from the halcyon campus of the University of Michigan: "Fascism has taken another goose step forward with the sell-out of Czechoslovakia by Tory Prime Minister Neville Chamberlain," starts a lengthy piece that acutely analyzes this dire situation in Europe with a Jewish angle in mind.[342] Lastly, we are also informed in this issue that a newly instituted Hillel Foundation Loan Fund had become available starting this academic year: "Men and women in need of funds are invited to take advantage of this opportunity."[343]

The November copy of *Hillel News* revealed to us immensely useful results pertaining to the geographic origins and religious preferences and orientations of Hillel members. Buried on the paper's last page under the odd headline "Did You Know?" and hailing from a student census that the University of Michigan was conducting at the time, we learn that 132 Hillel members indicated their preferences for Friday evening Reformed services, 81 favored Conservative services, and 44 favored Orthodox services. We also learn that Hillel members hail from more than 200 different towns, "making an average representation of five students per town; that next to Michigan in state representation come

341. Ibid.
342. Ibid.
343. Ibid.

New York, Illinois, New Jersey and Ohio; that the largest number of students (163) come from Detroit; that 77 students come from New York City and 60 from Chicago; that 39 students come from Brooklyn alone."[344]

In an otherwise cheerful editorial labeled "Saturday We Dance" and featuring sentences like "we were all one gang of happy Jewish kids having a heck of a swell time," the reader is simultaneously reminded that there also exists an ever-present "conscious or subconscious feeling of uneasiness that undeniably exists among Jewish people in a Christian world."[345] As if to reinforce the pervasive existence of this underlying insecurity, another editorial called "Sokolsky on Jews" exhorts the reader to "remember that one Jew to Gentile eyes, represents the entire Jewish people. Every word one may speak and every move one person may make, may be condemned or praised as a typical Jewish act. It is our duty to our people, as well as to ourselves, to remember the brand we bear."[346] Heavy stuff, this!

Because we are missing the December 1938 issue of *Hillel News*, we cannot bear witness as to how Hillel commemorated and accounted for Kristallnacht, which occurred on November 9 of that year. Indeed, Michigan students demanded that classes be canceled for one day so that they—as a community—could honor the victims of this Europe-wide atrocity and protest against its Nazi perpetrators. This actually happened on November 22.

## Exit Bernard Heller, Enter Isaac Rabinowitz

The theme of Jews' place in America continued to dominate the next issue of *Hillel News*, in which the lead article announced Dr. Bernard Heller's official resignation from the University of Michigan Hillel's directorship after having served nine years in that role.

344. *Hillel News*, Volume XII, Number 8, November 1938.
345. Ibid.
346. Ibid.

The fact that the Foundations' associate director, Dr. Isaac Rabinowitz, became Dr. Heller's successor assured continuity at this important Jewish organization at a leading American university in troubled times for Jews in the United States but especially in Europe.[347] Sure enough, two competing signed editorials offered very differing views on how to fight growing anti-Semitism and how to locate oneself as a Jew in these troubled times. In the first, called "Don't Hush Me," Ronald Freedman vehemently opposes what he perceives that some in the Jewish community—including *Hillel News*—advocate as a kind of "dignified" silence constituting the optimal strategy for Jews to pursue. Freedman argues that the notion of anti-Semitism being caused by some kind of fault in Jews' personalities and actions is deeply flawed and dangerous: "The causes of anti-Semitism are far deeper," he says. He argues that the "hush-hush school" seems not to realize that the current situation is far from embodying merely a "temporary deviation from the course of a perfect world. More and more we are realizing that we are at a critical turning point in the history of civilization. The lines of battle today are being drawn on the basis of a dichotomy of forces: on one side the democratic forces, on the other side the non-democratic forces (not all of which are fully fascist)." Furthermore, "the advocates of 'hush' confuse dignity with silence . . . No one will quarrel with the idea that reasonable decorum is necessary and desirable . . . What must be denied is the view that to prevent any adverse criticism we must live completely innocuous conventional lives, live according to accepted patterns, hold accepted beliefs . . . We must live not only in the dignity of good manners but also in the higher dignity of consistency with what we believe. Anything less is moral suicide. Anything less is to abandon religion."[348]

In his opposing editorial called "No, Not I!" Morton Jampel claims passionately that his position is decidedly not that of "Sha,

---

347. *Hillel News*, Volume XII, Number 9, January 1939.
348. Ibid.

Sha, Yid!" using a derogatory term for a Jew who is commanded to "shut up" and thereby deriding Freedman's "hush-hush" characterization of this serious issue. He grants Freedman the point that anti-Semitism has many deep causes—none more important than economic competition—that have nothing to do with Jewish behavior and attitudes. But then Jampel also states that he refuses "to say that 'personal idiosyncrasies' are not responsible in some part for anti-Semitic feeling . . . We still maintain that a great deal of Jewish hatred is aroused . . . by personal aggressive characteristics that many Jews maintain (and that even the most liberal Gentiles are wont to use for generalizations concerning Jewry in general) . . . There are many young Gentiles, neither Jew haters nor liberals, who are willing and ready to consider the Jew a fellow human being in all ways his equal. But after one unpleasant experience with a single Jew the Gentile leaves the border-line category and enters the class of potential anti-Semite. He is then ready material for men like Goebbels and Coughlin."[349]

In an article headlined "Anti-Semitism Is Widespread Survey Shows," the author, Leonard Schleider, summarizes the findings of an immensely interesting survey of Jewish students and professors at "sixty-three leading institutions of higher education in the United States" who were asked "to ascertain on their own campuses whether instances of religious prejudice have become more frequent in the past four years.[350] Results of the poll, when compared with previous questionnaires on the same subject, indicate a major increase in anti-Jewish feelings since the rise of Hitlerism in Germany. Those interviewed offered innumerable reasons and remedies for the ill-will manifested toward them by university

349. Ibid.

350. Unfortunately, like in our search for President Ruthven's mention discussed previously, in this case, too, our efforts to find this actual study proved futile. But we should point out that there were several surveys taken and published at this time that measured anti-Semitism in the United States. This was, we believe, due to the impact that Kristallnacht had on this issue even on this side of the Atlantic.

administrative officials, faculty members and students of other religions. Many blamed the tendency of Jews to concentrate in a particular school while others, chiefly Midwesterners, condemned 'New York Jews' and 'campus radicals' as trouble makers. A small minority was of the opinion that Jews should segregate themselves in all-Jewish universities and, especially, in separate professional schools."[351] Participants in the survey classified their institutions as follows: First, those with "none or little anti-Jewish feeling" in which there was—as would be expected—a highly disproportionate number of schools based in New York City and New York State, such as Brooklyn College, Bucknell University, CCNY, New York University (Washington Square division), Lehigh University, Union College, Rensselaer Polytechnic Institute, and Hunter College, but also non-New-York-based East Coast institutions, such as the University of Vermont, Amherst College, Connecticut State College, Bates College, and two non–East Coast schools with the University of Arizona and Vanderbilt University. The next category comprised schools in which there was "some anti-Jewish feeling." Here we find, among others, schools such as the Massachusetts Institute of Technology, the University of Alabama, the University of California, the University of Chicago, the University of Pennsylvania, Syracuse University, and the University of Nebraska. Then we have institutions in which there were "strong anti-Jewish feelings." Here we find schools such as New York University (University Heights division), Dartmouth College, Duke University, Harvard University, Indiana University, Princeton University, Stanford University, the University of Wyoming, and also the University of Michigan. The last category features schools in which respondents experienced "severe anti-Jewish feelings." Here we encounter institutions such as Carnegie Tech, Columbia University, Colgate University, Cornell University, Johns Hopkins University, University of Minnesota, University of Missouri, Ohio State University, Northwestern University,

351. *Hillel News*, Volume XII, Number 9, January 1939.

the University of Illinois, and Yale University.[352] While we have no idea how robust this survey's methodology was, it does give us at least a rough indication as to how Jews felt at these institutions of higher learning in the United States of the late 1930s. Justified or not, realistic or not, clearly Jews at the University of Michigan—the subjects of our study—expressed experiencing "strong anti-Jewish feelings" at this time.

In the subsequent issue of *Hillel News*, published in February 1939, three things stand out. First, the announcement that the University's President Alexander Ruthven will be present at the forthcoming testimonial banquet on March 7 honoring Dr. Bernard Heller's retirement from his directorship of Hillel and his nine-year service to the Foundation and thus the University of Michigan's community as a whole. This confirms yet again President Ruthven's deep commitment to Hillel and his views of the organization as the primary institution of the Jewish contribution to a meaningful representation on campus of what one could call an ecumenical and enlightened, yet also a self-assured, presence among what at the time were viewed as the three great religions of Protestantism, Catholicism, and Judaism.

The second, a crucial item indeed, informs us that this semester would see the Michigan Hillel assume a very rare, if not unique, position in American higher education—namely, as the purveyor of Jewish higher education based on the Oxford University tutorial system "in the form of an Honors Course of directed readings and studies in various fields of Jewish life and learning."[353] Personal interviews with Dr. Rabinowitz, in which each student's extant level of Jewish education was to be assessed, would provide the basis of acceptance to this course and decide the degree of complexity of the reading for each student. Special sections were to be accorded to students who had graduated from Hebrew high schools and Talmud Torahs (special Talmud-studying courses and

---

352. Ibid.

353. *Hillel News*, Volume XII, Number 10, February 1939.

institutions) and thus possessing an advanced level of knowledge in Jewish learning that graduates of regular high schools clearly lacked. Readings in Hebrew and English were to be offered in subject areas such as history, religion, philosophy, social sciences, Jewish scholarship, arts and letters, anthropology and travel, and Palestine and Zionism: "The Honors Course is aimed at meeting the problem of furnishing Jewish education on collegiate levels. Almost no such opportunities exist in the United States and virtually no organized approach to Jewish higher education is available to students in American universities and colleges . . . Michigan students may complement their general education by a broad, intensive Jewish training during their four years in Ann Arbor. It is hoped that this program will aid in solving the problem of cultural duality, with which the Jew is faced, in that this duality will be less one-sided."[354]

Apropos the duality of Jewish life in America, the third topic featured on the pages of this issue of the paper pertained to the continued acrimony and acerbity that informed the debates about anti-Semitism in *Hillel News*. None other than the new Hillel director, Dr. Rabinowitz, devoted the entirety of his extended "Director's Column" to an exposé on this topic. Concentrating his two points on refuting the arguments in the "No, Not I!" editorial penned by Morton Jampel, Rabinowitz first classifies such views as part of *Selbsthass* (using the German word for "self-hatred") in which by expressing their dislike for and disdain of fellow Jews, Jews hope to distance themselves from their coreligionists and thus be accepted by Gentiles as one of them: "'I don't like these Jews myself . . . and I can't blame Gentiles for being anti-Semitic so long as there are Jews like them' . . . What this really is, 'I would be anti-Semitic myself if I were a Gentile; we Jews are despicable.' And that, in turn, means: 'How I wish I were not a Jew! How much better to look down than be looked down upon, to be superior and not inferior!'"[355]

354. Ibid.
355. Ibid.

Rabinowitz does not dispute the fact that some Gentiles really dislike Jews for their alleged ill behavior and uncouth manners. But this only has meaning when it occurs in the context of other societal, economic, political, and historical factors that have created a deeply and widely present anti-Semitism that has nothing to do with personal characteristics such as manners and behavior. Rabinowitz continues: "The fantastic nature of the argument is further disclosed when we turn it around: whoever heard of any Gentile say he was a philo-Semite because he liked the way Jews combed their hair, wore their clothes, spoke English, etc.?"[356]

Rabinowitz's second point aims to refute the notion that "bad habits among Jews are bad because they bring anti-Semitism down upon us."[357] He argues that, curiously, those who most often hold that anti-Semitism is mainly attributable to the evil characteristics of the Jew "are not at all interested in combating evil itself. It is a curious coincidence, if indeed it is a coincidence, that this view of anti-Semitism emanates most frequently from circles which are not averse to the exploitation of labor or even the non-employment of Jews. And ironically, enough such folk defend their failure to hire co-religionists by the very same arguments which they use in advancing the view that anti-Semitism is caused by the badness of Jews i.e. 'personal aggressiveness,' 'unmannerliness,' 'loudness,' etc."[358] As we will see repeatedly, Rabinowitz astutely introduces the class-bound nature of this controversy, thereby giving voice to his obviously liberal predilections.

In an editorial entitled "For the People and of the People . . ." running alongside Rabinowitz's "Director's Column," Morton Jampel not only disputes Rabinowitz's points but uses this forum to further accentuate his own views. Jampel sees his refutation of Rabinowitz's *Selbsthass* argument as a statement of what he calls *Selbstlieb* (a slightly erroneously used version of the German

356. Ibid.
357. Ibid.
358. Ibid.

*Selbstliebe*, meaning "self-love"). This, in contrast to Rabinow-itz's characterizations, looks as follows: "'I don't like to see these obnoxious Jews hurting themselves. I am one of them and being glad of it, feel I have the right to advise to adopt means I happen to think best for preparing for the onslaught of a vicious and mili-tant anti-Semitism.'"[359]

In other words, Jampel couches his argument for accultura-tion and adaptation by Jews to Gentile manners and mores as the best strategy for the Jews' advancement in American society, most certainly for their protection, perhaps even survival, in it. Jampel phrases his argument in militaristic terms and speaks of battles and armies and discipline and armor, of which proper behavior and cultural adaptation are certainly the most potent versions: "As to what these standards of behavior are—well, we all know what is meant by obnoxiousness and personal over-aggressiveness . . . To put it tersely, when we talk about obnox-ious (to the Gentiles looking for a chance to criticize) Jews on campus, we mean that fraction of the Jewish student popula-tion that talks with a European Jewish intonation, that is loud, yes vulgar to the Gentile in dress, manner, and language. We repeat our previous editorials. There is absolutely no reason why American-born-and-bred boys and girls shouldn't be thoroughly American in behavior and habits. The truth may hurt, but it is our unpleasant duty to do the telling. We trust it is understood what is meant by American habits and manners."[360]

In Jampel's view, only a complete acculturation of Jews to mainstream America provides the sole potent weapon to fight the onslaught of anti-Semitism successfully: "The strong simi-larity between the condescending Jew who nervously tries to squelch his noisy brethren, and the Jew's Jew who is squelching his brethren, so that they will be better prepared to fight against anti-Semitism and for freedom is a similarity that must not be

359. Ibid.
360. Ibid.

confused. Suspiciousness and fear will readily confuse the latter with the former."[361]

President Ruthven appears mentioned in the next two issues of *Hillel News*. In the March issue, we learn of his speech at the banquet held in Dr. Bernard Heller's honor, in which the president praised the former Foundation director's work with Hillel in the highest possible way. Once again Ruthven reveals his admiration and approval of Hillel's presence on campus not only for the University of Michigan's Jewish students but also as a fine contributor to the university community as a whole. In the May issue (with the April one missing), President Ruthven's enthusiastic words in support of the local United Jewish Appeal (UJA) drive appear in full on *Hillel News*'s front page. It seems that in the 1939 UJA drive, the University of Michigan's Hillel Foundation performed in an exemplary fashion and was leading the nation: "During this period, Hillel is aiding refugee students, trying to help them obtain student visas and aiding them once they come to America. In 1939, Michigan had 9 refugee students on campus, more than any other Hillel [in the country]. Places were also found for 21 other students."[362]

That academic year's final copy of *Hillel News* announced the beginning of a new feature commencing with the fall semester of the 1939–40 academic year designed to enhance participation by Jewish students in Hillel—the creation of something called "affiliate membership." This was to be available for a yearly fee of $1.50. Successfully institutionalized at the Hillel Foundations of the University of Illinois, Indiana University, and Ohio State University, this initiative was to facilitate Hillel's institutional and cultural presence to students who wanted to avail themselves of the Foundation's resources without expressing a deeper commitment to the organization that a full membership entailed.

---

361. Ibid.

362. "B'nai B'rith Hillel Foundation at the University of Michigan, An Annotated Chronology," BHL-UM, Box 1.

Also in the spring of 1939, the Hillel Players resumed performing works of well-known playwrights and authors, in this case Irwin Shaw's *The Gentle People*. Staged on March 22 and 23 at the Lydia Mendelssohn Theatre, the performance was immensely well received. This production also ended a string of four years in which the Hillel Players performed plays written by students: *Unfinished Picture* by Theodore Kane Cohen '35, winner of the Hopwood Drama Award of 1935; *They Too Arise* by Arthur Miller '38, winner of the Hopwood Drama Award of 1936; *Roots* by Edith G. Whitesell '39, winner of the Hopwood Drama Award of 1937; and *Hospital Hill* by Harold Gast '39.[363] This newspaper article (bearing no author's name or date of publication) practically gushed at the outpouring of dramatic talent emanating from Ann Arbor: "Robert Sherwood, speaking in New York recently as President of the Dramatists' Guild, referred to Yale, Michigan, and Stanford as the places where our young dramatists are coming from. All of which should make you pretty proud of the University." Yale, of course, had the immense advantage of its proximity to New York City's theater and culture scene; the same was true for Stanford to San Francisco's: "But at the University of Michigan? Remember, Ann Arbor with Yale and Stanford as a dramatists' breeding ground in the United States. There have been only five student plays in public production in Ann Arbor in more than that many years. Four of them have been produced by Hillel (to its eternal credit), one by play production, and none during the drama season. Michigan has gained its fine reputation in the field of playwriting almost unaided by the encouragement of public production."[364] In addition to putting on plays at the Lydia Mendelssohn Theatre with regularity, the Hillel Players also toured the state in 1939 when they traveled to Jackson, Pontiac, and Flint to perform two one-act plays called *Two Goyem*

---

363. "Gulliver's Cavils by Young Gulliver," Hillel Players Scrapbooks, 1939–40, BHL-UM Hillel, Box 1.

364. Ibid.

and *Business Is Business*.[365] On April 29 and 30, the Hillel Players performed Albert Casella's *Death Takes a Holiday* at the Lydia Mendelssohn.[366]

The *Hillel News* of October 1939 opened with the banner headline in bold letters reaching across the entire front page of the paper: "Membership Enrollment Soars Over 830: TOTAL EXPECTED TO TOP 1,000 AS STUDENTS CONTINUE TO JOIN UNDER AFFILIATE MEMBERSHIP PLAN."[367] This made the Hillel chapter at the University of Michigan the country's largest. The text continues: "Of this number 245 are women students, representing a strong percentage of the less than 300 Jewish women on campus. Two hundred and fifty members came from fraternities and sororities, and the remainder were independents."[368]

While one editorial called "An Educational Program for Jewish Students . . ." listed an immensely impressive array of courses that Hillel offered in the context of its newly designed attempt to provide college-level courses to students interested in a variety of topics pertaining to Judaism ("The courses are designed not for Sunday School children nor for brotherhood group discussions, but for college people who wish to know more about the rich background from which they spring or who need guidance toward the unknown future"), another entitled "New Responsibility for American Jews . . ." brought the momentous developments of the outside world right to the University of Michigan's Ann Arbor campus in that the article made it crystal clear how the already commencing destruction of Polish Jewry was to make American Jewry the central locus and most important representative of the Jewish people: "We must face the future with the realization that

---

365. "Hillel's Wandering Minstrels to Visit Jackson, Pontiac, Flint," Hillel Players Scrapbooks, 1939–40, BHL-UM Hillel, Box 1.

366. "Casella Play to Be Given Tonight," Hillel Scrapbooks, Loose Materials, BHL-UM Hillel, Box 1.

367. *Hillel News*, Volume XIII, Number 2, October 1939.

368. Ibid.

the fall of Polish Jewry definitely places the center of gravity of Jewish life in the United States."[369]

But it was a letter published by Martin Dworkis in the "Mail Bag" section of the paper that fully articulated the political predicament Hillel had faced in 1935 and that it had never resolved with any lasting success in the ensuing four years. Since the Foundation's awkwardly subdued reaction in 1935 to the dismissal from the university of four radical students, all of whom happened to be Jewish, Hillel remained uneasy about the lasting presence of radical politics among certain Michigan students, a disproportionate number of whom were Jewish. With the Spanish Civil War, Italy's campaign in Africa, the beginning of the Sino-Japanese war, and the growing aggressiveness of Nazi Germany heralding an increased level of bellicosity that inevitably also affected the United States, the issue of American military engagement abroad became a hot topic in American politics and, of course, university campuses, Michigan's included. As has so often been the case before and since then, at this time, too, the radical left and right were in full agreement on a number of political items, none more so than insisting that the United States remain totally uninvolved in any wars abroad by maintaining its position of isolation and neutrality. According to Dworkis's letter, Hillel refused to send a representative to an all-campus peace meeting in the spring of 1939 "on the grounds that it was a controversial matter."[370] Dworkis continued: "Of course it was controversial but at the same time, it [the peace meeting] was the most important thing on campus at the time. The fact that the [Hillel] Council finally decided to send delegates who would vote as individuals and not as authorized speakers of the Foundation, shows the extreme and conservative caution that can be aroused. The Council cannot lock itself up in an ivory tower and watch the world go on its none-too-merry way. It must and can do something to add to the voice of

369. Ibid.
370. Ibid.

other campus groups in students' most essential problems today, problems which are everybody's not only students. As an example, may I point out, that an Armistice Day anti-war program is under consideration. It appears likely that the Council will refuse to have anything to do with the organization of such a program or with the program itself. The Foundation is an excellent means of expression for the Jewish student body, whether unanimous or in a majority. And yet? . . . It seems evident that the Foundation seeks to hide its head in the sand . . . The ostrich hiding its head in the sand is an excellent target for the marksman."[371] In his remarks, Dworkis made his full understanding of Hillel's predicament clear in that the Foundation's membership was far too diverse in its political views to allow unanimity on any topic. Still, Dworkis believed that Hillel as an organization had a duty to have its voice as a collective, as an institution, be heard and officially expressed in a debate of such political importance as America's potential involvement in wars abroad. He also thought it should grant its members the freedom to speak their minds on topics of such gravity not merely to themselves as individuals but also to Jews as a collective. Announcing a lecture by the well-known Zionist Ludwig Lewisohn on November 12 in which he will offer answers to "The Jewish Problem," the piece expresses deep worry about the rise of anti-Semitism "even in America" and voices the anxious query as to why the Jewish people cannot find any peace.[372]

Three further items in this issue are worthy of mention. First, there appears a fine piece by Foundation Director Isaac Rabinowitz in which—even at this juncture in terms of the tragic events befalling Europe's Jews—he carefully differentiates between Hitler and the Nazis on the one hand and the German people on the other. He also reminds the reader that one of the reasons for the Nazis' and Hitler's rise to power was the problematic

371. Ibid.
372. Ibid.

peace reached in the chateaus around Paris after the conclusion of World War I. Rabinowitz warns that "an unmerciful peace [following this war] would simply repeat the ghastly mistake of the last one. Worse yet, it would prove that there had been no genuine repentance, no genuine atonement, for that mistake."[373]

Second, under the headline "A Working Definition for Jews," *Hillel News* printed a lengthy passage from Kurt Lewin's article "When Facing Danger" that was published in the September 1939 issue of *The Jewish Frontier* in which Lewin recounts that he had "heard Jewish students in the Middle-West say that they feel more like non-Jewish Mid-Westerners than like Jews from New York."[374]

Lastly, we cannot help but marvel about the high intellectual level of at least some of Hillel's students gauging by the quality of authors and books that the library received that month (e.g., Sigmund Freud's *Moses and Monotheism* and Thomas Mann's *Joseph in Egypt*), augmenting an already impressive stock of works by the likes of Marx, Lassalle, Spinoza, Einstein, Odets, Asch, Tolstoy, Dostoyevsky, and Proust.[375]

The next issue demonstrated that journals of equivalent intellectual quality to these books formed what was truly a gem of a library. Under the title "Hillel Boasts Collection of Periodicals," we learn that the Foundation classified the magazines and papers to which it subscribed under four categories. The first was "literary-sociological," in which we find, among others, Anglo-Jewish magazines like *The Menorah Journal*, *The Jewish Frontier*, *The Reconstructionist*, *Jewish Education*, *Jewish Spectator*, *Jewish Social Studies*, *Journal of Oriental Studies*, and *Jewish Quarterly Review*. The second was "general," which included publications like *The New York Times*, *Current History*, *The New Republic*, *The Nation*, and *The American Scholar*. The third comprised Yiddish publications such as *Der Forwaertz*, *Die Freiheit*, *Yiddisher Kampfer*, and

373. Ibid.
374. Ibid.
375. Ibid.

*Hadoar*, "from which students may gain a rich insight into the living, idiomatic Jewish world and appreciate the cultural progress, the richness of the Jewish and Hebrew vernacular."[376] The fourth included Anglo-Jewish papers such as the *Detroit Jewish Chronicle*, *Chicago Reform Advocate*, *Indianapolis Jewish Post*, *Cincinnati American Israelite*, and *Hartford Jewish Courier*: "Also available at the Foundation is an exceptional news service, known as the Jewish Telegraph Agency (JTA) which is received daily."[377] We also read about the bevy of classes offered by Hillel in that fall term, ranging in topic from Jewish ethics to conversational Hebrew and from Biblical reading to Yiddish literature taught in Yiddish.

Of course we also find a response to Martin Dworkis's critical piece penned by Ronald Freedman. The author refutes Dworkis's point that Hillel proved deficient in its commitment to democracy by refusing to endorse political positions as Hillel—the institution, the collective—rather than leaving it up to each individual member to do as he or she pleases. Instead, Freedman argued, Hillel's existence as a general-purpose organization for all Jews prevents it from voicing such positions in its official capacity that, if it did, would make Hillel profoundly undemocratic, since this would inevitably mean that it privileged one group of its members over others: "To label the [Hillel] Council 'undemocratic' because it limits its activities to the functions for which Hillel was established is unfair."[378] Isaac Rabinowitz offers a learned analysis of the Hitler-Stalin pact, which he denounces for its cynicism. But he also worries that the left's obvious mistakes and shortcomings—which, in his view, led in part to this pact—will in all likelihood enhance the voice and stature of the right.

Two unusual articles appear in this issue. The first delineates a plan by Morris Zwerdling, son of Osias Zwerdling—Ann Arbor

---

376. *Hillel News*, Volume XIII, Number 3, November 1939.

377. Ibid.

378. Ibid.

furrier, chairman of the state Hillel Committee, and without a doubt the most prominent member of the Ann Arbor Jewish Community at the time—to enlarge the Hillel membership via a "friend of Hillel" system, "whereby adults throughout the state will nominally join the local chapter and in return receive the Foundation publications, the National Hillel Digest, and some sort of weekend in Ann Arbor. Such a weekend as suggested would include free tickets to the annual play of the Hillel Players, a luncheon, and a program of cultural lectures and seminars."[379]

The second is an editorial under the title "Jobs for Jews . . . ," which openly pleads for Jewish students to consider vocational options as careers even though such was (and remains) so contrary to predominant Jewish culture. What makes the piece particularly interesting is that its gist not only rests on advocating individual students' welfare and possibly beneficial career options but, in so doing, also provides an untried but hopeful venue that might perhaps help reduce, if not eliminate, existing anti-Semitism: "The occupational mal-distribution of the Jews is a well-known phenomenon. Jews are crowded into the 'white-collar' occupations. For the Jewish people as a whole, this has had far reaching consequences. It has stamped upon them the characteristics of the urban-dweller, the 'white-collar' worker, the 'rational' cosmopolitan. It is one of the factors that helps produce anti-Semitism. Insofar as there is any deep-seated resentment against the Jew, it is in part a resentment against the urbanism of the Jew." To make this development a reality, Hillel established a career clinic that was to help Jewish students on campus find jobs in vocational fields: "This agency [the career clinic] is prepared to offer a complete vocational guidance service including considerations that the factors that affect Jewish youth alone [sic]. Every Jewish student on the campus should take advantage of this rare opportunity to secure expert help in making an important decision. Let

---

379. Ibid. We mentioned already the Zwerdlings' pivotal role in Ann Arbor's Jewish community at the time.

the Hillel Career Clinic help you find the vocation in which you want to spend your life."[380]

The last issue of *Hillel News* published in December 1939 featured a scathing critique of Ludwig Lewisohn's Zionist lecture of November 12. Written by Robert Solomon, it argues that the Zionist argument rests on a willful distortion of the situation for Jews in America. Even though anti-Semitism exists in the United States, this in no way should lead Jews to depart from this country and travel to a situation of total uncertainty and danger: "It is true that there are discriminations against Jews in this country. But shall we run away from them to Palestine? There is also discrimination towards negroes. Shall they go back to Africa? Again and again, Mr. Lewissohn points out that we are a poor people. Let us try to attack the problem more directly. Is there no chance of improving our lot here in America? Shall we run? . . . It is right here that we American Jews can have equal rights as Americans and Jews. Let us strive to improve our position rather than run away. We question Mr. Lewissohn's answer."[381]

Additionally, there is an interesting proposal by Rabbi Rabinowitz to introduce the Kalla: "Long ago in far-off Babylonia, the makers of the Talmud created a splendid institution. This institution was known as the Kalla. Briefly, the idea of the Kalla was this: twice each year laymen from all over the region would come to the great schools of Sura, Nehardea, Pumbethita, and Mahora where in the week before the spring and autumn festivals, public seminars and lectures on matters of Jewish law and life would be delivered. Modern universities have institutions similar to the Kalla: I refer, of course, to the various 'homecoming' celebrations and alumni reunions . . . [which are] more often than not . . . merely the glorification of a particular football game; but lately, some universities have inaugurated the wise custom of holding

---

380. Ibid.

381. *Hillel News*, Volume XIII, Number 3, December 1939. It is a tad disappointing that in every single case Ludwig Lewisohn's name is mentioned in Hillel publications, it is always misspelled as "Lewissohn," just like in the quote here cited.

classes and seminars for alumni during commencement week or other suitable occasions, thus unconsciously reproducing the pattern of the ancient Jewish Kalla. Is there room for such an institution in American Jewish life? I think there is." Rabinowitz then uses the rest of his presentation to delineate how the Hillels on the country's university campuses could become the focal points for the creation of such loci for Jewish learning and affirmation.

Lastly, an article entitled "Jews Penned in Huge Ghetto: Mass Migration Under Way" constitutes the first report in this Hillel publication—merely four months into World War II—that describes the horrors befalling the Jews in Nazi-occupied Poland and what was to become known as the Holocaust.[382]

The war in Europe and the role of the United States toward it dominated the January 1940 edition of *Hillel News*. An editorial entitled "Minorities and the War . . ." spends most of its space berating Britain and France to the point of equating them to Nazi Germany in their culpabilities for causing the war and their moral failures to deal with key problems that remain central to it.[383] Above all, the piece derides Britain and France for their unwillingness and inability to deal with their minorities as well as their deficient approaches toward small nations in Europe. The editorial then demands that policies addressing these problems in the postwar period be issued as soon as possible to differentiate these two countries from Nazi Germany: "If the Allies are to be distinguished from Hitler in any respect, it should at least be on the question of minorities. Consequently, the governments of France and England should amplify their statement that they are fighting 'Hitlerism' and state specifically the solutions that they propose and are fighting for, as far as minorities are concerned . . . In short, what plans, or aims have England and France towards a decent solution of all, or most of Europe's important problems? If they would state

382. Ibid.

383. *Hillel News*, Volume XIII, Number 5, January 1940.

these, it would be much easier to make clear for ourselves our position in regards to the War, and provide the Allies with some justification for prosecuting it."[384] The article's arrogance that Britain and France commit themselves to performing totally unspecified beneficial acts on a postwar European continent not in their own right and for their own sake but to justify an American entry into World War II is quite baffling. But more surprising still is the complete misreading of the real nature of National Socialism and the German people's support for it. The equating of the Allies' nature and cause with those of Nazi Germany (i.e., British imperialism and French colonialism being every bit as evil and reprehensible as German National Socialism) were common fare on American campuses in those days well beyond the radical right's and left's isolationism.

But this editorial was not the only text in this issue that dealt with the war. Under the title "War and Peace," two opposing views of the current war and the United States' relation to it confronted each other. Constructing his contribution in response to the self-posed question "Why World War II?" Martin Dworkis hopes not to repeat the mistakes of the previous war, which drew the United States into a conflict whose resolution "introduced a decade of misery, deprivation and social stagnation for most of central Europe. From these conditions arose the dictatorships and the cause of the war of 1939." Worse than that, Dworkis continues, "today the imperialist rulers of England are fighting to preserve their world markets and raw materials in the interest of profits for the industrial monopolists. The people of England and France have been led to believe that they are fighting a holy war against the devil of Fascism. Rather they are fighting to preserve the profit-yielding markets and colonies which provide their meager employment and doles."[385] Dworkis ends his contribution with

384. Ibid.
385. Ibid.

a sentence unmistakably asserting his desire: "The year 1917 must not be repeated."[386]

This standard view articulated in the habitual language of anti-imperialism and anticapitalism employed by most left-wing isolationists opposing the United States' entry into the war met its challenge in a piece written by Joseph Bernstein entitled "The Present War." The author accuses Dworkis of "having been asleep for the past 25 years as far as his approach to international problems is concerned."[387] Bernstein faults Dworkis for ignoring completely fascism's aggressions both in Europe and in Asia throughout the 1920s and 1930s, which, Bernstein says, provided the main cause for the current war. To buttress his argument, Bernstein lists examples from Japan's, Italy's, and Germany's behavior of the previous decade. While he grants that England and France are capitalist powers with imperial interests, Bernstein argues in a sophisticated manner in which he demonstrates how fascism, though anchored in capitalism economically, is an altogether different animal in its aggressive rapaciousness. Citing relevant books, Bernstein writes: "German imperialism is a positive evil, if it is successful, then its ideas or storm troopers threatens [*sic*] the entire world."[388]

Showing how strong the antiwar and anti-Ally—thus de facto pro-German—position was on the Michigan campus at the time is the theme of *Hillel News*'s editorial of February 1940 in which the paper takes the *Michigan Daily*'s antiwar stance to task. Under the headline "News and the 'Michigan Daily,'" the editorial accuses the *Daily* of "'throwing out the baby with the bathwater'" by labeling all news about German brutalities in Poland as "'war propaganda' too unreliable to merit publication. The stand of these papers[389] is ostensibly that these reports are created by

---

386. Ibid.

387. Ibid.

388. Ibid.

389. The editorial mentions "many other American newspapers" in addition to the *Daily*.

pro-Ally agents who wish to draw the United States into the war . . . Although it is true that many stories about German atrocities are false or exaggerated, it is also true that there is good reason to believe that many of them are true."[390]

The *Hillel News* editorial makes it crystal clear that it in no way endorses any policy that would use German atrocities as a pretext to have the United States enter the war. Even though the paper expresses great caution on this matter and emphasizes its neutral stance on any American step concerning the war, the editors make clear that some atrocities committed by the Germans had been well reported and documented and are thus facts that should not be denied by the *Michigan Daily* or any other American newspaper. In a response to this editorial entitled "Yes, Germans Have Been Persecuting Jews. But . . . ," Elliott Maraniss, editor of the *Michigan Daily* at the time, thanks *Hillel News* for according him the space and courtesy of responding to the editorial, after which he proceeds to equate Daladier and Chamberlain with Hitler on all evils, including their treatment of Jews. Maraniss cites a long list of atrocities committed by Britain and France, from behavior in Ireland and India in the case of the former to the maltreatment of Spaniards and German Jews in concentration camps run by the latter.[391]

On a much happier note, we read in an article written by Joanne Cohen labeled "3 'B's'—Brahms, Bach, Benny Goodman on Hillel Records" how the Foundation has made arrangements that both "the classical and swing camps" can listen to their favorites at the same time without interfering with one another's pleasures, since "one faction can seek the seclusion of the victrola in the ping-pong room." We also learn that Hillel just added Tchaikovsky's Fourth and Beethoven's Sixth Symphonies as well as several Wagner records and Weber's "The Overture to Oberon" to its already impressive record collection.[392]

390. *Hillel News*, Volume XIII, Number 6, February 1940.
391. Ibid.
392. Ibid.

In addition to listing the acquisition of yet another immensely impressive array of new books for the Hillel library by authors such as Fyodor Dostoyevsky, Sigmund Freud, Bernard Shaw, Henrik Ibsen, Eugene O'Neill, Charles Horton Cooley, Hans Kohn, Max Lerner, Mortimer Adler, and Thomas Wolfe, among many others; announcing the winner of an oratory contest who prevailed with the topic "I Want to Be an American Jew"; and promoting a lecture with accompanying slides on the controversial subject "Is There a Jewish Type?" *Hillel News* ran an editorial called "Ours Is to Ask and Reason Why" in which the paper addressed head-on the political issues confronting Jewish students at the University of Michigan as well as in American society and the world at large.[393]

The editorial starts by declaiming the era as being a pivotal one in history that needed clear thinking. Instead, the public had been confused by its muddy variety of which not only the "masses" are at fault but—perhaps even more so—"the scholar, the writer, the college student and many others who are generally considered to be 'professional thinkers.'"[394] It is these whom the editorial addresses. It divides this group into "rightists," "liberals," and "leftists." After dismissing the first as pathetic defenders of the status quo who, by dint of their normative position, basically forego the act of thinking and thereby "either tacitly or explicitly accept a position of indifference, of apathy, and finally of retrogression and reaction," the editorial devotes most of its space to addressing the world of "liberals" and "leftists."[395] Concerning the former, the editorial sees them as "too proud of their past, too oblivious of the present, and much too aware of a far-distant future, in a world that is being dizzily whirled about in the present and which is seriously questioning whether

---

393. *Hillel News*, Volume XIII, Number 7, March 1940.
394. Ibid.
395. Ibid.

it is to see any future at all."[396] Invoking the liberals' Hamlet-like removal of themselves from action "until society reaches a point where ITS decline and THEIRS is equally inevitable," the editorial implores liberals to jettison their usual equivocation and act now.[397]

The "leftists" receive much more space than the liberals. Here, too, criticism surpasses approval: "But criticism of them should NEVER take the form of Dies persecutions, or F.B.I. raids; criticism of their position must come from an appreciation of their work in labor and politics, and from an understanding of the profound motivations that impel many of them. However, the Soviet leftists, who include splinter groups of Lovestoneites and Trotzkyites, as well as Stalinists, are now liable to fundamentally the same criticism that was directed against the rightists. Theirs is now the position of an essentially LAISSEZ FAIRE attitude, an attitude of faith, in regard to the Soviet Union. In many ways they have gone into bankruptcy; they are demonstrating to an unbelievable degree, for some of us, the slavish, imitative, and distorted thought that can follow from too close an alignment with a suspect leader such as Stalin or can follow from any uncritical alignment. If the major portion of this editorial seems to be devoted to them, it is because on this campus they influence and lead, or mislead, those who are socially conscious and alive (for the most part). Once and for all they must stop follow the leader, when the leader is following Hitler."[398] This editorial fully revealed Hillel's liberal-leftist sympathies coupled with its deeply held antipathies toward radicals, especially of the Stalinist variety. It also added a crucial voice to a campus that was riven by ideological antagonisms at the time, which—as we will present shortly—assumed deeply troubling dimensions in the summer of that year.

396. Ibid.

397. Ibid. The all capital letters in *ITS* and *THEIRS* appear in the original text.

398. Ibid. The all capital letters in *NEVER* and *LAISSEZ FAIRE* appear in the original text. "Dies persecutions" refers to the Jews' being persecuted for their alleged role in having caused the Black Death.

Two main themes preoccupied the last two issues of *Hillel News* in the academic year 1939–40. First, Hillel's celebrating its Bar Mitzvah on the Michigan campus with a large banquet on May 9, at which President Ruthven was to be one of the speakers. (As will be recalled, even though one can technically date the founding of the University of Michigan's Hillel Foundation to December 1926, its de facto operational beginning happened in 1927. Hence the Bar Mitzvah celebrations in 1940, thirteen years after 1927.) And second, the continued urgency of the deteriorating situation for Jews both in the United States and abroad. Pertaining to the former, many of the Foundation's past accomplishments were feted, none more than the contribution of the Hillel Players. Additionally, the Hillel Service Cup (also known as the Hillel Fraternity-Sorority Service Trophy) was awarded at the banquet to the "organized house" that had best cooperated with Hillel in the past academic year. With Alpha Epsilon Pi having won the trophy the two previous years, winning it a third year in a row would mean that this fraternity would get to keep the cup for good. And so it did before Zeta Beta Tau resumed its own winning ways in May 1941. But far and away the most interesting thing that happened at this Bar Mitzvah celebration was the content of the speech delivered by President Ruthven, which was reprinted in its entirety in the November 1940 issue of *Hillel News*.[399]

Ruthven decided to make his speech a deeply substantial one, foregoing the vacuous praises that are common at such occasions: "I should tonight, I suppose, say some nice things about the Hillel Foundation and sit down, but I would really like to be rather critical. Please let me indulge for once and speak quite frankly. If you do not like my remarks, I assure you that your sufferings will be of brief duration. Remember, too, that I am not talking about you who are here tonight."[400] Ruthven continued: "Concisely, I am disappointed with our Jewish students. If it is any comfort to you, I

399. *Hillel News*, Volume XIV, Number 2, November 1940.
400. Ibid.

am also disappointed with our Christian students, Mohammedan students, and with those of other faiths on campus. Education must have a religious foundation or it is not education in the best sense of that term." Thus Ruthven displayed the core of his beliefs, which held that the deep knowledge of any and all religions and the necessity of their forming the basis for the study of all subjects offered a humanizing dimension to education and ethics that nothing else could.[401] Ruthven then singles out Jews by appealing to the special role of learning that informs Jewish identity by asking: "Do we not have a right to expect that at least our Jewish students will try to learn and heed the lessons read by their own teachers?"[402] Ruthven concluded his remarks by praising the Hillel Foundation for having played a crucial role in this educational endeavor of which he would like to see more, not only on Hillel's part, but on that of other organizations at the University of Michigan: "I congratulate the Hillel Foundation on its work during the past 13 years. I hope it will continue to inculcate an understanding of, and devotion to, the Principles of Jewish Ethics. This should be its principal objective, because the Jewish religion is above all universal, not national or racial. If this work is faithfully performed, then the Foundation will be serving not only the Jewish student, but also the University, because it will be assisting all students."[403] Equating Judaism with a strong sense of universalism characterized Ruthven's deeply held views of Jews being agents of learning and enlightenment, a core value widely shared by Protestants of Ruthven's persuasion at the time.

As to the issue of increasing efforts to organize against anti-Semitism in the United States and abroad, there appeared a powerful editorial in the April 1940 issue under the telling title "Jewish Unity Is Essential Need in Present Crisis."[404] While welcoming

401. Ibid.

402. Ibid.

403. Ibid.

404. *Hillel News*, Volume XIII, Number 8, April 1940.

the creation of something called the Joint Council in 1938, which comprised such key institutions of American Jewry like the American Jewish Committee, the American Jewish Congress, the B'nai B'rith Anti-Defamation Committee, and the Jewish Labor Committee, the editorial comes to the conclusion that "after two years of existence, the Joint Council has completely failed. The reasons for this are obvious. The Council was not representative of American Jewry, it was a close-knit organization, it never completely agreed upon the scope of its activity, and most important—the Council had no functional power. It was doomed to failure at the outset."[405] The editorial then lists a long array of Jewish organizations that will need to be included to give this creation the chance of any success. The editorial concludes by stating that "the situation facing Jewery [sic] today is tragically similar to that of 1918. By unifying for the preservation of Jewish rights, American Jewery [sic] can play a tremendous role in the maintenance of its own position, as well as the position of all minority people."[406]

The May issue of *Hillel News* features a lead article in which the paper announces that town and gown will join forces to make the just-opening United Jewish Appeal drive as successful as possible. Rabbi Rabinowitz was to lead the University contingent with Osias Zwerdling representing Ann Arbor's Jewish community. In the same issue, we see the first photograph published in the paper of Jews in Nazi-occupied Poland. Entitled "The Yellow Patch of Degradation," we see three women "wearing the yellow patch on the back of their garments in accordance with Nazi regulations."[407] We also learn that Elliot Maraniss and Joseph Bernstein, the two prominent antagonists holding opposite views on the most desirable action by the United States regarding the war, were to head a panel discussion on precisely this topic on May 10.[408]

405. Ibid.
406. Ibid.
407. *Hillel News*, Volume XIII, Number 9, May 1940.
408. Ibid.

Just as Jews on campus were beginning to focus more intently on the fate of their coreligionists in Europe, the summer of 1940 also brought back unpleasant memories closer to home. In June 1940, following an angry address in which he effectively called for the removal of students from campus, Ruthven dismissed seventeen students, most of whom were from the East Coast. Judging by their last names, we are reasonably confident that almost half of them were Jews and all were members or fellow travelers of the NSL's successor organization, the American Students Union (ASU).[409] While these new dismissals were not exclusively targeted at Jews, they *do* appear to have been spurred, in part, by outside pressure from well-known anti-Semites, especially Henry Ford. To wit, Ruthven seems to have been pressured by Harry Kipke—Michigan football coach from 1928 to 1937, member of the Board of Regents beginning in January 1940, and friend to Henry Ford's hatchet man,

409. We cannot be certain as to the exact number of Jews among the dismissed students because their religious affiliations were never listed on any documents, which means that we had to rely on last names and the students' geographic origins as data that allowed us to form educated guesses. Here are the students' names and their places of origin: Abraham Stavitzky from Newark, NJ; Hilda Rosenbaum from Milford, CT; Howard Moss from New York, NY; Joan Geiger from Woodmere, NY; Nathaniel Rinzberg from Brooklyn, NY; Hugo Reichard from South Plainfield, NJ; Roger Lawn from Radburn, NJ; and Morris Gleicher from Detroit, MI. The percentage of Jewish students at the University of Michigan at this time was just shy of 10 percent. Jews constituted a bit less than 4 percent of the population of the United States in 1940. In 2016, there were approximately 4,500 Jewish undergraduate and 1,500 graduate students at the University of Michigan (out of a total of 28,312 undergraduates and 15,339 graduate students), making the percentage of Jewish students among the University of Michigan's undergraduate population almost 16 percent, with the Jewish ratio among graduate students just under 10 percent. In the same year, Jews comprised about 2.2 percent of the population of the United States. The current numbers for Jewish students at the University of Michigan are, of course, approximations because nobody really knows the exact figures unless every student identified her or his religious affiliations officially. The number for the Jewish undergraduates is—according to Hillel—a much more solid and reliable approximation than the one for graduate students, which is really unknown.

Harry Bennett—to dismiss members of the ASU before the start of the 1940–41 academic year.[410] Bennett's memoirs make it clear that Kipke wanted information about radical activities on campus.[411] These dismissals occasioned far more of a public outcry than those of 1935, to the point that Ruthven was given a mock trial in November 1940 by the Michigan Committee of Academic Freedom, which had been formed by prominent Detroit-area progressive leaders like the Reverend Owen Knox and labor lawyer Maurice Sugar. These dismissals were part and parcel of an attempt to crack down on all radical activity on campus, including bringing the *Michigan Daily*—whose editorial line had shifted from conservatism in the mid-1930s to a more left-wing stance by 1940—to heel.

The *Daily*, moreover, was perceived as dominated by Jewish students, and Kipke especially wanted to see more faculty representation on the Board of Student Publications, which served as an oversight body. In a slight contrast to parallel events in 1935 when Bernard Heller, Hillel's director at the time, wrote an extensive editorial as to the implications for Jewish students on campus, and even Jews in general, of the involvement of Jewish students as leaders of radical politics, Hillel remained silent in this case in 1940 with no equivalent editorial penned by Director Rabinowitz paralleling Heller's. This was no doubt in part because Ruthven had ordered the *Michigan Daily* not to print anything about the dismissals (the paper eventually did in October 1940) so as

---

410. This certainly appears to be what many students believed, and there is corroborating evidence in the Ruthven files that Kipke was forwarding secret reports from agents spying on Michigan students' radical activity. For a student perspective, see the letter written by Robert Copp in the January 6, 1941, issue of the *New Republic*, pp. 23–24, where he claims that Kipke handed Ruthven a list of one hundred names he wanted to see expelled. In a December 2015 interview with Copp, he could not recall where he heard about this list or if it even existed. For evidence that Kipke was receiving reports on Michigan students' political activities and forwarding them to Ruthven, see the Bentley Historical Library's Alexander Ruthven Archive, Box 28, Folder 20, and especially the typed report dated October 15, 1940.

411. Harry Bennett, *We Never Called Him Henry* (New York: Fawcett, 1951), p. 127.

not to be associated with the ASU's particular radical activity on campus. For an organization like Hillel that sought to represent *all* Jews on campus, and whose wide-ranging activities covered issues that would by and large not rankle the University's administration, wading into this second dismissal controversy could bring no benefit.

## Exit Isaac Rabinowitz, Enter Jehudah Cohen

Consequently, with the start of the 1940–41 academic year, *Hillel News* stuck to internal matters rather than voicing any sentiment about the second, and more controversial, round of dismissals. The first two issues of *Hillel News* commencing the academic year of 1940–41 featured articles announcing Dr. Isaac Rabinowitz's resignation from the Foundation's directorship and his replacement by Rabbi Jehudah M. Cohen, formerly of Los Angeles. In his first "Director's Column," Rabbi Cohen offered his ambitious visions for Hillel well beyond the Foundation's Michigan chapter by stating that more than thirty thousand Jewish students countrywide were being served by Hillel on their respective universities' campuses, with the rabbi hoping that "within the next few years more than half of the 100,000 American Jewish university students will undoubtedly have affiliated."[412] We also learn that Dr. Rabinowitz was tapped by Dr. Abram L. Sachar, national director of the Hillel Foundation and very much a member of this institution's founding generation at the University of Illinois, to become the director of the newly found Hillel chapter at Brooklyn College, the first such institution on the East Coast: "Hillel has come to Brooklyn, the largest center of Jewish life in America. It has come to a campus where, of a registration of 13,000, 8,000 are Jewish students. This is the largest challenge that the Hillel technque [*sic*] has ever encountered . . . The permanent director will be Dr. Isaac Rabinowitz, who was transferred from the Michigan Foundation to

412. *Hillel News*, Volume XIV, Number 1, October 1940.

take charge of the unit. He will have the personal collaboration of Dr. A. L. Sachar, the National Director, who has taken a leave of absence from the Illinois Foundation for one semester. Dr. Sachar will establish temporary National headquarters in Brooklyn and operate from there so as to help get the new unit underway."[413]

Three interesting pieces appeared in the December issue of *Hillel News*. An editorial entitled "Hillel, Great Teacher . . ." offers a fine biographical exposé of Hillel, the great teacher, born around 100 BCE in Babylonia, and emphasizes the man's qualities and priorities, which became the main reasons that the founders of this university-based institution chose his name for their big-tent-oriented student-centered educational organization. Hillel's brilliance of mind—but, more important still, his commitment to lifelong learning and teaching—and the simplicity in the conduct of his life made him and his values prime candidates to have an educational mission centered on Jewish students at institutions of postsecondary learning honored with his name.

The second item concerns the summary of a lecture on anti-Semitism delivered by the renowned scholar Rabbi Mordecai Kaplan who made it very clear that anti-Semitism was not the Jews' problem, it was the Gentiles'. He argued that nothing the Jews will—or won't—do will weaken anti-Semitism. Kaplan said that anti-Semitism's pervasive existence, alas, was independent of Jewish behavior and actions. Jews had to live their lives steeped in the ethics of their religion, culture, and tradition and make no concessions based on the hope that such will somehow lessen anti-Semitism. Kaplan concluded that a learning process that only the Gentiles can and must accomplish on their own will render anti-Semitism less potent. The third piece, written by Herm Epstein, puts forth an excellent argument for the paying of college athletes well over seventy years before this issue became such a ubiquitous topic on American college campuses.[414]

413. *Hillel News*, Volume XIV, Number 2, November 1940.
414. *Hillel News*, Volume XIV, Number 3, December 1940.

An editorial entitled "A Positive Program for Democracy" touts the many benefits that refugees from fascist Europe can bring to the city of Ann Arbor and the University of Michigan campus. This editorial accompanies news accounts that describe how "campus" and "townspeople" unite as efforts to raise funds for refugees under the aegis of The Refugee Student Campaign and the Ann Arbor Jewish Committee approach their conclusion at the beginning of 1941: "What can the refugees do for the campus, the community, and the nation? They bring to the campus a cosmopolitanism that is bound to influence those American students and faculty who come into contact with them. Their life and their tragedy brings home to us the need for a dynamic democracy. As students, their experience forces us into asking how can we stop the same forces here that drove them from their native lands. The community benefits from them. They add knowledge and experience to our communal life . . . In our interest as Americans and democrats and Jews, in the humanitarianism that is the best in people, let us put our hearts in the helping of these who are our brethren as human beings."[415] As the February 1941 issue of *Hillel News* informs us, the Ann Arbor Jewish Committee ended up raising $4,300, which was an impressive sum of money at the time. Martin Dworkis led the students' effort; Professor I. Leo Scharfman, the faculty's; and Osias Zwerdling, the "townspeople's."[416] The conclusion of this committee's work was announced in a policy statement that read, in part, "Ten refugee students will be enabled to complete their university education through funds raised by the Ann Arbor Jewish Committee in a campaign which closed this week. The campaign resulted in the collection of the equivalent of $4,300.00 in cash contributions and offers free room and board . . . All Jewish fraternities and sororities (numbering eleven on the U. of M. campus), Avukah, and the Katharine Pickerill Girls' Co-operative (non-sectarian) supported the campaign. The Ann Arbor Jewish

415. *Hillel News*, Volume XIV, Number 4, January 1941.
416. *Hillel News*, Volume XIV, Number 5, February 1941.

Committee was organized two years ago under the auspices of the University of Michigan B'nai B'rith Hillel Foundation . . . No Gentiles were solicited, but Dr. Edward Blakemon, University Religious Counselor, and Mr. Kenneth Morgan, Director of the Student Religious Association at the University of Michigan, sent in contributions 'because they wished to help.' Since the formation of the Ann Arbor Jewish Committee, and with the arrival of five new refugee students, a total of twenty-five refugees will have been aided by the Committee. Two of the new students, Esther Torczynor, formerly of Vienna, Austria and Henry Proskauer, formerly of Breslau, Germany, have already arrived on the campus and have registered at the University."[417] And once again, the acquisition of more than two dozen books by authors such as Franz Werfel, James Joyce, Andre Simone, Otto Tolischus, and Lewis Mumford truly impresses.

In the very next issue of *Hillel News*, the literary sophistication of at least parts of the Hillel membership exhibited its musical counterpart, which, too, was nothing short of impressive: Brahms's violin concerto in D Major performed by none other than Jascha Haifetz under the baton of Serge Koussevitzky; Beethoven's First Symphony conducted by Arturo Toscanini; Grieg's piano concerto in A Minor performed by Wilhelm Backhaus; *Ballad for Americans* performed by Paul Robeson; Rachmaninoff, Mozart, Mussorgsky, Bach, Ravel, Verdi, Puccini, on and on![418]

And yet again we are treated to a fascinating intervention about the state of Jews in America in this issue of *Hillel News*. Under the headline "Knowledge of History, Culture Would Help American Jews," Sid Sachs bemoans the fact that Jews, more than any other group, are "anti-religious" and "modernist" and uninterested in their own culture and ways: "And speaking of Jewish culture, why aren't there more [Jewish students] enrolled in the classes of

417. "Publicity Release, Released by B'nai B'rith Hillel Foundation, University of Michigan, Ann Arbor, February 16, 1941," Hillel Scrapbooks, Loose Materials, BHL-UM Hillel, Box 1.

418. *Hillel News*, Volume XIV, Number 5, February 1941.

Jewish interest which the University offers? The excuse 'lack of time,' often given for non-attendance at Hillel's extra-curricular classes cannot apply here. Three courses were given on the Bible the first semester, for example . . . It is a safe guess that most Jewish students here know less about it than they do about Hemingway's latest opus. There must be hundreds of Jewish students enrolled in French, German, Latin, Greek, Spanish and other language courses, but in the course in elementary Hebrew there were two entered last semester. There seems to be little appreciation of the beauty of Hebrew as a language or of the culture which a knowledge of Hebrew can help one understand."[419]

The centrality of this topic carries over to the March issue of *Hillel News*, in which an editorial called "The Future of Judaism Depends on Education . . ." continues in the pessimistic tone expressed in Sid Sachs's contribution, adding, if anything, an almost fatalistic hopelessness: "The enemies of effective Jewish education in America are legion. One is indifference, born out of a lack of understanding as to what we need to save Judaism in America. Another is the point of view that charges that Jewish education is too Jewish. Then there is the heavy hand of tradition which would rather break Jewish education than bend a millimeter . . . To make the brew a wee bit more bitter, there is the tension between the professionally trained educator and the 'volunteer' who adds a little to the confusion. There are still several too many lay boards of education who insist that the burden of Jewish education should be a labor of love, and should not be vulgarized by having associated with it the tawdry motives of 'professionalism.' And finally there is the parent who really doesn't care but for the sake of neighbors and goes through the motions of providing her children of tender age with what passes for Jewish education."[420] Alas, there is literally not one sentence or thought in this lengthy piece that would suggest to the hopeful reader how this apparently dismal situa-

419. Ibid.
420. Ibid.

tion could ever be overcome. But there are some positive reports in this issue of *Hillel News* that could be summarized under the heading "fraternities to the rescue": Thus we learn that a refugee named Robert Contini, "who is now at Columbia on a scholarship," was aided by the Sigma Alpha Mu fraternity during his time at the University of Michigan, where "he made a straight 'A' average" while attending its engineering school.[421] We also read that the "Phi Epsilon Pi fraternity last year placed seventeen exceptional refugee students in fourteen chapter houses."[422]

This academic year's last two issues of *Hillel News* reflected a growing concern on campus with the increasing possibility of the United States' involvement in World War II. Many worried that the question of America's participation would never be put to a vote by the American people, the vast majority of whom, as "the polls of public opinion show conclusively . . . do not want to participate in this war." Irving Zeiger, in his piece "Do the People Want to Go to War . . . ," argues passionately that this "popular opinion must be kept alive until all the issues on this war are clear. No individual or group has a monopoly on the truth. We cannot make the horrible mistake of sending men to die unless we are completely certain of both the issues and risks . . . On the Michigan campus many students want to keep this public opinion alive. As this paper goes to press, preparations are being made to hold two peace meetings, one a demonstration by the students, and a second a more formal meeting with little student participation. Without arguing the case for either of these two meetings, I am certain that they are both deservant of wide attendance."[423]

In the next issue of *Hillel News*, the ubiquitous Martin B. Dworkis (with coauthor David Crohn, in this case) offers a reply to Zeiger's piece in which, though agreeing with some of Zeiger's points, Dworkis seems to have departed from his previous isolationist

421. Ibid.
422. Ibid.
423. *Hillel News*, Volume XIV, Number 7, April 1941.

views. Entitled "In Reply . . . ," Dworkis and Crohn take Zeiger to task for his "ill-considered attacks on the democratic process," which will neither strengthen "national confidence" nor offer minorities "better consideration by protesting national policy in a subversive manner." But then Dworkis and Crohn state that "it is equally true that national unity should not be secured by bludgeoning dissenters and silencing criticism. Mr. Zeiger could have done more by objecting to the administration's program as not being wise or realistic. He might even have challenged our administration's right to lead the country to the brink of war . . . However, without openly using such a challenge, thus implicitly accepting the present order, one must not charge a government with treason, as Mr. Zeiger seems to imply. This would only lead to national confusion and anarchy."[424]

The issue of *Hillel News* welcoming the students to campus in the fall of 1941 confronted them with not only the scourge of fascism and war in Europe but also the growth of pro-fascist and anti-Semitic movements and sympathies here in the United States: "Are the young people of America prepared to know a 'false prophet' when they hear one? Are they immune to the seductive flutings of Latter Day Pied Pipers? German and Italian youth succumbed to the sweet music, the pot-of-gold promises. Now a million lean, long-limbed, fresh-faced youngsters are rotting on every battleground in Europe. They were seduced, betrayed. They gave up their liberties, rubbed out their integrity . . . The foul excrescence, the witches' brew, whipped into being in Italy and Germany is blowing our way. A storm of pro-Fascist, anti-Semitic ravings is blowing up here in America. It's a whirlwind of danger. It looks mighty like the stuff that blew over Germany before Hitler took over."[425] The article, though unsigned, appears under the headline "New Students Welcomed by Rabbi Cohen, Hillel Director" alongside a photograph of the rabbi. After setting the stage of the

424. *Hillel News*, Volume XIV, Number 8, June 1941.
425. *Hillel News*, Volume XV, Number 1, October 1941.

existing dangers posed by fascism's and anti-Semitism's increasing appeal in the United States, the piece uses this to urge students to join Hillel, which the article sees as being an essential bulwark in fighting these evils: "Hillel, with sixty foundations operating on as many campuses, and cooperating with thousands of other liberty-loving Americans, can do a lot to keep those banners [of freedom and against tyranny] flying. But you've got to do your share. Before the day is over join-up with us. Our great movement is named after one of the most magnificent, one of the most beautiful characters in history . . . Candidly, I find it hard to believe that Hillel knew Herbie London and Millie Gerson personally. Yet he was a man of immense vision. Perhaps he did have an idea that this year they would be heading our membership enrollment. At any rate, he wanted to wish them well and did nothing less than give them their slogan. Now it belongs to you. 'If I am not for myself, who will be for me? But if I am for myself alone, what am I? And if not NOW, WHEN?'"[426]

In an editorial entitled "New Editorial Policy . . . ," *Hillel News* recognizes the urgency of the day presented by global developments. And yet again, it invokes the age-old intra-Jewish debate between Jewish particularism and Jewish universalism as being the most ethical but also the most expedient strategies to confront these enormous existential problems for Jews and others as well: "A course for Jews today is a highly controversial subject. No person or no group can arbitrarily determine for us a policy. Have we even any right to talk of things specifically Jewish in regards to the vast problems facing the world? Dare we agitate for a course of action for Jews, or must we stop thinking in those terms? Should we take a more active part in the policies of the day, or should we for our own good make our presence less felt in the leadership of public affairs? Some feel that the situation today has finally proved the Zionist case. Others are just as sure that the situation today proves that Zionism was all wet from the start. One way or another

---

426. Ibid. The words *NOW* and *WHEN* appeared in capital letters in the original.

we must think clearly on these important issues. Physical chaos we may not be able to avoid. Mental chaos it is our duty to avoid."[427] To debate these immensely important issues, the paper decided to open its pages for pro-and-con-style debates starting with the November issue, for which the topic was to be, as we will soon see, the always controversial "'shall Jews take a more or less active part in the affairs of the day?'"[428]

We learn from this issue that the new school year's second Friday Evening Fireside Discussion at Hillel was led by none other than W. H. Auden, "one of the greatest living English poets."[429] His topic was "The Adjustment of Youth in a Changing World." The notice introduced Auden, among others, in the following manner: "He has been a liberal throughout his life. He fought in the Spanish Civil War. His wife is Erika Mann, noted author and daughter of the great German writer Thomas Mann."[430]

There appears a short obituary mourning the death of Justice Louis Dembitz Brandeis, retired Supreme Court Justice, at the age of eighty-four: "Brandeis was not merely the first Jew to attain the honor of occupying a seat on the High Tribunal; he occupied that place in public life in such a manner as will make his name immortal in the history of Jurisprudence, indeed in the history of our country. Brandeis was a great American. He was a great Jew. His life was an unending crusade for the little man."[431]

This issue of *Hillel News* also presents an impressive array of courses that the Hillel Institute of Jewish Studies planned to offer during the 1941–42 academic year. The list includes, among others, Elementary Hebrew, The Bible, Modern Hebrew Literature, Yiddish, Yiddish Literature, The Jew in the World Scene, and Marriage and Family Relations. Long gone were the days when the

427. Ibid.
428. Ibid.
429. Ibid.
430. Ibid.
431. Ibid.

Foundation (in the early 1930s) refused to teach Hebrew, defer-
ring all didactic authority to the University of Michigan in terms
of teaching that subject. We also learn that, at last, Hillel established a Fraternity and Sorority Cooperation Committee that was
to create a much better liaison between the Greek organizations
and the Foundation and make the latter a much more attractive
place to students drawn to Greek life on campus: "If Hillel has
been able to build itself up with only the minimum of aid from
organized groups, think what it could be with the whole-hearted
cooperation of these groups. Give the Foundation a chance and
then, decide for yourselves its worth. Seek out the activities which
are of great interest to you and make them a vital part of your college education."[432] But as if Hillel simply could never shed its fear
of and contempt for the fraternities' frivolous and anti-intellectual
priorities, here comes Hillel's passive-aggressive warning to the
very groups that it was trying to woo with the creation of this
committee, lest their members only consider Hillel as yet another
source for fun and games: "Remember that the importance of the
Foundation lies not merely in amusements, but largely in new
contacts. Do not allow yourselves to be satisfied with one group
or clique of friends. Broaden your experience and widen your
scope by making new connections."[433]

Two interesting pieces continue the debate about anti-
Semitism in the United States in the November 1941 issue of *Hillel
News*, the last one published before Pearl Harbor. In the lengthier
article, entitled "'Our Place in the Sun,'" Gerry Davidson commences by stating that "American Jews are increasingly concerned
with the threat of American anti-Semitism. First, let's see what
we are getting so frightened about and then let's try to find out
what to do about it."[434] Davidson then proceeds to delineate two
kinds of anti-Semitism. The first he sees as anti-Jewish feelings

432. Ibid.
433. Ibid.
434. *Hillel News*, Volume XV, Number 2, November 1941.

and hatreds that have existed for centuries emanating, among others, from "Christian folklore," "unscientific Fascist thinking," and "forms of jealousy." Such resentment "has always been with us and there is no prospect of its eradication until the general world status of Jews is radically changed by a non-minority center somewhere . . . The important thing is that we did not cause it and no amount of conservative clothing, soft speech and mimicry of non-Jewish culture patterns is going to stop it. The less attention given it, the better."[435] Davidson discerns the second strain of anti-Semitism as an expression of contemporary American politics that, he believes, is new to America. He squarely places this anti-Semitism's origins in the popularity of fascism in Europe and elsewhere in the world, which has clearly bled into the discourse of American politics: "The would-be American men-on-horseback are trying to do exactly what their German counterpart did so successfully. Anti-Semitism is the spearhead of the Fascist movement in the United States. It is a method for the destruction of American democracy."[436]

Davidson then discerns two woefully inadequate reactions by Jews to these dangerous developments. First, "some people (the hush-hush Jews or ostriches) put their heads firmly into the sand and hope that by thus being inconspicuous the whole matter will blow over. The other reaction has been somewhat deeper. It begat several large national organizations that publish pamphlets, saying, 'We are not, (1) International bankers, (2) Communists, (3) middlemen, and (4) whatever else you call us.'"[437] The only correct and effective way to fight anti-Semitism, according to Davidson, is for Jews to align themselves unequivocally with all progressive forces in American society, none more so than the labor movement, which is the bulwark for a better democracy: "The moment we start to run or only defend with 'We are not'

435. Ibid.
436. Ibid.
437. Ibid.

pamphlets we are fighting a losing battle. We are not only against Fascism, but what's important, we are going to FIGHT FOR a BETTER Democracy. There is disaster in the status quo, safety in progress."[438]

Right alongside Davidson's piece, there is a shorter contribution by Loren Hart. Entitled "Let's Go Easy . . . ," the article basically calls on Jews, who furnish but 3 percent of the population of the United States, to shut up and not give the Lindberghs of the world and other anti-Semites reasons to vilify them. Above all, Hart decries the existence of a "handful of outstanding Jewish politicos, uncommissioned to speak for the Jewish people, but whose opinions, willy-nilly, are accepted by their Gentile neighbors as representative ones of the group as a whole. Washington has been filled with a highly overproportionate number of Jews, lobbyists, key men in defense, committee advisors—men lending violent ammunition to the Lindberghs and others, men serving to imprint on the minds of the American people the fact that the flames of this war are being fanned by Jewish interests . . . When three percent of the population attempts to create twenty-five percent of public opinion, whether that opinion be for or against war, that three percent is exposing itself needlessly to vilification and attack."[439]

Positively linking America to Jews and vice versa is the appearance of a quote attributed to the late Justice Brandeis, who once said, "'The twentieth century ideals of America have been the ideals of the Jew for twenty centuries.'"[440] Alas, the linkage between America and Jews has remained an uninterrupted staple of conservative and right-wing European anti-Americanism and anti-Semitism since the founding of the United States in 1776. In the course of the twentieth century, particularly with the rise of

438. Ibid. The all capital letters in *FIGHT FOR* and *BETTER* appear in the original text.
439. Ibid.
440. Ibid.

the New Left in the 1960s, similar linkages between Jews and America have also entered the discourse of big parts, though not all, of the global left.[441]

And then the morning of December 7, 1941, changed everything. The front page of the January 1942 issue of *Hillel News* informs us of the formation of a Defense Committee by Hillel's Student Council "to coordinate all of the Foundation's defense activities."[442] Even a cursory reading of this article reveals the prominence of women in the leadership of this new endeavor: Mildred Gerson became the chair of the new committee, and Marjorie Teller and Ina Mae Rabinovitch, leading figures of the Hillel Student Council's Social Welfare Committee and Ann Arbor Jewish Committee, respectively, also joined. These three women outnumbered the two men, Sam Rosen and Dan Seiden.[443]

Also on the front page of the paper, we are told about a conference at the University of Illinois to be held on February 14 at which all the regional Hillels are to gather to plan their activities addressing the new situation for American Jewish students and American Jews caused by America's entry into the war. The editorial, aptly entitled "Hillel and Its Obligations . . ." and written by the University of Michigan Hillel's director Rabbi Jehudah M. Cohen, offers a scathing view of those who want to use their war obligations to neglect—or defer—matters that continue to remain relevant to Jews, such as culture, learning, and other constructive activities comprising the core of the Hillel Foundation. Engaging in activities that help the war effort cannot impinge on the Foundation's regular work, which Rabbi Cohen sees as offering precisely the stuff that will help both materially and spiritually in supporting the new situation caused by the war. Interestingly, Rabbi Cohen also uses his editorial to complain about Churchill's

441. For an extensive presentation of this topic, see Andrei S. Markovits, *Uncouth Nation: Why Europe Dislikes America* (Princeton: Princeton University Press, 2007).

442. *Hillel News*, Volume XV, Number 4, January 1942.

443. Ibid.

and Roosevelt's omission of any mention of the Jewish people as victims of the Nazis and fascism: "When Churchill and Roosevelt met on the high seas, they named all the wronged peoples who would be restored as a result of an Allied victory. Of all the peoples wronged by the Nazis, the Jewish people, obviously the most bitterly hurt and the people most vitally concerned in the favorable outcome of the struggle, were not even mentioned. This is a tragedy that hurts too much to dwell on. This was not merely an oversight on the part of these two great figures. This is the tragedy of Jewish life."[444]

There is a commentary by Sid Sachs, invoking the works of Franz Kafka, Reinhold Niebuhr, W. H. Auden, and Søren Kierkegaard, that calls on Jews to use these trying days to learn from their Judaism, indeed to revel in their Jewishness as a means to strengthen the communal bonds that are so important in dire situations such as these. We learn of two Hillel members, Herb London '43 and Marvin Koffman '43L, having joined the Army Air Corps. In a powerful concluding piece on the last page of this issue of *Hillel News*, Rabbi Cohen makes a strong case for the Jews' remaining in Europe after the war because Jews have every right to live on the continent where they had lived for centuries. Zionism and its argument of a Jewish homeland have a definite place in the discussion, but they cannot replace the Jews' right to remain in Europe if they so choose. Cohen concludes his piece in the following way: "Let's work for Zion as the legally recognized for those who feel the need to live their lives in a 'non-minority Jewish center.' But we must cease to give hostages to the enemy by proclaiming that the Jews of Europe live in Europe by sufferance and not by right."[445] It is amazing how, even at this late date, the enormity of the Holocaust and the massive success of the Nazis' initiative to eradicate much of continental Europe's Jewry seemed simply beyond the rabbi's—and many others'—comprehension and imagination.

444. Ibid.
445. Ibid.

In the very next issue of *Hillel News*, David Crohn offers a detailed and impassioned response to Rabbi Cohen's argument that Jews will need to remain in Europe after the war. Crohn believes that Rabbi Cohen's faith in the Atlantic Charter, which promises "'peace, freedom and security' for all peoples, including the Jewish people," is a chimera: "When victory finally comes, as it certainly will, the Jews of Europe will be physically and spiritually bankrupt, millions will have been so uprooted and degraded by a generation of propaganda, so economically severed from what was once their homes, that their re-establishment will be well-nigh impossible. Of course we fight for 'Freedom, security and peace,' but let us not be so unrealistic as to believe that a new peace treaty, a new spirit of exaltation after this war, will quickly settle all the Jewish problems. Assuming all the good will which must follow the final defeat of Hitlerism, is there some hidden miracle which will restore everyone to his own fig tree and to his own birthplace? . . . Century after century, the Jews have put their trust in movements of world emancipation. Time and again, they were disappointed and left to the mercy of the world about them . . . In the light of present world opinion as to the nature of the post-war world, and in view of our historic disappointments, we feel that the burden of proof lies on the other side. Meanwhile, we must face the consequences of the statement, that 'in all probability several million Jews will have to leave Europe.' At this point, the statement would appear to be the truth, and facing the truth has always been the soundest policy."[446] While not mentioning the words *Palestine* or *Israel* or *Zionism* in his piece, Crohn's plea for the Jews' exit from Europe is pretty emphatic, if also despondent.

Robert Warner contributes an article in a similar vein in that, he, too, does not anchor his solution for the postwar situation of Jews in an openly Zionist option, even though he makes it clear that Jews will only face security and peace in a construct in which

---

446. *Hillel News*, Volume XV, Number 5, March 1942.

they enjoy full political sovereignty.[447] In notable contrast, Gerald Davidson offers an unvarnished plea for the Zionist solution. He states strongly in his powerfully worded piece that no solution other than the departure from Europe to Palestine will exist as a realistic option to give the Jews the semblance of a secure and sheltered existence. He ridicules all the hopes that some Jews have placed in socialism: "To those that tell us 'Socialism is coming,' and 'we won't have to worry about depressions,' the only answer is that they don't know how to face realities. They assume that economic factors are the sole cause of anti-Semitism. Really they are only the catalyst. Anti-Semitism is with us in good times, too."[448] Rabbi Cohen provides an impassioned article indicting all appeasers and the erstwhile spirit of Munich.

Lastly, in his "Commentary" column, Sid Sachs touts Hillel's great relevance for the situation at hand. In so doing, he offers a wonderful encapsulation of Hillel's all-encompassing mission that does, in fact, feature items for most, if not all, interests exhibited by Jewish students on campus. But reading between Sachs's lines, it is also clear that he is fully aware that Hillel's very variety might be construed as a failing as well: To secular Jews, it might be too religious. To non-Zionists, it is viewed as too Zionist. To Conservatives, the presence of *The Nation* and *The New Republic* on its library shelves offers prima facie evidence of Hillel's radical inclinations. Perhaps Sachs's ending words offer Hillel's most essential and endearing as well as ecumenical features: "It [Hillel] is a campus home. It is a place to sit around and talk and meet people. It is a place where you can hear the best music, and play ping-pong and dance and read. (And where can you find a better library than Hillel's?)"[449] Having closely mined this monthly Hillel publication for eighteen years (from 1927 to 1945) and having witnessed the music and book collection that this organization

447. Ibid.
448. Ibid.
449. Ibid.

acquired during this period, we wholeheartedly agree that there were probably few, if any, places on the University of Michigan campus that featured better books and records than the University of Michigan's Hillel Foundation.

Rabbi Cohen's "Facing the Wind" leads the front page of the April 1942 issue of *Hillel News*. In this piece, the Foundation's director offers a fine universalization of Passover to oppressed peoples over time and space: "When the Haggadah praises the rebellion of Jewish slaves in Egypt, it is also speaking for the serfs of the Middle Ages and for the men who made the American, French and Russian revolutions. And all have been obedient to God for they have been rebellious against tyranny . . . It was a Spanish Loyalist who proclaimed that she and her people would rather 'die on their feet than live on their knees.' The tortured but courageous Serbs still cry out to their Nazi executioners, 'It is better to be in a grave than live as a slave.' And the Joads of the world and the Chinese peasants and Russian guerilla fighters are saying in substance, 'You may kill us, but you can't kill the millions upon millions of men who will win freedom, or die fighting for it.'"[450] The Hillel director's profoundly universalistic interpretation of the Passover story, in which the Jews' exodus from Egypt is barely discussed in its own right but used instead as a catalyst to invoke the iniquities befalling peoples in the contemporary era, represents a long Jewish tradition that, of course, thrives in our contemporary world. Remember that Rabbi Cohen wrote these words when the Nazis had already embarked full blast on their "Final Solution" to the Jewish problem by institutionalizing their mechanized murder of millions of Jews. Of course, Rabbi Cohen had no inkling of the infamous Wannsee Conference that occurred in January of that year, in which fifteen Nazi officials (Adolf Eichmann among them), gathering over tea, coffee, and pastries in a beautiful villa overlooking Berlin's most

---

450. *Hillel News*, Volume XV, Number 6, April 1942. Rabbi Cohen refers to John Steinbeck's famous *Grapes of Wrath* with his mentioning of "the Joads of the world."

picturesque body of water, took the necessary steps to implement the total destruction of European Jewry. And Cohen did, as we showed, address the plight of Europe's Jews in one of his previous columns. We are not blaming Cohen for what we believe to be a tepid statement of solidarity with European Jews. Indeed, we will soon see how explicit he became in articulating the horrors of the Nazi genocide of the Jews. Rather, in this instance, we wanted to emphasize how deeply the universalization and extrapolation of Jewish suffering to that of other collectives (nations, classes, ethnicities, and religions) represents an integral part of authentic Jewish identity.

Apropos universalization being an essential ingredient of a certain manifestation of essential Jewishness, William Schumer addresses yet again, in an insightful piece entitled "Twofold Problem . . . ," the ageless polemic of the complex coexistence of American and Jewish identities that we encountered in our reading of this Hillel publication since the Foundation's inception in 1926 and that, in a more muted form, continues to this day. Schumer claims that the two identities are deeply symbiotic by comparing General Douglas MacArthur to Judah Maccabeus and that American Jews are fighting this war both as Americans and as Jews. Moreover, to Schumer, the Jewish struggle is identical with the democratic struggle, and since the United States is a democracy, it thus coincides also with an American struggle, which also includes labor's struggle: "Just as it would be treachery to break the labor movement in the name of democracy, so would it be treacherous to curtail Jewish activities under the cloak of a false patriotism."[451]

Sid Sachs holds nothing back in his frontal attack on various expressions of selfishness on the home front. Many were trying to profit from the war, be it Standard Oil or a corrupt inspector who said, "'This ordinance inspection thing can become a swell racket. I ought to be able to make a nice rake-off from manufacturers by

451. Ibid.

putting my O.K. on munitions not quite up to standard.'"[452] Sachs also inveighs against Father Coughlin, "our neighbor, [who] is making statements that could be read word-for-word over Berlin radio."[453]

This academic year's last issue of *Hillel News* features a number of articles celebrating the Foundation's fifteen-year existence at the University of Michigan. A major regional B'nai B'rith confer-ence honoring the Foundation was held on May 10 at the Michi-gan Union Ballroom. Something called "Hillelzapoppin'," a kind of variety show in which the Jewish fraternities played a leading role, was presented at the Lydia Mendelsohn Theatre. This event also served as a successful fundraiser for various war-relief agen-cies that Hillel supported. The paper also announced in this issue that Hillel was to move into a new home in the coming fall: "A 23-room mansion will be Hillel Foundation's home next fall. The new home located on the corner of Hill and Haven, is being pur-chased for the Foundation by B'nai B'rith, the Foundation's parent lodge. This purchase, the first by any Foundation in the country, will provide greatly enlarged facilities. The new building, when open, will have chapel lounges, a library, offices, a kitchen and liv-ing quarters."[454] The exact address of this building was 730 Haven Avenue, one block and a half from the main Michigan campus. This house was not only the very first Hillel structure that the Hillel Foundation at the University of Michigan bought outright rather than rented; it represented a novelty for all Hillels nation-wide, since none of them at this time owned their own facilities: "Though the National Office helped out with the mortgage, the fundraising was done by a non-profit corporation, the 'B'nai B'rith Hillel Foundation at the University of Michigan, Inc.,' which had been formed for that purpose. The house had 30 rooms."[455] The

452. Ibid.

453. Ibid.

454. *Hillel News*, Volume XV, Number 7, May 1942.

455. "B'nai B'rith Hillel Foundation at the University of Michigan, An Annotated Chronology," BHL-UM, Box 1.

location of this wooden-framed structure was very close to the space presently occupied by the University of Michigan's Hillel Building at 1429 Hill Street. However, it was not until after World War II—in September 1951, to be exact—following the demolition of the aforementioned wooden house, that a one-story redbrick building, constructed by the Detroit architectural firm Lerner-Linden, was inaugurated to become the University of Michigan Hillel Foundation's permanent home at 1429 Hill Street.

Rabbi Cohen uses his column "Facing the Wind" to heap praise on Hillel's numerous accomplishments in its fifteen-year presence on the University of Michigan campus: "For fifteen years, through the efforts of thousands of youthful and zealous hands and brains, a fellowship of Jewish students has been formed at Michigan which has molded character, developed talents, provided human companionship, created opportunities for self-fulfillment."[456] But Cohen also addressed the stark realities of the times: "Some of our sons are traveling to distant lands to defeat the military enemies . . . Their jobs completed, the Norms and Marvs and Herbs and Martys will return to us. Awaiting them must glow the Torch of Democracy, warmer and more luminous than when they went away. Less than this we dare not do for those who march away to die if necessary, so that humanity may endure."[457]

In his "Commentary," Sid Sachs writes a thoughtful plea for Zionism that, he hopes, will at least catch the attention of the "emancipated students" on campus whose disdain for this movement is evident "by the looks on their faces," which betray the negative stereotype that they associate with Zionism.[458] In his hope to make Zionism perhaps a tad more interesting and attractive to at least some Michigan students, Sachs touts the Histadrut's activities, policies, and approaches to his readers:

456. *Hillel News*, Volume XV, Number 7, May 1942.
457. Ibid.
458. Ibid.

"Histadrut has a great cooperative marketing society, a wholesale purchasing organization and a communal unemployment fund providing work and relief."[459]

The first issue of *Hillel News* published in the new academic year of 1942–43 featured the following note by University President Alexander G. Ruthven in the center of the paper's first page: "It has been a very gratifying experience to follow the history and observe the development of the B'nai B'rith Hillel Foundation at the University of Michigan. Under intelligent leadership and with enthusiastic co-operation from its student membership the Foundation has throughout its history been a constructive agency in the religious, intellectual, and social life of our campus. I am sure that all those who know the University join in congratulating the Foundation upon its acquisition of a new home and the opportunities for even broader and more valuable activity thereby presented."[460] We learn that none other than Dr. Abram L. Sachar, in many ways Hillel's cofounder at the University of Illinois and surely its most prominent national representative, was the keynote speaker at the inauguration of this new home. We also learn that Osias Zwerdling, "pioneer Ann Arbor resident, whose aid, both spiritually and materially, was in this case, as in all others, invaluable," played a key role in Hillel's acquisition of this new home.[461] Given the exigencies of the times, the new Hillel home was immediately harnessed for various activities assisting the war effort.[462] Inside the paper, Rabbi Cohen uses his column "Facing the Wind" to argue for the compatibility and symbiosis of Americanism and Judaism, invoking the aforementioned saying by

---

459. Ibid. The Histadrut, founded in 1920 as part of the labor Zionist movement, was perhaps the most important institution in the Yishuv, the Jewish "settlement" preceding the founding of the state of Israel in May 1948. Thereafter it became the country's powerful trade union federation and remains so to the present.

460. *Hillel News*, Volume XVI, Number 1, November 1942.

461. Ibid.

462. Ibid.

Justice Brandeis: "The twentieth century ideals of America have been the ideals of the Jews for twenty centuries."[463]

In the "Commentary" column, Zav Schumer summons a full-blown attack against any attempts to assimilate, which he finds not only futile but essentially immoral.[464] We encounter for the first time an outright appeal for Avukah, the Zionist organization on campus, in the pages of *Hillel News*. Under the heading "Avukah," Elise Zeme and Elyse Gitlow argue with verve and vigor for Jews to become Zionists, which in no way compromises their democratic loyalty as American citizens: "Avukah does not ask you to give up an iota of your democratic loyalty as an American citizen, but it does ask that you share that security with the millions of Jewish refugees that seek a home."[465] Lastly, Harvey Miller praises Hillel's library, which, as we argued before, was nothing short of amazing: "One of the most attractive rooms at our new Hillel is the library . . . We are proud of our books and believe that we will have even more reason to be proud. There are novels and plays that make you think, philosophy to deepen your appreciation of life; there are books on economics, on history, and on sociology . . . There are books on many aspects of Jewish life . . . You will find books here to help you in your courses, as well as to aid you in the solution of your personal problems."[466]

The war's presence in Hillel's daily life becomes evident on the front page of the December 1942 issue of *Hillel News*. We read that Hillel men are busily helping in the harvesting of beets that are so crucial for the production of sugar. We also learn that soldiers are heartily welcomed to the Hillel Jamboree that is to commence on December 12.[467] In a fascinating symposium triggered by the publication of a book entitled *Washington Is Like That* authored

463. Ibid.
464. Ibid.
465. Ibid.
466. Ibid.
467. *Hillel News*, Volume XVI, Number 2, December 1942.

by W. J. Kiplinger, the sensitive and long-standing topic of quotas for Jews limiting their access to and participation in various aspects of American public life and some of its institutions—not least, of course, universities—became center stage in the pages of *Hillel News*. Kiplinger argued that "the self-imposition by Jews of quotas . . . contribute[d] toward the stabilization of the position of the Jews in the communities in which they live" and thus provided a "practicable" and "desirable treatment of the Jewish problem."[468]

Under the headline "Quotas Called Undemocratic," Ted King argues emphatically that a "numerus clausus" that is self-imposed by the Jews not only is undemocratic and profoundly unmeritocratic but will actually not shelter the Jews from the wrath and envy of parts of the Gentile population. This strategy will not diminish, let alone alleviate, anti-Semitism: "But today there are still those who wish to place temporary expediency above ideals. They believe that the murmurs of protest against the current status of the Jews is a natural thing and that there is nothing we can do about it. They do not realize that they are playing into the hands of those who would rejoice in seeing a four percent Jewish numerus clausus as an important step in the total elimination of Jews in all fields of competition."[469] King's piece is followed by one written by Sanford Ross bearing the unmistakable title "'Numerus Clausus' Defended." Ross writes: "Gentiles have few sources of information about Jews. What they know is what they pick up through hearsay; chance acquaintances with a Jewish salesman, and infrequent references in the newspaper . . . Thus, when a Gentile meets Jews who are loud and vulgar or sharp in business, an immediate and often permanent impression is formed . . . Jewish prominence in public life has grown to an alarming degree. War-time is the wrong time to throw kindling on the fires of race prejudice. Unity is the need of the moment in America at War. The

468. Ibid.
469. Ibid.

average American will view with fear and envy the striking role Jews are beginning to play in Washington. This cannot but have a harmful effect upon national morale. The hard facts of reality demand that a 'numerus clausus' be applied to Jews in the public service."[470]

David Crohn is the third author of this symposium. In his piece called "Quota a 'Patent Medicine,'" Crohn writes: "There is a dangerous fallacy implicit in our acceptance of a 'numerus clausus' that has serious implications from the Jewish point of view. Inherent in such a policy is the idea that the problem of anti-Semitism can be appreciably alleviated by a 'hush-hush' policy. Some are still of the opinion that if we will be less obnoxious, tread more softly, make ourselves less evident, etc. then we will be well on the road to solving or at least lightening the problem of anti-Semitism. The 'numerus clausus' as a method of dealing with anti-Semitism reeks of the 'patent medicine' policy. A patent medicine may often be fatal, not so much because it does positive harm, but because valuable time may be wasted while the dread [sic] disease enters an incurable stage. So, too with the Jewish problem. Anti-Semitism has its root buried deep in the social, economic, and political forces of our culture. Jews must think in these terms when dealing with the Jewish problem . . . The very least we can do is refrain from adopting a policy which by its very nature presupposes that free opportunity for all groups will not be a part of the future world."[471]

In a different section of the paper, we learn that Pearl S. Buck, in an article chastising Kiplinger's book for advising Jews to restrict their participation in American society via a self-imposed "numerus clausus," opposed such measures emphatically and categorically. Highlighting yet again Rabbi Cohen's interpretation of Jewish values as being most effective when universalized to issues of human emancipation and social justice well beyond

470. Ibid.
471. Ibid.

the particularistic concern of Jews only, there appears an impassioned essay by the Foundation director in his "Facing the Wind" column. Here he pleads for racial equality in American society; for the immediate desegregation of restaurants in Ann Arbor; for the repeal of the poll tax in many states of the Union, particularly in the South; and for the cause of farm workers in Salinas, California. This was arguably Rabbi Cohen's most impressive essay among an array of very fine ones.

Soldiers at Hillel are the main features of the January 1943 issue of *Hillel News*. Articles on visiting soldiers dominating the "Second Annual Fall Frolic, a two-day jamboree" and on a gala dinner honoring men who leave for the war feature on the front page among other pieces describing the Foundation's deep involvement in aiding the war effort by helping soldiers of all sorts (already serving and about to serve).[472] In the "Commentary" section, David Crohn offers his last published words in this forum before assuming his commission in the infantry. Crohn's piece, perhaps his most impassioned and tautly presented, calls on the United Nations to defeat the scourges of not only anti-Semitism but also imperialism and colonialism. But the article also represents Crohn's most pronounced expression in support of the creation of a Jewish homeland, which he sees as indispensable in the hoped-for reduction, perhaps even elimination, of anti-Semitism. Crohn ends his piece with a thoughtful note that is worthy of mention in its entirety: "This column is the last which I shall write for the *Hillel News*. This semester is for me, as for a good part of the Hillel's membership, my last on campus. Therefore, I have tried to make the column an expression of what I, as a Jew, feel should be kept in mind as the war goes on, and what I feel should occupy the thoughts and motivate the actions of those who go with me and those who remain here."[473]

Right alongside Crohn's column is a piece authored by Herbert Edelhertz entitled "A Thing to Remember." The title is completely

472. *Hillel News*, Volume XVI, Number 3, January, 1943.
473. Ibid.

enclosed by a bold black margin the likes of which we had not seen in any of the previous issues of the paper. The piece is in fact the very first one in this publication expressly describing the Nazis' systematic extermination of the Jews: "They [the Jews] have been killed in the concentration camps, executed with their backs to Ghetto walls, and murdered in their own homes by the ruthless application of hunger and cold. Jews have been torn from the miserable hovels which were left to them as homes, packed into unheated, filthy cattle cars, and shipped across the continent without food or rest, the survivors to be dumped like so many pieces of coal into the pest holes of Poland which have been marked as execution pens for the rich culture and personality of European Jewry"[474]—a pretty good description of what later became known as the Holocaust.

To be sure, Edelhertz feels compelled to cite his sources and bona fides to a world—surely including Jewish students at the University of Michigan as well—that simply could not (or refused to) comprehend the singular magnitude of the Nazis' genocidal project: "The accusations which we direct at Hitler and his Gauleiters have firm foundation. They are based upon facts and figures given out by the American State Department. Vice President Henry A. Wallace denounced the Nazis for these atrocities in an address delivered before a protest meeting in New York, and messages were read at that same meeting from President Roosevelt and Prime Minster Churchill. If there is anyone who still doubts the intentions of Hitler let him 'look at the record.' It stands in one of the best-sellers: 'Mein Kampf.'"[475]

Rabbi Jehudah Cohen devotes his entire "Facing the Wind" column to a graphic depiction of the Nazi genocide's nefarious methods. This piece is partly written in the first-person plural as somebody brutalized by these atrocities were the Nazis to be successful in invading and occupying any part of the United States:

474. Ibid.
475. Ibid.

"We might be loaded on a 'caravan of death' and shipped to an 'extermination center' where our execution could take place 'quietly.' But we probably wouldn't arrive alive, because the sealed box-cars in which we travelled would be sprinkled with chloride of lime. There would be no water or food during the trip. Only asphyxiating fumes. We might be burnt alive in a synagogue, a Jewish center or a Hillel Foundation. Or our end might come from carbon monoxide gas from the exhaust of a Nazi army truck. But if we were lucky we might be saved to serve in a slave gang. And if we were luckier still, we might survive a month despite the sulphur fumes in the mines where we worked, the lack of heat in the barns or stables where we were quartered, and the starvation diet we were grudgingly dished out. We would not survive even the month if we fell ill during that period. If fatigue or lack of food felled us for as much as two days, we'd be put to death as 'useless'"[476]—an even more accurate description than Edelhertz's apt one mentioned previously of what later became known as the Holocaust.

In a short announcement of the recent publication of a pamphlet that approvingly depicts "hatred" to children, entitled *Children in Wartime* and written for the Child Study Association of America, its author, Dr. Caroline Zachry, is approvingly mentioned for her advocacy of hatred that is directed by weaker nations against stronger ones and hatred directed at the suppressors of freedom. The reason, according to the author, is that some things are worse than war and bloodshed. These are slavery and degradation.[477]

Despite the newly created challenges for Jews in general and Jewish students at the University of Michigan in particular, Hillel's high level of cultural involvement and offerings did not diminish one iota. We learn that "Hillel's already well-stocked library of classical records has been augmented by the purchase of five

476. Ibid.
477. Ibid.

new albums and seven albums of replacement."[478] Dmitri Shosta-
kovich's Fifth Symphony, Pyotr Ilyich Tchaikovsky's Fifth Symphony as well as his Nutcracker Suite, and Jean Sibelius's Second
Symphony were among the acquisitions of new works by Hillel,
whereas previous recordings of Ludwig van Beethoven's Third,
Fifth, Sixth, and Ninth Symphonies had to be replaced with new
purchases because the sound quality of the old records had diminished substantially due to the extensive wear and tear caused by
the frequency of listening to them. This is not at all surprising
in a culture in which, as we mentioned already, Brahms's and
Debussy's music was considered and treated as "pop." On the
book front, more than fifty new works had arrived at Hillel: Franz
Neumann's soon-to-become-famous study of German National
Socialism entitled *Behemoth*, Alfred Rhys Williams's *The Soviets*,
Franz Kafka's *The Castle*, and Lion Feuchtwanger's *Josephus and
the Emperor* among them. Lastly, the Hillel Foundation continued
to offer an array of classes on topics such as Hebrew and Yiddish language and literature, socialism, communism, Zionism,
and even on the Jews' possible disappearance by extermination
or assimilation.[479]

While women played important roles in the Hillel Foundation's
early years on the University of Michigan's campus—just recall Josephine Stern's prominence in the early 1930s to which we referred
frequently—it was due to the mass exodus of men because of the
war that women assumed leadership positions in Hillel on both a
national and a local level. Thus we are informed in the March 1943
issue of *Hillel News* that "for the first time in its history, Hillel has
selected a woman to serve as National Field Secretary. Her name
is Sarah Lee Meyer, and she has been secretary to Dr. A. L. Sachar,
national director of the Hillel Foundations, since 1939."[480] On the
front cover of the paper, we see photographs of Estelle Sager and

478. Ibid.
479. Ibid.
480. *Hillel News*, Volume XVI, Number 4, March 1943.

Elyse Gitlow, both of whom became new student directors of the Michigan Hillel. Nothing made this profound change clearer than the editorial in that issue of *Hillel News* called "Hillel's New Role." The piece commences: "As our nation enters the period of total war, the American college campus is rapidly 'changing over.' Women, always far more capable than we gave them credit for, are 'taking over.' Among other things, this war will prove the fallacy of 'male chauvinism.' . . . Women students are everywhere where men held sway a few short weeks ago. The bulk of the top Student Council positions are being ably administered by women. Two new student directors have been appointed, both women [the aforementioned Estelle Sager and Elyse Gitlow]. Avukah's new president, the Forum Committee chairman, the Council's second vice-president . . . all women.[481] And it is likely that when the Editor of the *Hillel News* puts on his uniform in a few days his successor will also be a member of the fairer sex. President Roosevelt, when submitting his budget message to Congress in January, said, 'In total war we are all soldiers, whether in uniform, overalls, or shirt sleeves.' He might have added 'skirts,' for the skirted ones are really finding themselves these days. And we're lucky we're finding out about them, and all the hitherto unrevealed skills they possess."[482]

Case in point: right alongside this editorial, there appears a lengthy review by Elyse Gitlow on the writings and thought of Mordecai Kaplan, professor at the Jewish Theological Seminary of America and founder of the Reconstructionist movement and the Society for the Advancement of Judaism. Gitlow's exposé discusses eloquently Kaplan's notions of "self-hood," "other-hood," and "God-hood," to which she also adds her own notion of "country-hood," which attains particular salience in time of war: "Every American today is fighting for freedom and country-hood.

481. Indeed, in the Avukah Notes of the same issue of the paper, written by Elise Zeme, we are provided a lengthy list of only women's names who have come to assume every position of leadership in Avukah.

482. *Hillel News*, Volume XVI, Number 4, March 1943.

In terms of what the country is to the individual lies the meaning of God-hood. God should have the self-same personality that we connect with our country. The way to find an answer to this worldly salvation is through a faith in God which is a belief in reality and the definition of it as such."[483]

As seems to have been his wont since the entrance of the United States into the war, Rabbi Jehudah Cohen, the Foundation's director, once again uses his "Facing the Wind" column to write about the war and macropolitics rather than anything pertaining to Hillel or Jewish students at the University of Michigan. In a piece with repeated references to events featuring George Washington, Abraham Lincoln, and Franklin Delano Roosevelt, Cohen praises the summit meeting at Casablanca between President Roosevelt and Prime Minister Churchill. But he reserves perhaps his most pronounced praise for Joseph Stalin who "didn't go to Casablanca because he was personally directing the military operations which resulted in the greatest United Nation victory of the war—the victory at Stalingrad. That victory may shorten the war by many months, perhaps years. That victory will mean that tens of thousands of our brothers who might otherwise have fallen will be alive to return to us when the war has been won. Washington laid the foundations for the United States. Lincoln saved them from destruction . . . A few days ago President Roosevelt, in proclaiming Brotherhood Week, revealed how deeply the lessons taught by Washington and Lincoln have influenced his thinking, for he wrote, 'The American conviction in war and in peace has been that man finds his freedom only when he shares it with others. We are fighting for the right of men to live together as members of one family rather than as masters and slaves.'"[484] We get a list of "Hillelites in the Armed Forces" that includes the names of six young men, David Crohn's—a major contributor to *Hillel News* whose articles we have repeatedly mentioned in our

---

483. Ibid.
484. Ibid.

study—among them. Lastly, the Hillel library received works, among others, by Friedrich Nietzsche, Will Durant, and Somerset Maugham and volumes of poetry by Judah Halevi and Solomon ibn Gabirol.[485]

In the last issue of that school year's *Hillel News*, we learn that women are to live at Hillel: "Hillel is becoming completely feminized. Resulting from the depletion of males from the civilian campus of the University, Hillel has been informally approved by the office of the Dean of Women as a girl's residence house for the coming semester . . . Eight girls will live on the third floor at Hillel and the house mother will live on the second floor. Although girls are being accepted only for the summer semester, the Foundation will probably continue to house women students for the duration."[486] We are quite certain that this was welcome, though perhaps a tad belated, news to Jewish women attending the University of Michigan who, as we mentioned previously, faced considerable housing shortages throughout the period of our study, not least because these women suffered from open discrimination on the part of Ann Arbor–based landladies who refused to rent rooms to these students merely because they were Jewish.

We read that 155 Jewish students and soldiers attended the first night of Seder on April 19, 1943, organized by the Foundation. But we also read the first obituary for a fallen friend. Under the heading "Did Schiraga Die in Vain?" we encounter words of desperation and pain such as "the death of a friend and fellow cooperator knocks the complacency out of our slow-thinking minds and it burns the question deep into our hearts: 'Did Jack die so that we might live in a better and freer and purer world?' If there are any among us who love life more than did Jack who despised the world for which Hitler and fascism and all reaction stand, can we stand by and merely mourn the death of a fellow mortal?"[487]

485. Ibid.

486. *Hillel News*, Volume XVI, Number 5, May 1943.

487. Ibid.

In the same issue of the paper, ten names appear on the list of "Hillelites in the Armed Forces" right alongside an announcement as to how Sergeant Jack Schiraga died in a plane crash on March 22 "near his station at the Harlingan Army Gunnery School in Harlingan, Texas."[488]

Rabbi Jehudah M. Cohen once again reveals his progressive political preferences in his "Facing the Wind" column in which, on the one hand, he welcomes the impending formation of the American Jewish Conference, a new institution that was to encompass all major Jewish organizations to give a single unified voice to American Jewry in this hour of need for the Jewish people. On the other hand, he simultaneously bemoans the fact that perhaps the most progressive constituency of American Jewry—that is, Jewish trade unionists—remains woefully absent: "To the extent that Jewish workers are not represented, the Conference will be without the vigor and determination of the most anti-fascist element within the Jewish fold."[489]

Perhaps one of the most impressive—actually quite moving—editorials among the many that we read in our study appeared in this issue of the paper. Entitled "Let Us Bring Democracy Home . . . ," it addresses the rampant racism in the United States, which clearly mars the democratic mission that Americans saw as perhaps their most important guiding principle in their war against Nazi Germany, fascist Italy, and militaristic imperial Japan: "One of the seemingly apparent aims of the current fight against Fascism and all its manifestations is the abolition of anti-Semitism, Jim Crowism, and other forms of religious intolerance. But today in our own Congress—in the House of Representatives—where the leadership for a nation at war should be provided, we find instead a number of narrow, bigoted politicians who are still using the race myth to further their political aims or to squelch the political aspiration of others. The main example of this, of course, was the

488. Ibid.
489. Ibid.

attack made on David Ginsburg, OPA counsel, by Rep. J. W. Flanagan of Virginia, who declared that he did not want 'any Ginsburg' to be in charge of his son in the army. He followed up this assertion in another discourse on governmental Washington which he discovered to be 'full of Jews' today. The request of Robert Nathan of the economics planning board for immediate induction into the army is indicative of a similar condition. But these are not the only examples of intolerance on the part of our legislators. These same men who opposed the repeal of the Poll Tax Bill continue with their Jim Crow line like Rep. Rankin of Mississippi who lashed out against the Justice Department for 'persecution' of the 'white people' throughout the South . . . It's easy to talk about bringing democracy to the rest of the world, but who is going to accept the judgement of these men in guiding a post-world war [*sic*; it is obvious that the editorial's text meant to say postwar world]? It is up to us to provide ourselves with the best men now regardless of race, color, or any other rabble-rousing stigma."[490]

Our concluding account of the remaining war years relies on scant evidence, since we were able to gather only four copies of *Hillel News* covering this era. It is clear that the paucity of this number rests mainly with Hillel's publishing fewer copies of the paper on a much less regular basis during these trying times than had been the case for the previous fifteen-plus years. This is evident, for example, by the fact that the paper's first issue of the 1943–44 school year was not published until February 1944; it was absent during the entire fall semester of 1943. This paper's front page features a photograph depicting Hillel's student governing body, the Student Council. We see the presence of fifteen young people, nine of whom are women. Also on the paper's front page, we are informed that "there are approximately 700 Jewish servicemen stationed on the campus and more than fifty percent of these take advantage of the Foundation."[491]

490. Ibid.
491. *Hillel News*, Volume XVII, Number 1, February 1944.

Rabbi Cohen uses his "Facing the Wind" column this time to give detailed accounts of several Hillelites' whereabouts and feats on the war's many fronts. And true to form, the Foundation's director succeeds in invoking labor and trade unions in his text, further augmented by two major icons of the American left at the time: "Some of Irv's [Irv Zeiger '41, former Hillel resident student director] pals at his far away station include . . . Bill Eubank, a nephew of Paul Robeson, who fought with the Lincoln Brigade in Spain."[492] But in his contribution, the rabbi also addresses a topic that was particularly acute at the time and is alive and well today: the consistent myth that Jews shirk their duties by avoiding to serve in the country's military, particularly during wars: "Rabbi Bernstein [Rabbi Philip Bernstein speaking at a meeting of the Jewish Welfare Board (JWB) in Detroit] also declared that on the basis of all studies made thus far, Jews are in the armed forces beyond their proportion to the general population. High army officials and psychiatrists stationed at embarkation points have observed that Jewish servicemen display as much or more courage than other groups just before troop transports shove off to sea for unknown ports."[493] The rabbi concluded his piece with a funny note that is worth quoting, since it testifies to the difference and tension that existed at the time between Jewishly identified Jews and their assimilated coreligionists, a schism that has persisted to this day: "One of the humorous highlights took place when Dr. Moe Chaseman, regional supervisor for the J.W.B., pointed out that Lox and Bagel Clubs are being formed at many USO centers throughout the country, and that when he can't make assimilated Jews

---

492. Ibid. The Lincoln Brigade, comprising Americans who fought against the fascist rebels invading the Spanish Republic during the Spanish Civil War (1936–39), was an icon for and of the American left at the time and remains so to this day. So was, and still is, Paul Robeson, the African American singer, actor, football player, and civil rights activist.

493. Ibid.

understand what a bagel is, he tells them that it's merely a doughnut with *arterio Sclerosis* [*sic*]."[494]

*Hillel News* of April 1944 announced on its first page that Stanford Wallace, president of the Hillel Student Council, was appointed to head the Speaker's Bureau for the United Jewish Appeal (UJA) drive. The year before, Wallace headed the drive along with Herb Levin "and succeeded in setting an all-time high of $1,600 collected, the new goal for the year."[495] Indeed, the across-the-front-page headline in bold letters reads "UJA Drive Quota Is $1,600."[496] We are also informed that noted author Maurice Samuels will speak at Rackham Auditorium on his specialty, which focused on the interpretation of Jewish values. He was also the author of a well-received bestseller called "'The World of Sholem Alechem,' a recently published volume depicting the atmosphere and environment surrounding this great Jewish humorist."[497]

The paper's editorial deals, not surprisingly, with the 1944 UJA Drive. Under the headline "Dig Deeper: 1944 UJA Drive Needs Enthusiastic Support of All," the editors run a quote from President Franklin Delano Roosevelt himself: "'The United Jewish Appeal is one of the agencies through which the American people can make their contribution to the fight for decency, human dignity, and freedom for all to live in peace. The work of relief and reconstruction here and abroad envisaged by the appeal is an important part of the humanitarian front.'"[498] Note—at least in the passage quoted in *Hillel News*—the president's universalizing language omitting any particular reference to Jews, thereby, we presume, trying to broaden the UJA's visibility and legitimacy to a larger audience way beyond the Jewish community.

494. Ibid. Italics appear in the original text.
495. *Hillel News*, Volume XVII, Number 2, April 1944.
496. Ibid.
497. Ibid.
498. Ibid.

In a very interesting review of Ben Hecht's *A Guide for the Bedeviled*, a book about anti-Semitism and anti-Semites, Henry Popkin takes the author to task for offering a mistaken interpretation of anti-Semitism in the United States. While agreeing with Hecht that the situation for European Jews is much worse than it is for American Jews, Popkin argues that Hecht contradicts himself in his discussion of the latter: "Early in the book he launches a tirade against the many types of discrimination in the United States. Toward the close, however, Hecht takes Professor Kennedy of Yale to task for saying that anti-Semitism is an important problem in the United States. He chooses not to read about the Messrs. Raukin and Hoffman, not to wonder about the Congressmen who laughed when Raukin called Winchell a kike. And when Hecht vows that what he does not choose to see cannot exist, he is wantonly belittling the problem he has set out to analyze."[499] We also learn of a new study group that was formed to study anti-Semitism and that Professor Mentor Williams from the English Department gave a lecture on "Labor and the Post War World" in which he "reviewed the growth of organized labor in America, the anti-labor reaction after the last war, and the rejuvenation of unions during the depression. He charged industry with conducting an organized campaign to turn public sentiment against not only labor, but all present social security measures as well."[500] Even during the war, progressive politics did not abate at the University of Michigan's Hillel or on its campus.

The headline for the May 1944 issue of *Hillel News*, that academic year's last, announced that council elections were to be held on Thursday and Friday of May 11 and 12.[501] What makes the list of candidates rather special and offers a fine testimony to the times is that among the top fifteen names, only three belong

499. Ibid.
500. Ibid.
501. *Hillel News*, Volume XVII, Number 3, May 1944.

to men. The editorial entitled "Poland's Anti-Semitic Fascists Must Be Smashed" got our attention due to the awkward timing of such an exhortation when, at this time of the war, Poland's politics surely must have taken a backseat to anybody worrying about World War II in the European theater—most certainly every Jew—compared to the Nazis' occupation of the country since 1939 and the Red Army's successful advances against German-occupied Poland. In the spring of 1944, the Red Army had reached Poland's eastern borders and, with its Operation Bagration, was about to clear eastern Poland of all German forces between late June and the middle of August in that year. So why this venomous attack on Polish fascists at this particular juncture? Apparently, a movie called *In Our Time* had been shown locally in which there is a conflict between "the good, peasant-loving, Nazi-hating Poles (like Paul Henried) and the wicked, boar-hunting, peasant-hating Germanophile Poles (like Victor Francen). At the end, in 1939, the wicked Poles were fleeing the country, discomfited and chastened, while the good Poles were staying carrying on their fight."[502] The editorial continues to argue that "quite a few people have been looking for these 'good Poles' with magnifying glasses and microscopes and have not been able to find them. They know all about the Poles who have spent the 1920s practicing the anti-Semitic devices that Hitler perfected; they have heard of the Poles who backed Hitler's coups in Czechoslovakia and helped dismember that last Central European democracy; they know of the Poles who, a few years ago, demonstrated in the streets of Warsaw, shouting 'lead us to Kovno!' We, personally believe that there are good Poles—the Poles who fought and stayed in Poland—the Polish Jews who sold their lives dearly in the ghetto of Warsaw—the Poles who formed a new government in the U.S.S.R.—men of good will like the late General Sikorski and the late Ignace Jan Paderewski. The difficulty is that the western democracies evidently prefer to deal with the 'Victor Francen

502. Ibid.

Poles,' the boar-hunters, the Jew-haters, the Nazi-lovers."[503] The editorial then proceeds to label as Polish fascists Polish anti-Semites, whom Western powers, according to this piece, preferred as their interlocutors for postwar arrangements of Poland over Polish liberals, Social Democrats, and Communists: "If the American and British governments are sincere in their opposition to fascism and their loyalty to the Four Freedoms, they will support the cause of the Jews against the anti-Semitic Poles."[504]

The assertive tone of the editorial continues in Rabbi Jehudah Cohen's "Facing the Wind" column, in which he extols with great pride the thousands of Jews that were fighting the Nazis on all fronts, from the ten thousand that rushed from Palestine to join the British Army in building the defenses at El Alamein to the "40,000 Jewish partisans of Poland who have given battle to the Nazis at Lemberg and Tarnov and Lublin."[505] Cohen glowingly mentions a twelve-thousand-man-strong Jewish brigade fighting alongside "Marshal Tito's Yugoslav armies" just as he rejoices "that in Bulgaria and in Romania, in Hungary and Czechoslovakia, in Belgium and Holland, the meek and the gentle, the scholars and the dreamers, have been transformed into barricade fighters."[506]

The last piece of note in this issue of *Hillel News* presents Maurice Samuel's views on the causes for anti-Semitism. In his lecture "The Jew in the World of Tomorrow" held on April 16, Samuel "castigated those Jews who continually bemoan the sorrowful fate that has fallen upon their race throughout history and more recently in Europe. It is true, he said, that the Jews have suffered more than any other group, but grieving over their tragedy will get them only pity from the world, and not acceptance as partners by other people."[507] Introducing the well-established link between

---

503. Ibid.
504. Ibid.
505. Ibid.
506. Ibid.
507. Ibid.

Jews and democratic forces and democracy, Samuel argued that "one reason for anti-Semitism is that the negative forces of this world see in the Jewish tradition a great democratic force. We are the bearers of a tradition that is the complete negation of the Nazi dream . . . The American Jew must realize his part in shaping American democracy and in working for a democratic homeland in Palestine. Only on this constructive level, Mr. Samuel concluded, will the Jews win what they want, a chance for a fuller, more creative life."[508] Even at the height of the Holocaust, prominent speakers at the University of Michigan's Hillel found ways to castigate Jews whom they deemed too self-centered, too particularistic, too wallowing in their misery instead of finding hope in the only possible route to salvation—that of universalistic democracy. Quite remarkable!

The next issue of *Hillel News* represents a unique case in our collection in that its publication date lists August 1944. The paper was thus published during the summer and not the regular school year. Perhaps for that reason, this issue of the paper is the only one that appears in a mimeographed format, thereby giving its appearance a decidedly amateurish hue. The lead story on the front page announces that David Crohn, now Lieutenant Crohn, was wounded in Normandy but was recovering at a hospital in England. His injuries seemed to have been under control and the prognosis for a full recovery was encouraging.[509] Netza Siegel offers a dire view of what she calls "intellectuals," by which she means "the people best equipped by brains and education and by the opportunity to attain the political leadership of country."[510] In other words, Siegel is disappointed by a group that we in our current parlance and understanding associate with college graduates and professionals rather than intellectuals. Indeed, she addresses

508. Ibid.

509. *Hillel News*, Summer Edition, August 1944 (no volume and/or issue numbers appear).

510. Ibid.

"the college students of the present," whom she grants a level of "inspiring interest" but also blames for featuring a "frightening lethargy": "The Post War Council, the Inter-Racial Association, Michigan Youth for Democratic Action, Hillel Forums draw their regular groups who want to learn, to discuss, to listen or to participate. How many at each meeting? Twelve, or fifty, or two hundred out of six thousand who during the course of the year take an hour now and then with the realization that they may have something to say in determining it [the future]."[511] We also learn that under the auspices of the B'nai B'rith Lodge of Battle Creek and the Jewish Welfare Board, "thirty-five Michigan coeds journeyed by special bus to Battle Creek on Sunday, August 13, to spend the day with convalescent soldiers of the Percy Jones Hospital."[512]

The November 1944 issue of *Hillel News*, back to its usual format and with proper date, volume, and issue numbers, includes a small note about Lieutenant Crohn, who, apparently fully recovered from his Normandy injuries, was now commanding a platoon of "convalescents" at a hospital in England: "Very soon, the entire unit, all infantrymen, expect [*sic*] to land on the coast of France for the second time."[513] But far and away the most important news—blasted in bold headlines across the front page of the paper—was the announcement of a huge gathering of more than five hundred guests from a dozen states on Sunday, November 26, for the occasion of burning of the Foundation's mortgage for the building that Hillel had "acquired a brief two years ago. Hillel directors from twenty Hillel foundations and counsellorships are expected to attend a district conference which will take place in Ann Arbor on Friday and Saturday, November 24th and 25th. Dr. Abram L. Sachar, national director of the Hillel Foundations, will preside at the sessions."[514]

511. Ibid.
512. Ibid.
513. *Hillel News*, Volume XVIII, Number 1, November 1944.
514. Ibid.

With a profoundly optimistic editorial entitled "Faith of Jewish People Has Kept Them Alive," Stanford Wallace, the new president of the Hillel Student Council, argues that the "secret weapon" of the Jews has been the dominance of right and reason as their overarching guiding principle: "Within this abounding faith of all peoples [that of dignity gauging from earlier parts of Wallace's piece] is a core that is peculiar to the Jewish people. Has it not been they who suffered the most and longest? Has it not been they who have felt the oppressor's heel with the greatest severity? But for them, there has always been a deep faith in the ultimate dominance of right and reason. That has kept them alive and virile. That has been their 'secret weapon.'" According to Wallace, it has been this belief in right and reason that has helped the Jews survive all their trials and tribulations over their lengthy history, has bridged the divisions that have beset the Jewish people forever, and will furnish "the time tested formula [that] might well be the signal for success or failure for our postwar dreams."[515]

Rabbi Cohen uses his "Facing the Wind" column to offer a most enthusiastic panegyric for President Franklin Delano Roosevelt and his policies, both domestic and foreign. He also cites approvingly a study published in *Public Opinion Quarterly* that found that in the 1940 presidential election, 85 percent of the Jewish citizens voted. While Cohen does not mention how much of this Jewish vote favored the president, it is clear that the Hillel director sees this datum as a sign of a mature sense of citizenship on the part of the Jews that others in the country might not have: "This is obviously higher than most other groups in the country."[516]

Next, in a segment called "Past and Future," Edythe Levin, the new student director at the Foundation, offers the optimistic hope that if the economy will perform positively in the postwar period, anti-Semitism will diminish, possibly disappear. According to Levin, it would be a big mistake to have the dark images of

515. Ibid.
516. Ibid.

the past cloud the bright hopes for the future: "There are those who look at the past with a mournful eye and, when they face the future, have equally dark visions superimposed over the whole picture. The view of darkness obscures their hopes so thoroughly that they are unable to give the chances for future betterment a fair examination."[517] Right beneath Levin's article we find the following little dictum: "Where the Jews have been the allies of the progressive, creative forces of a historical period, they have been candidates for survival. Where they are not—they are candidates for extinction.—Waldo Frank."[518]

Lastly, a piece authored by Helen Alpert entitled "Student Directors Take Charge of Activities at Hillel Foundation" presents an introduction to the female foursome of Sonya Heller, Zena Etkin, Judy Jacobs, and Edythe Levin, "four energetic and enthusiastic young women who will be in charge of the activities at the Foundation this year."[519]

The last issue of *Hillel News* available to us during the time frame of our study hails from December 1945.[520] It features the full-page headline of the welcome news that "Hillel Membership Campaign Hits Top," with one of the subtitles announcing that "90% of Jewish Students Enrolled during Drive" and the other subtitle indicating that this was a "First Record of Its Kind Reported Here—May Top All National Reports for Year."[521] The article under these headlines begins as follows: "Boasting its largest membership enrollment in history, the B'nai B'rith Hillel Foundation can proudly announce that over 90 percent of the Jewish student body on the University campus have joined. Betty

517. Ibid.

518. Ibid.

519. Ibid.

520. We were able to locate one issue of *Hillel News* in 1946, two in 1947, two in 1948, and one in 1950. Thereafter, we found no issues of *Hillel News* at all. We decided not to use these scattered issues of the immediate postwar era, preferring to end our study with 1945.

521. *Hillel News*, Volume XIX, Number 1, December 1945.

Korash, President of the Student Council, announced that in previous years the enrollment had never exceeded 80 percent. New members are being added to the lists daily, and the Foundation hopes to announce that it has the largest student membership of any Hillel Foundation in the country."[522]

522. Ibid.

There simply is no better ending to our story, which commenced with the modest, even shaky, establishment of a new institution under totally uncertain conditions in 1926–27 and flourished to organize 90 percent of Jewish students on the University of Michigan campus, thereby becoming the largest branch of any Hillel Foundation at any North American institution of higher learning less than twenty turbulent years later. The overall tally must be gauged a rousing success, all the more so because the Michigan Hillel Foundation was able to thrive in an era and a geographic environment in which anti-Semitism was not only rampant but indeed accepted in public discourse. Let us remember that during the period of our study, southeastern Michigan was the home of two of the most vocal and virulent anti-Semites in the United States. First, there was Henry Ford. Whereas the very last issue of *The Dearborn Independent*, Ford's most pronounced medium for the dissemination of his vile anti-Semitism, replete with all the common stereotypes of this ancient human hatred—from the venal to the subservient, from the Communist to the capitalist, from the cowardly to the devious Jew forever engaged in all kinds of conspiracies designed to spread his evil and conquer the world—appeared for the last time on December 31, 1927 (the end of the Hillel Foundation's first year on the Michigan campus), Ford's anti-Semitism, which was integral to his vast reach in Michigan and beyond, did not diminish at all in subsequent years. If anything, his influence over important political

developments on the University of Michigan campus via his oper-
ative Harry Bennett's close connections to Michigan's football
coach and subsequent Regent Harry Kipke increased in the second half of the 1930s, lasting well into the 1940s. Ford's profound
connections to the University of Michigan in this era cannot be
overstated. Then there was Charles Edward Coughlin, better
known as Father Coughlin, a Canadian-born Roman Catholic
priest, whose weekly broadcasts, filled with the vilest anti-Semitic
bile extolling the policies of Adolf Hitler and Benito Mussolini,
reached up to thirty million listeners throughout the 1930s. One
should also mention in the context of this area's national prominence in anti-Semitic discourse and virulent antipathy toward
Jews the presence of Gerald K. L. Smith, a clergyman and right-
wing political organizer who founded the America First Party in
1943 and was a serious voice on the American right and a pro-
lific advocate of unbridled anti-Semitism, which he coupled with
his hatred of communism. Both of these sentiments formed the
core of Smith's authoritarian isolationism and his wish "to build
a moral America based upon Christian morals, good citizenship, and patriotism—but with an authoritarian leader."[523] Smith
moved to Michigan in 1939, where he came to base his operations
during World War II. He established close relations with Henry
Ford who, initially, admired Smith considerably and supported
him financially before Smith wore out his welcome with Ford.
Smith entered politics by running for a seat in the United States
Senate representing Michigan as a Republican in 1942, though this
proved unsuccessful.[524]

As to the atmosphere on campus, our study could not gauge
the actual acuity and concrete acerbity of anti-Semitism during
this time. But it is clear that it existed and did so in the open. After
all, Jewish students at Michigan responded to that nationwide

523. Glen Jeansome and Gerald L. K. Smith, *Minister of Hate* (Baton Rouge: Louisiana
State University Press, 1997), p. 70.
524. Ibid., pp. 70–75.

survey in 1939 that attempted to assess how Jewish students at an array of American universities categorized their institutions' feelings toward them. "Strongly anti-Jewish" was the verdict of the Michigan respondents. To be sure, it could have been worse. "Severely anti-Jewish"—the most negative of the four categories provided by the researchers—was reported by Jewish students at a number of the University of Michigan's peer institutions, among them universities of foremost prominence such as Columbia. Then again, it could have been two grades better by providing an atmosphere on campus that the Jewish students at Michigan would have characterized as exhibiting "none or little anti-Jewish feelings" or showing only "some anti-Jewish feelings." As we stated in the passage describing this survey, we have no idea of its methodological robustness and cannot vouch for its solid grounding in the social sciences of the era. But given the large number of universities appearing in the reported results of the study, which thus permits some degree of comparison, we are reasonably certain that this classification of the Jewish students' perception of the atmosphere toward them at the University of Michigan in 1939 as being "strongly anti-Jewish" has some validity. This leads us to voice some thoughts on President Alexander Ruthven's relations to Jewish students in general and Hillel in particular. There can be no question that the president had nothing but great respect, even affection, for Hillel, which he saw as far and away the most important—indeed possibly the only legitimate—representative of Jewish students on campus. This all occurred in the context of Ruthven's great admiration for and love of the Jewish people. Recall how enthusiastically the president praised the theatrical production of *Romance of a People*, depicting two thousand years of Jewish history, when this show finally reached Detroit in April 1934 (having been performed earlier in Chicago, New York, Philadelphia, and Cleveland), an event that had absolutely nothing to do with the University of Michigan other than its staging in a city close to it. The careful reader will remember the many instances that Ruthven visited Hillel, mostly, though not exclusively, for some festive occasion. The president regarded Hillel as so important to the University of Michigan that he went out of his way to procure funds for the Hillel Foundation during a period of dire need. In 1933, Hillel faced near bankruptcy due to the cascading effects of the Great Depression. Ruthven actively lobbied on Hillel's behalf by reaching out to Jewish alumni of the University to get them to make monetary donations to Hillel. Although we do not know how much money was raised by this effort, it is safe to say that Ruthven's intervention saved Hillel either from outright foreclosure or from experiencing a financial crisis that would have seriously curtailed its activities on campus. In Ruthven's view, Hillel had an important part to play not only as a center for Jewish life on campus but also as one of the pillars of Ruthven's ecumenical vision of a religiously pluralistic University of Michigan. Indeed, we see Ruthven's assessment of Hillel as being completely congruous with what Hillel saw as its own ideal: a big-tent, broad-based, multipurpose organization that provided a home for Jewish students; was their most effective representative on campus toward all the University's constituencies; and remained deeply committed to being a place of learning, ideas, debates, reading, writing, and acting—in short, an organization that cultivated the mind and was worthy of its surroundings furnished by the University of Michigan. Ruthven seemed not to have had similar affect for the Jewish fraternities and sororities mainly on account of their emphasizing their role as primarily social institutions rather than intellectual ones, an issue that also posed a problem for Hillel as we have seen throughout our study. Lastly, Ruthven certainly had few, if any, sympathies for Jews who happened to have been radicals of one sort or another, particularly if they were members of Communist-affiliated organizations and hailed from the East Coast. On this count, too, our study demonstrates ample instances in which Hillel assumed a stance similar to the President's.

It is in this context of ecumenicalism, so dear to Ruthven's heart and his vision of a proper university, that Hillel's regular engagement with institutional representatives of Protestantism and Catholicism needs positive mention. As we saw repeatedly throughout our study, the Foundation made a concerted effort to reach out to these two faiths by organizing joint lectures, hosting jointly sponsored events, and engaging in regular contact. There is no question that this positive dynamic existed on the level of these institutions' leadership. Alas, we do not know how deeply this reached into the world of regular Michigan undergraduates, meaning how closely students of these faiths actually interacted with each other beyond establishing superficial acquaintances in the classrooms and lecture halls.

In conducting this study, Hillel's very being reminded Markovits, the political scientist, of what in that field's literature on political parties has come to be called a "catch-all party." So coined by the great German-Jewish émigré Otto Kirchheimer, eminent scholar of comparative politics at Columbia University from the early 1940s until his death in 1965, the "catch-all party" represents a big-tent, broad-based, multipurpose party that disdains ideological purity, spurns radicalism of any kind, and exists for the sole purpose of helping as many people as it possibly can by winning elections. As such, compromise and pragmatism are its guiding principles. Knowing that they can never fulfill the wishes of ideologically pure minorities, catch-all parties, by their very nature, never seek to maximize desires; rather, they aim to "satisfice" needs (to use Nobel laureate Herbert Simon's apt terminology for this case). Recall the words we cited from the *Hillel News* of October 1938, which describe this catch-all nature of the Foundation superbly: "An invitation to express your Jewish interests through the agency of Hillel is not a call to join a few narrow pre-digested activities. It means that you are given an opportunity to experience here and develop here all the factors which enter into the eddy and swirl of living as a Jew in the modern world. As a democratic Jewish community center Hillel can invite you to help it be a cross-section of the Jewish life outside." We award the Hillel Foundation at the University of Michigan an A+ for satisficing the needs of thousands of Jewish students during the eighteen-year span of our study. This, of course, inevitably means that on some subsidiary, but very important and urgent, issues of maximization, our grading of Hillel's work would be much less generous and, in some cases, sink perhaps even to the B– range.

In order to assist our assessment of Hillel's performance during the first two decades of its existence at the University of Michigan, we thought it appropriate to gauge how Michigan's Hillel Foundation fared on the five guiding principles that the founders of this organization, Benjamin Frankel and Abram Sachar, decreed in Urbana-Champaign in 1923 (with subsequent major assistance from Boris D. Bogen and Alfred M. Cohen away from campus). Though we mentioned these in some detail in our introduction, here they are in an abbreviated version to refresh the reader's memory: (1) Hillel Foundations will need to be run by a permanent, professional staff that is led by a Hillel director. (2) Hillel Foundations need to be the home to all Jewish students, regardless of their theological orientation, their ideological predilections, or their knowledge of Judaism. (3) Hillel Foundations must be educational institutions with a high degree of intellectual sophistication. They cannot be "frozen on the Sunday school level" and have to be cognizant in their intellectual programming that they are part of an institution of postsecondary education. (4) Hillel Foundations cannot only commit to being the conduits of Jewish knowledge but must also be the purveyors of Jewish values. (5) Even though, per the first principle, Hillel Foundations must have a director with a staff, the actual governing of the organization has to be completely and solely the students' purview. This means that students must staff all committees, write all publications, decide all programs, book all speakers, organize all dances and socials—in short, students have to be in charge.

From our vantage point, there appeared to be no problems with the first and fifth principles. While our evidence is scant on these two dimensions, we have no reason to doubt that the work of the four men whom we encountered as the Michigan

Hillel Foundation's directors—Adolph Fink, Bernard Heller, Isaac Rabinowitz, and Jehudah Cohen—were at the very least competent, perhaps much better than that. We simply cannot say. These directors addressed with eloquence and some frequency the salient issues that concerned the Foundation, the University, Jewish issues beyond the academy—indeed, topics related to politics and philosophy—during their incumbency; they seemed to have good relations with President Ruthven (we have no idea as to Director Adolph Fink's relations with University of Michigan President Clarence Cook Little, which, however, lasted less than three years); and they appeared to be omnipresent at the most diverse activities, from religious services to lectures. Equally, we have no indications whatsoever that students failed to run the Foundation's affairs properly. Gauging from the breadth and the bevy of offerings in terms of lectures and talks and concerts and plays and debating contests, we think that the students did a fine job. We were particularly pleased to see the participation of women in leadership positions from Michigan Hillel's early days in the 1930s. Remember Josephine Stern's ubiquity and obvious star role in the Foundation. This became even more pronounced in the early 1940s when—*faute de mieux*, of course—the war transformed Michigan Hillel into a veritable matriarchy.

We believe that Michigan Hillel excelled off the charts in terms of the third principle. On any metric measuring Hillel's cultural offerings, there can be no doubt that they attained a very high level of sophistication fully in accordance with the standards of a leading institution of postsecondary learning. We need to mention first and foremost the Hillel Players who, from what we can surmise, must have been a truly extraordinary troupe of actors throughout the nearly two decades that our study covered. We would not be surprised if indeed the Players were among the leading amateur theater company in the Midwest, perhaps the nation. The Players' annual gigs at the Lydia Mendelssohn Theatre were campus and Ann Arbor–wide events of genuine importance. Perhaps to the players' greatest credit, they staged four student-written plays yearly in the late 1930s, Arthur Miller's *They Too Arise/No Villain* among them.

Possibly to the reader's slight irritation, we offered solid evidence in our study regarding the Foundation's cultural sophistication by our repeated mention of Hillel's acquisition of books, periodicals, journals, magazines, and newspapers. We were truly impressed with Hillel's obvious commitment to culture. We believe that the quality and quantity of these items that Hillel ordered as a matter of course for its library must have rivaled that of a small college's. From Kafka to Werfel, from Freud to Marx, from Mann to Feuchtwanger—just to keep it among authors producing their original work in German—Hillel's acquisition of books authored by towering intellectuals of culture-defining writing is truly impressive. We have no way of knowing how many of the Foundations' members—or students in general—actually bothered to read these major works of Western civilization. Perhaps they were just parked on Hillel's shelves gathering dust. But somehow we doubt this for two reasons. First, our research gave us the impression that the Hillel library was a major locus of socialization for many students. Kids just hung out there, meeting each other, having tea, schmoozing. But second, we believe that the cultural capital in which many of these students grew up and which they brought to the University of Michigan as students featured a certain well-rounded *Bildung*, in which at least some knowledge and appreciation of literature of this kind constituted social currency. It was "cool" for many of these students to have read Tolstoy and know Dostoyevsky. Ditto, we believe, was the case with music, which, if anything, impressed us even more than the printed material that Hillel possessed. Somehow we do not believe that the Hillel Foundation would have continued purchasing records of the works of Sibelius, Mahler, Wagner, Brahms, Mendelsohn, Schubert, Dvorak, and many others had the students not shown keen interest in consuming them. We do know for a fact that students listened to a number of Beethoven symphonies with such frequency that Hillel had to replace these records with new ones on account of their getting worn out. The snippet "be it Count Basie or Count Beethoven" mentioned earlier best encapsulates the impressive musical catholicity that Michigan's Hillel students had in this era. This, after all, was a milieu in which the music of Brahms and Debussy, Mendelsohn and Schumann were considered "pop" and thus essential to quotidian common knowledge and *Allgemeinbildung*. Lastly, let us not forget to mention in this musical context the Hillel Choral Group, which, though perhaps not as prominent as the Hillel Players, certainly contributed to the depth and breadth of Hillel's cultural offerings on campus and beyond. The Hillel-organized lectures by invited speakers from across the country as well as by faculty of the University of Michigan all exhibited a high level of expertise and sophistication by the invitees. There were lectures on a wide range of interesting and demanding topics, from philosophy to history, from current events in the United States to developments abroad. Finally, of course, Hillel—by its very nature and mandate—provided a bevy of courses on many Jewish topics, from Hebrew and Yiddish language to literature in both, from Talmud studies to that of the Bible, from Jewish history to Jewish philosophy. As we mentioned in our study, Hillel's offerings on Jewish subjects were broad and deep. They fully accomplished what Hillel's original mandate stated—namely, that such an educational effort "not remain frozen on the Sunday school level," that "the development of a college approach to Jewish life and experience [be] the raison d'être of a mature program for Jewish college students," and that this effort require "the use of educational methods and the development of resources which are geared to the intellectual needs of the academic community."[525]

Remember the Honors College based on the Oxford tutorial system that Hillel created? This in essence became a kind of parallel university to Michigan's, teaching subjects on Jewish topics that the University most certainly did not. The Hillel Foundation

525. Jospe, *Jewish Students and Student Services*, p. 30.

at the University of Michigan was quite possibly the only such institution in the country engaged in such a high level of education. Again, we have no idea how many students availed themselves of these offerings. But it is clear that there must have been some need for them on campus among some Jewish students, since the regular curriculum at the University offered very few, if any, courses on any of these topics. Those that it did, like courses on ancient Hebrew, were hardly attended by Jewish students, even though in its first few years, Hillel encouraged all Jewish students interested in learning Hebrew to take precisely such courses taught by the University that, at least in Hillel's judgement, were of such quality and expertise that Hillel at the time did not see the need to teach Hebrew. This changed in the course of the 1930s, especially because most Jewish students, who by then were interested in learning Hebrew, chose to do so at Hillel rather than at the University, where they much preferred to study French, German, or Spanish to fulfill their language requirement. The Hillel Foundation at the University of Michigan created in essence a small version of what a few decades later, particularly following the massive changes in American higher education propelled by events of the late 1960s, came to be known as centers of Jewish studies.

This leads us to a discussion of the much more complex topics relating to the second and fourth founding principles: Hillel's role in the thorny thicket of Jewish identity, assimilation, dissimilation, religion, ethnicity, communism, isolationism, and internationalism, to mention just a few. Let us begin by discussing briefly Hillel's consistently complex relationship to the ten Jewish fraternities (though we found mention of an eleventh in a *Hillel News* article in 1941) and two Jewish sororities on the Michigan campus: From the get-go, these Greek organizations were an irritant to Hillel. Basically, Hillel found their purpose and participants shallow on all levels that mattered to Hillel. The students belonging to these organizations were simply not sufficiently Jewish or, put differently, wrongly Jewish in Hillel's eyes. By featuring their Jewishness primarily in a social manner, the Greek organizations irked Hillel on a number of dimensions. Being social was fine for Hillel; after all, part of its mandate was precisely that—to provide a social organization for Jewish students. But Hillel's "social" was a completely different proposition from the Greeks' "social." Whereas the former saw its social mission firmly anchored in Jewishness, it perceived the latter as displaying a culture in which Jewishness played a secondary role or, perhaps even worse than that, a role solely based on exclusion from Gentile Greek life. So the Jewish fraternities and sororities suffered a double stigma for Hillel: their Jewishness was only grounded on their not being accepted by the Christian world—that is, on the negativity of exclusion rather than on the conscious agency of voluntary joining. For Hillel, the students belonging to the Greek system represented a hybrid for which Hillel had little patience. In Hillel's eyes, the fraternity and sorority members wanted to jettison the Judaism that Gentile society and culture would not allow, thereby resorting to the creation of a world in which they emulated the shallowest aspects of the dominant outside world, hoping that those aspects would be mastered in their four-year stay at college and would eventually become their reliable ticket to a much-desired entry into what at the time were closed places. Worse still, the actual lived Jewishness in which the fraternities and sororities engaged was insufficiently Jewish for Hillel on a number of levels, most profound among them on the intellectual. Hillel disrespected the anti-intellectualism of the fraternities and sororities, which it also perceived as being detrimental to living a meaningful Jewish life. There is also no question that another reason for Hillel's tension with the Jewish fraternities and sororities hailed from its seeing these Greek organizations as direct competitors for the attention and ultimately the adherence of the so-called independent Jewish students at the University of Michigan that did not formally belong to any organization. Throughout the period of our study, Hillel had to navigate these treacherous waters dividing it from the Jewish fraternities and sororities that, let us remember, comprised the absolute center for Jewish social life at America's universities of the era.

Then, of course, Hillel had to balance the constant battle of how best to confront anti-Semitism, which instantly raised the cognate topic of what it meant or took to be a real Jew. On the one hand was a conformist view that did not call for an all-out assimilation of Jews to American society and thus the Jews' disappearance in it, but that hoped that a less-explicit expression of Jewishness would be to the Jewish community's benefit in the United States. This issue was these conformists' sole concern, as they had given up on Europe's more vicious and ultimately murderous anti-Semitism. Indeed, the essentially benevolent and tolerant culture of America formed the basis for this view. Students subscribing to it believed that—at least in part—anti-Semitism was a function of the Jews' doing, pertaining particularly to their overtly Jewish mannerisms, behavior, comportment, and language, which, to no one's surprise, Gentiles disliked (as did, of course, most of these "conformists"). Giving this voice further complexity (and power) was a generational and regional dimension that identified first-generation East Coast Jews—New York Jews in particular—as the most egregious representatives of these overtly Jewish mannerisms. If only the Jews would shed all these (East European accents, loud speaking voice, gesticulation with arms and hands just being a few among many), anti-Semitism would abate. If Jews would only become more American as defined by Gentile, mainstream Anglo-Protestant America, anti-Semitism would diminish, if not disappear. Remember how this strategy seems to have been pursued by a large group of Jewish students well beyond the Greek system at the University of Michigan (and elsewhere in America of the time and of the present) whom their opponents called derisively "hush-hush Jews" (or, in its more aggressive Hebrew/Yiddish version, "sha sha Yids"). As a small vignette in the October 1938 issue of the *Hillel News* stated with no attribution at all, "Assimilationists are Jews who associate only with Jews who don't associate with Jews." This strategy and path represented the most pronounced "loyalty" option.

Opposing this conformist view were equally emphatic voices arguing that anti-Semitism's presence had nothing to do with Jews' behavior, mannerisms, and language. Anti-Semitism, in this analysis, had many reasons, from economic to religious, from political to cultural; it had existed for a long time regardless of the Jews' actions. We were surprised not to have read any piece arguing that this most historic of hatreds thrives on imaginary, not real, Jews, that anti-Semitism exists—indeed, thrives—without the necessity of having any Jews, as Paul Lendvai's work has so eloquently informed us. The question then became how to assert one's Jewishness. We witnessed many expressions of this assertion in Hillel's world that one can categorize as "voice" options.

The first could best be characterized as the "democracy-is-a-Jewish-value" option. Like the previously mentioned conformism, this strategy, too, extols America not by dint of its wealth or culture or consumerism or any other trait associated with macro America but by virtue of its democratic institutions. The argument holds that nothing is more Jewish than democracy, that the two have been compatible and are symbiotic. (Recall Justice Brandeis's point of the twentieth-century ideals of America having been the ideals of the Jew for twenty centuries.) In other words, the essence of a Jewish identity coincides with America's ideals. This version also is assimilationist and conformist in a way, though exactly in the opposite direction from the one previously mentioned: in the earlier case, it is the Jew that needs to conform to America; in the case at hand, it is as if America had to conform to Judaism, with its millennia of democratic values and universalistic ideals, as opposed to the former's mere two centuries.

The next option enhances the scope of democracy and America's virtues to include labor. This Social Democratic version of Jewishness experienced a serious representation among Hillel's voices, none more pronounced than Director

Jehudah Cohen's, who repeatedly emphasized the importance of featuring labor in any politics that presumes to be progressive and—crucially—beneficial to the Jews.

Taking things a step further becomes the most pronounced of the "voice" options, which, as we know, often departed from that path, assuming a clear "exit" strategy instead. That, of course, was the radical (mostly, but not exclusively Communist) strategy that, in a way, saw as its task to raise its voice to such a level as to depart frequently from—indeed reject—both America and often Judaism as well. Our study did not analyze the many reasons Jewish students and intellectuals played such a disproportionally large role in this particular exit option. It is well known that in Europe, too, Jews played a most prominent role in the myriad manifestations of the political left, from the varied version of social democracy to the different faces of communism. It is interesting to note that perhaps more than members of any other ethnic group, Jewish intellectuals and members of the intelligentsia came to identify a deep commitment to universalism—in other words, their conscious rejection of their Jewish particularism—as a necessary ingredient of their progressivism. Whereas a proud expression of any group's ethnic (or linguistic or religious) particularism has been a sine qua non for any radical politics in the United States (e.g., African American, Native American, Latin American) and actually in much of the developed world—never mind its developing counterpart where such particularistic identities are sine qua non for any radical politics—the exact opposite has been the case for the Jews throughout much of the twentieth century. Remaining too Jewish, too particularistic, was often identified as being too clannish, too ethnocentric, too unenlightened, indeed retrograde and reactionary. Few expressed this notion more emphatically than Rosa Luxemburg in a letter to Mathilde Wurm, a prominent member of Germany's Social Democratic Party (SPD) and one of its parliamentary representatives in the Reichstag, whom the famed revolutionary chided for what she believed to be Wurm's excessive adherence to Jewish particularism: "I have no room in my heart for Jewish suffering . . . Why do you pester me with Jewish troubles? I feel closer to the wretched victims of the rubber plantations of Putumayo or the Negroes in Africa with whose bodies the Europeans are playing catch ball . . . I have no separate corner in my heart for the ghetto."[526] To be sure, the Jews' striving for universalism—in other words, shedding their alleged Jewish particularism—did not save them from anti-Semitism, as the well-known Communist (as well as other left-wing) accusation of the Jews being "rootless cosmopolitans" has amply confirmed. This predicament has remained very real for Jews throughout the twentieth century and was a big issue for Jewish students at the University of Michigan in the 1930s. On the one hand, they were considered too clannish, too particularistic, too self-absorbed; on the other hand, they were seen as too cosmopolitan, too universalistic, too other-directed. Damned if you do, damned if you don't.

Suffice it to say that the leftist "exit" option became a major problem for the Hillel Foundation on the University of Michigan campus twice in the period of our study, in 1935 and 1940. In both cases, a disproportionately large number of Jewish students hailing from the East Coast—New York Jews, in certain instances—were expelled by the University for their on- and off-campus activities in radical politics involving organizations close to or part of the Communist Party. While being tepidly critical of the University's actions in 1935, Director Bernard Heller's editorial made it clear that he (and thus the Hillel Foundation at the University of Michigan, whose leader he was) would have preferred that Jews not be the leaders of such organizations—though they could be their avid followers and sympathizers—since by holding leadership positions, they will not only suffer the consequences but also cause problems for the larger Jewish community, which,

---

526. Rosa Luxemburg to Mathilda Wurm, February 16, 1916, in Rosa Luxemburg, *Briefe an Freunde*, ed. Benedikt Kautsky (Hamburg: Europaeische Verlagsanstalt, 1950), pp. 48–49.

as a minority, must always be aware of its precarious standing in a Gentile-dominated world. Despite Hillel's silence concerning the events in 1940, there can be no doubt that among the three grand options that Hillel delineated in an editorial published in that same year—"rightists," "liberals," and "leftists"—Hillel was ideologically and normatively closest to the "leftists," among whom, however, it emphatically disdained the Stalinists. According to Hillel's thinking and that of many others then and since, this group perverted and abused the true identity of the left. Let us remember in this context Hillel's immensely progressive positions on women that the Foundation expressed as early as April of 1928 when it identified itself as "feminist" in its "militant advancement" of women's rights. We found repeated instances where Michigan Hillel defended women's rights and advocated for their causes.

The most pronounced "exit" option was, of course, Zionism, which saw no possibilities for Jews to improve their lives in the Diaspora—the United States included—via either the "loyalty" or the "voice" option. Zionists saw both of these as completely futile because Gentile society desired and permitted neither.

The Hillel Foundation at the University of Michigan had to integrate all these disparate voices and wishes. As a "catch-all" organization, it had to pursue a balancing act that, we believe, was immensely difficult throughout the two decades of our study and remains so today as well. But at the end of the day, Hillel proved a worthy institution that—without any doubt—enhanced the Jewish experience for thousands of students at the University of Michigan in often troubled times. What the exact content of that experience was—or should have been—remains unclear, as it still does in the world of today's Hillel Foundation. We think it is best that way.

# ABOUT THE AUTHORS

Andrei S. Markovits is the Karl W. Deutsch Collegiate Professor of Comparative Politics and German Studies and an Arthur F. Thurnau Professor at the University of Michigan. He holds professorships in the University's Department of Political Science and the Department of Germanic Languages and Literatures, as well as a courtesy appointment in its Department of Sociology.

Kenneth Garner received his PhD in history from the University of Michigan.

# INDEX

Notes are indicated by *n* after the page number.

www.ingramcontent.com/pod-product-compliance
Lightning Source LLC
Chambersburg PA
CBHW060011050426
42448CB00012B/2701